THE AGITATED MIND OF GOD

The Theology of Kosuke Koyama

Edited by
Dale T. Irvin
Akintunde E. Akinade

ORBIS BOOKS

Maryknoll, New York 10545

The Catholic Foreign Mission Society of America (Maryknoll) recruits and trains people for overseas missionary service. Through Orbis Books, Maryknoll aims to foster the international dialogue that is essential to mission. The books published, however, reflect the opinions of their authors and are not meant to represent the official position of the society.

Library of Congress Cataloging in Publication Data

The agitated mind of God : the theology of Kosuke Koyama / edited by
    Dale T. Irvin, Akintunde E. Akinade.
        p.   cm.
    Includes bibliographical references.
    ISBN 1-57075-084-X
    1. Koyama, Kosuke, 1929–   .   I. Irvin, Dale T., 1955–   .
II. Akinade, Akintunde E.
BX4827.K68A35   1996
230'.044'092—dc20   96-32930
                                                                              CIP

Contents

Part Three
Neighborology

Kosuke Koyama

Foreword

DALE T. IRVIN AND
AKINTUNDE E. AKINADE

The past one hundred years have witnessed a radical change in the composition of world Christianity. Gone are the days when Christianity was predominantly a European religion. The age of the Christian West is over, and with it Christianity's captivity to ecclesial-cultural forms belonging to the North Atlantic world. Certainly remnants of colonial and neocolonial mind-sets that dominated global Christianity for so long remain, but Western ecclesial hegemony has been broken. Christian churches in every continent are becoming increasingly grounded in the life and culture of their own particular situations. New forms of contextual liturgy and theological discourse are emerging that reflect the character of these "localizing" Christian communities. A reconversion to the life of the people is taking place, enabling churches to discover new dimensions of their ancient ecumenical vision of faith.

Such a decisive transformation did not just happen, without direction or reflection. One of the key architects of this ecumenical endeavor to contextualize theology is the Japanese-born theologian Kosuke Koyama. For over three decades Koyama has been a keen observer of the changes taking place in the global Christian landscape, helping the churches to respond to the changes that are taking place in the contours of Christianity and contributing to theological reflection that arises out of the warp and woof of life. The impact of his work has been felt most directly within the fields of missiology and ecumenical theology, but Koyama has not confined himself to these arenas of study and action. His work has ranged across several intellectual disciplines. On several continents, through a wide variety of formats, he has sought to articulate in fresh ways the message of Christian faith. His poignant images and short meditations have revealed a distinctive Asian mode of theology. At the same time, his theological reflection has never lost sight of its global horizon.

Since 1960, when Koyama first went to Thailand as a missionary from the United Church of Christ in Japan, his theological pilgrimage has taken him to the peripheries of modern history, where he has encountered God amid the brokenness of the world. It is the agitated God to whom Koyama has turned time and again in his journey—the God who is at work in the world, struggling against injustice and oppression, confronting the idolatries of the false gods of the modern world, and seeking the *shalom* of the cities. Amid the brokenness of the modern world, Koyama has discovered the agitated mind of the God who is "hot," expressed most clearly in the person of Jesus Christ, the one who "affirmed his centrality by going to the periphery."[1] The cross of Jesus Christ is for him the "strange center" which is in fact the "denial of self-centeredness." At the periphery of history, Koyama finds Christ revealing the passion of God, who is pouring out the divine self for salvation among those who are broken as Christ was.

The theme of brokenness was concretized for Koyama in his own life during his teenage years when he experienced the U.S. firebombing of Tokyo in 1945. He witnessed the city transformed into a wilderness, evoking for him the haunting words of the prophet Jeremiah. Crisis followed upon crisis as the cities of Hiroshima and Nagasaki were destroyed by atomic bombs, and then came the radio broadcast of the emperor declaring the end of the war. Following the war, Koyama journeyed to the imperial land that had dropped the bombs on Tokyo, Hiroshima, and Nagasaki, pursuing his theological education first at Drew Theological School, where he earned the B.D. in 1954, and then Princeton Theological Seminary, where he earned the Th.D. in 1959. Upon graduating from Princeton with a dissertation on Luther's interpretation of the Psalms, he was sent by the United Church of Christ in Japan as a missionary to Thailand. There he found himself exploring a theology that began not with Thomas Aquinas, Martin Luther, or Karl Barth, but with the needs of the farmers among whom he worked. Out of this commitment to being a neighbor to the northern Thai farmers was born the "waterbuffalo theology" that would permanently enter the name of Koyama in the register of twentieth-century contextual theologians.

Over the next several decades Koyama's unique methodology of walking among the persons with whom he would seek to engage in theological reflection (a "three-mile-an-hour God" he would later call it) would serve him well. Wherever he went, Koyama remained a student and active learner. Along the way his reputation as a missiologist and theologian grew immensely. In 1980 he accepted the chair as the John D. Rockefeller Professor of Ecumenics and World Christianity at Union Theological Seminary in New York, a position he has occupied for sixteen years. With a distinctive style that is imagistic and aphoristic, he has engaged in theological reflection amid the social contradictions and cultural contrasts of the twentieth century. In his own life he has witnessed the contextual theology he pioneered in Asia, along with other modes of liberation theologies, become firmly entrenched in the theological curriculums they originally sought to challenge. Koyama is numbered among the generation of missiologists who have altered the framework of theological discourse in Asia and across the world. Even now his work remains full of surprises, awakening "the minds of people to the living reality of God and God's work in the world."[2]

The following essays have been presented to Koyama on the occasion of his retirement from Union Theological Seminary in New York. In them, colleagues, friends, former students, and admirers celebrate and respond to his work in a number of ways, reflecting Koyama's own enthusiasm for open dialogue and conversation. Collectively, the essays gathered here represent an outstanding tribute to the life and thought of this major twentieth-century Christian theologian.

The book is organized into three main sections, "Global Community," "The Crucified Mind," and "Neighborology." The first of these themes emerges from Koyama's own life as a Christian raised in a predominantly Buddhist and Shinto religious context. Throughout his career he has carried on a deep theological dialogue with Buddhism. He has also engaged for a number of years in the study of Judaism and Islam, Christianity's closest relatives from West Asia. Time and again, Koyama has returned to reflect upon the theme of the encounter between East and West, drawing upon the insights of Mircea Eliade regarding cosmology and eschatology but taking these insights in new directions.

Dr. K. C. Abraham's essay, "Globalization and Liberative Solidarity," opens the first section of the volume by examining inequalities in the present global political economic system and posing the alternative of a global mission of liberative solidarity. Fr. Tissa Balasuriya next engages in "Christian rethinking on God," doing so likewise in light of the global structural inequalities but also drawing upon particular resources found within the religious heritages of Asia and the Christian tradition. In the third essay of this section, Augustine Musopole draws upon the resources of African historical consciousness and anthropology to develop an African Christian spirituality for the religious global village. In the final essay in this section, Michael Amaladoss, S.J., provides a positive theological basis for embracing religious syncretism through the concept of *kenosis*, paying attention to the criteria for distinguishing legitimate syncretism from more improper forms.

Several of these authors in the first section make reference to Koyama's theology of the cross. Indeed, one need only to have a passing acquaintance with Koyama's ideas or take a brief glance through his published works to recognize his profound engagement with the theme of the crucified one. Among the more enduring images found in his work is that of the "crucified mind of Jesus Christ," a kenotic image of self-denial at the center of Koyama's theology of mission. From the perspective of the crucified mind of Jesus Christ, the one who has gone to the utter peripheries of history, Koyama has developed a powerful and sustained critique of idolatry in the modern world.

The image of the crucified God and the cross as the framework for mission are themes Mary Motte, F.M.M., explores in her essay on St. Francis of Assisi. In it she examines the life experience of St. Francis as a hermeneutical focus on the redemptive mystery of the incarnation through which God inhabits the space of the poor and accepts vulnerability. Lars Lindberg's essay explores Koyama's development of the theology of the cross in the Japanese context and engages it in dialogue with the contemporary Swedish social context. Echoing Koyama's biblical themes, Humberto Alfaro explores the spirituality of the critique of idolatry from a Salvadorian perspective. David Kwang-sun Suh's essay continues the theme of the critique of idols, doing so from the perspective and experience of Korea. In the essay that concludes this section of the volume, James M. Washington boldly embraces the task of revisionist history as a critque of idols, in this case the racialist ambience and tribal ideology of Western church historiography by which Western church history masquerades as both universal history and the bearer of the revelation granted to the church universal.

The essays in the second section raise from a variety of perspectives the question of God's involvement in the experiences of those who are marginalized, poor, suffering, or oppressed. For Koyama, this contextual theological endeavor requires of missiologists and theologians a radical commitment to the life of the people. In the opening pages of *Waterbuffalo Theology* he described his own "conversion" through his work among farmers in northern Thailand:

> I decided to subordinate great theological thoughts, like those of Thomas Aquinas and Karl Barth, to the intellectual and spiritual needs of the farmers. I decided that the greatness of theological works is to be judged by the extent and quality of the service they can render to the farmers to whom I am sent. I also decided that I have not really understood *Summa Theologiae* and *Church Dogmatics* until I am able to use them for the benefit of the farmers. . . . Do I mean to say that I dare to give priority to the farmers over Thomas Aquinas and Karl Barth in my theological thinking? Yes. The reason is simple: God has called me to work here in northern Thailand, not in Italy or Switzerland. . . . God commanded me to be a neighbor to these farmers.[3]

Throughout his career, and in a variety of contexts, Koyama has returned to what he calls "neighborology," which is for him a divine imperative for missions and theology. It is also the title we have given to the third section of these essays, which all deal with themes of neighborology, hospitality, and home.

In the first essay in this section, Victoria Lee Erickson explores the social theoretical dimension of Koyama's concept of neighborology, demonstrating its compatibility with the more formal sociological practice of ethnomethodology and celebrating his unique ethnomissiology. Dale T. Irvin then draws upon the biblical theme of Christian hospitality as a missiological practice creating new options for faith. Akintunde E. Akinade examines the Aladura churches of Yorubaland as African Independent Churches in which people have created a place to enjoy Christianity and feel at home. In her contribution to the volume, Mercy Amba Oduyoye draws upon her experiences as an African woman to reflect upon the marks of neighborliness, the implications of the whole earth as a neighborhood, and the place of unacknowledged neighbors. Larry Rasmussen concludes this section by examining a neighborology of *oikos* that incorporates environmental justice.

The final essay of the book is a personal tribute provided by Donald W. Shriver, Jr., who, as former President of Union Seminary, was instrumental in bringing Koyama to that institution. Professor Shriver's personal tribute is followed by a bibliography of Koyama's published works.

Koyama once remarked that one reason he enjoyed reading a particular work by Thomas Merton was that he could pick it up and begin reading anywhere, in any direction, and the book still made sense to him. Koyama found in Merton's work a profound circularity in which beginning and end met in a cosmological rather than eschatological way. The logic was not linear and progressive but circular and unfolding. Perhaps the same can be said of the writings and life of Kosuke Koyama. It is an unfolding message he has sought to offer, circulating from the global to the local and back to the global dimensions, comfortable with dancing between the cosmological and the eschatological dimensions of religious life, yet doing so with a certain agitation as he seeks to follow the God who spoke from the Mountain.

NOTES

1. Kosuke Koyama, *Mount Fuji and Mount Sinai: A Critique of Idols* (Maryknoll, NY: Orbis Books, 1985), p. 252.
2. Masao Takenaka, *God is Rice: Asian Culture and Christian Faith* (Geneva: WCC, 1986), p. 10.
3. Kosuke Koyama, *Waterbuffalo Theology* (Maryknoll, NY: Orbis Books, 1974), p. viii.

Contributors

K. C. Abraham, a Presbyter of the Church of South India, is Director of the South Asia Theological Research Institute, Bangalore, India, and President of the Ecumenical Association of Third World Theologians (EATWOT).

Akintunde E. Akinade, an ordained deacon in the Anglican Church of Nigeria, has served as Adjunct Professor at New York Theological Seminary. He is Assistant Professor of Religion at Highpoint University in North Carolina and a member of the International Association for Mission Studies (IAMS).

Humberto Alfaro is pastor of the Church of God (Cleveland) in Hempstead, New York, and Professor of Ministry at New York Theological Seminary.

Michael Amaladoss, S.J., is the President of the International Association for Mission Studies (IAMS) and Professor at Vidyajyoti College of Theology in Delhi, India.

Tissa Balasuriya, O.M.I., is Director of the Centre for Society and Religion in Colombo, Sri Lanka, and a member of the Ecumenical Association of Third World Theologians (EATWOT).

Victoria Lee Erickson is University Chaplain and Associate Professor of the Sociology of Religion at Drew University, New Jersey. She is an ordained minister in the United Church of Christ.

Dale T. Irvin, Professor of Theology at New York Theological Seminary, is an ordained minister in the American Baptist Churches.

Lars Lindberg is a Senior Lecturer in Systematic Theology in the Stockholm School of Theology, Stockholm, Sweden. A pastor of the Mission Covenant Church of Sweden, he is a member of the Faith and Order Commission of the World Council of Churches and a former member of the Executive Committee of the World Alliance of Reformed Churches.

Mary Motte, F.M.M., is Director of the Mission Resource Center of the Franciscan Missionaries of Mary, Rhode Island, and a member of the Board of Trustees of the Overseas Ministries Study Center.

Augustine C. Musopole is a member of the Presbyterian Church and Director of Christian Publications in Malawi.

Mercy Amba Oduyoye, from Ghana, has served as Deputy General Secretary of the World Council of Churches and as the Luce Professor of Ecumenics at Union Theological Seminary, New York. She is currently serving as Professor at Immanuel College, Toronto.

Larry L. Rasmussen is the Reinhold Niebuhr Professor of Social Ethics at Union Theological Seminary, New York, and a member of the Evangelical Lutheran Church of America.

Donald W. Shriver, Jr., President of the Faculty, Union Theological Seminary in New York (1975-91) and William E. Dodge Professor of Applied Christianity (1975-96), is an ordained minister of the Presbyterian Church (U.S.A.).

David Kwang-sun Suh is Professor of Theology at Ewha Womans University in Seoul, Korea. He has served as Dean of the College of Liberal Arts and Sciences, the University Chaplain, and Dean of the Graduate School.

James Melvin Washington is Professor of Church History at Union Theological Seminary, New York, and an ordained minister in the American Baptist Churches.

PART ONE

GLOBAL COMMUNITY

1

Globalization and Liberative Solidarity

K. C. ABRAHAM

Globalization is the magic word today. Economic development in the Third World countries, we are told, is possible only if they link up with the global economy through the global market. Globalization is also a cultural as well as political reality for many in this world. Ecological crisis, information technology, and other aspects of modern life know no boundaries. They are global issues. Therefore it is not surprising that theological thinking and mission praxis in recent years has been influenced by globalization. The euphoria with which it was greeted by many theological colleges in the United States indicated its importance for theological education. This paper is an attempt to analyze the phenomenon of globalization and to raise some issues that are pertinent in facing its challenges. It suggests a model of Christian response, liberative solidarity, that is rooted in the experiences and spirituality of the poor and the message of the cross.

GLOBALIZATION: AN ANALYSIS OF THE PHENOMENON

Modern communication has converted the world into a "global village." TV brings events in far-off lands into your living room, drawing you closer to the gruesome war in Bosnia or the tribal massacre in Rwanda. Air travel is fast. You have your breakfast on one continent and lunch on another. And there is hardly a major city in the world that cannot provide you with a Chinese restaurant, a hamburger, or a Japanese car.

Political and economic changes that take place in one corner of the world affect the life of people far away. Seldom do we realize that a drop of a few cents in the stock market in New York has drastic effects on the economy of major cities in the Third World. A United States decision not to purchase raw rubber can unsettle the economy of Malaysia, for example.

We may briefly mention three aspects of this process as they are pertinent for our discussion.

First, the process is an inevitable consequence of certain historical as well as structural factors at work in the last three to four hundred years. Travel across the sea provided opportunity for closer relations between countries. Travel was not for pleasure or adventure alone, but also for trade. Spices, minerals, and other commodities of Asia and Africa created new trade routes from the West to the East. Soon they needed to be protected from competition from rival powers. Slowly colonial powers began to exert military and political control over most of the countries in Asia, Africa, and Latin America. This colonial rule, as is well known, provided the cheap raw materials for the industrial expansion in the countries of Europe and a ready market for their finished goods.

Second, from the beginning the process of globalization was fraught with competition, conflict, domination, and exploitation. Certainly there has been an exchange of ideas and customs between peoples of different countries, and this has been mutually beneficial, but the ambiguous character of the process of globalization is quite obvious.

Colonialism was perhaps the most blatant form of exploitation during this period of globalization. Several consequences of colonial rule are now well known. It is now evident that the industrial development of the West would not have been possible without the cheap raw materials and labor of the colonies. Cotton, iron, gold, and minerals of all kinds were taken out of the countries, sometimes arbitrarily with the use of force and at other times with the enthusiastic support of the local elites. Not only did the colonies provide cheap materials, but they became ready markets for products manufactured in the West. The textile industry is a case in point.[1] Built into this practice is a process of double exploitation, and the historical roots of poverty in the Third World can be traced to this colonial exploitation.

Colonialism has inflicted more serious damage on the colonized people. Frantz Fanon, in his famous analysis of colonialism, has brought out the condition of colonized minds. "Those who internalize the colonial mentality," wrote Fanon, "suffer a systematic negation of personhood. Colonialism forces the people it dominates to ask themselves the question constantly, 'In reality who am I?' The defensive attitudes created by this violent bringing together of the colonized man and the colonial system form themselves into a structure which then reveals the colonized personality."[2] Perhaps many erstwhile colonies have not recovered from this.

Science and technology have accelerated the process of globalization. For one thing, they have created "rising expectations" about development and faster economic growth. While they have promised opportunities for expansion of human potential, they have also unleashed new forces of destruction. Ecological crisis is the most serious crisis brought about by modern technology.

Third, today there is a sense of urgency when we talk about global realities. Nuclear threat raised the possibility of total annihilation of the world. This threat has drawn us together. Ecological crisis has brought to our awareness the need for preserving this fragile earth which is our common home. Life is endangered, and we need all our resources to preserve it.[3]

Any consideration of globalization should keep these three aspects in mind: inevitability, ambiguity, and urgency.

GLOBALIZATION AND THE THIRD WORLD

The global village has provided new opportunities for the enhancement of life of our people. No doubt we need to affirm the positive side of this development, but many in the Third World look at this process with apprehension. They look at the global village as an order or mechanism for greater exploitation and political oppression. In this discussion, we enter into the modern period of globalization.

When the Third World nations became independent of colonialism after long periods of struggle, they embarked on massive efforts to develop their reserves and eliminate poverty. Development by economic growth based on rapid industrialization was the magic word. The three ingredients of this program were local elites (rulers), external resources (aid from the developed world, multinationals), and trade. The goal was not only to eliminate poverty, but also catch up with the First World in modernization, but the net results of the past few decades of development have been well summarized by the cliché of the poor becoming poorer and the rich becoming richer.

On the global level, the gap between the rich nations and the poor nations has increased. The average per capita income of the developed world is $2,400, and that of the developing countries is $180. The gap is widening. The United Nations tried to change this trend, but failed. In 1970 the United Nations suggested that 7 percent of 1 percent of the total GNP of rich nations should be made available for development assistance. But actual help declined from 52 percent of 1 percent in 1975 to 32 percent of 1 percent in 1976. This downward trend continues, and what is more distressing is that the First World countries confirm that they have increased their military expenditure. The existing trade patterns are inimical to the well-being of developing nations. The aid that supposedly helps the growth of the Third World always comes with strings attached and is used as a tool for continuing the First World dominance over the economic growth of the Third World.

C. T. Kurien points out that the countries of the Third World regard the 1980s as a "lost decade in terms of their development opportunities." He writes,

> The prices of many of the goods they export came down, the richer countries kept them out of their markets and the terms of trade turned against them. As is well known, many of them have come to be caught in the "debt trap." Less well known is that the decade came to be one of net resource transfers from the South to the North. And the gap between the rich and the poor countries (measured by per capita income) widened.

Kurien further notes:

> The integration of the global economy has brought to the fore a new set of actors who have played an increasingly important role in it: the transnational or multinational cor-

porations (TNCs or MNCs). These first attracted comment in the 1960s, grew rapidly in the 1970s and emerged as powers to be reckoned with in the 1980s. Some even argue that by the dawn of the next century they, rather than national economies, will be the principal actors in the emerging global economy and that we are already well into the "transnational stage" in the development of capitalism.[4]

The TNCs' role in the Third World has now been subjected to serious analysis by economists. These large corporations know no national boundaries, and their products find their way to the remotest corner of the world. Between 300 to 500 TNCs control an enormous portion of the world's production, distribution, and marketing processes. The sales of an individual corporation is bigger than the GNP of many developing countries. According to the figures supplied by the United Nations in 1981, Exxon has sales of $63,896 million and General Motors, $63,211 million, whereas the GNP of Nigeria is $48,000 million, Chile $15,770, and Kenya $15,307.

The power of global corporations is derived from their unique capacity to use finance, technology, and advanced marketing skills to integrate production on a global scale in order to form the world into one economic unit, a "global shopping center." They do not bring a large amount of capital to the host countries, but they take out huge profits. They do not generate more employment, as their technology is not labor intensive. Profit maximization is their goal, not development. They decide where people should live, what they eat, drink, or wear, and what kind of society their children should inherit.

Their primary goal is to safeguard the interests of developed countries, not the developing countries. In the recent discussion on conserving the world's biological diversity,[5] the behavior of MNCs has again been criticized by the Third World leaders. The Malaysian delegate to the 1990 United Nations General Assembly made the following pertinent observation:

> There are various instances where transnational corporations have exploited the rich genetic diversity of developing countries as a free resource for research and development. The products of such research are then patented and sold back to the developing countries at excessively high prices. This must cease. We must formulate mechanisms for effective cooperation with reciprocal benefits between biotechnologically rich developing countries and the gene-rich developing countries.[6]

Local elites are also agents of globalization, and their role in development should be recognized. When the countries became independent, leadership was naturally transferred to the local elites. They have developed interlocking interests with the western industrial elite. The development model which the newly independent countries accepted has helped them, and they exert considerable pressure on the policy decisions of the Third World countries on globalization. The priorities are determined by the demand of the market—often greed, not need, becomes the controlling factor.

TV was considered a great symbol of modern development, but in an informal survey conducted by a sociologist it was revealed that the people who benefit most from TV are our industrialists. They have increased the sales of their products, many of which are not essential to the life of ordinary people.

The growing inequality between rich and poor nations and between the rich and the poor in each nation is a fundamental threat to global harmony. Globalization and marginalization go together. This contradiction needs special attention and can be illustrated by the economic situation in India.

GLOBALIZATION AND THE INDIAN ECONOMY

In 1991, the government of India introduced drastic reforms in its economic policies that have far-reaching implications for the life of the country. The involvement of the World Bank and International Monetary Fund was acknowledged as crucial in the structural adjustment. It was a deliberate move to take the country right into the process of globalization. MNCs are allowed to come into the country in a big way by liberalization of the earlier stringent regulations regarding types of industry and the profits they are allowed to take out of the country. It is perhaps too early to evaluate the full impact of these policy changes. These reforms have helped to revive the sluggish economy and to discard some unproductive bureaucratic controls. But some of the inevitable consequences of these reforms are quite alarming. The indebtedness of the country (internal and external) has now reached the staggering figure of $90.6 billion. C. T. Kurien, who has made a careful analysis of the trends in the present economy, has concluded:

> If the economic reform measures in India have therefore been sponsored by a tiny, though exceptionally powerful and influential, minority which is pursuing them to safeguard and promote its own narrow interests, they are unlikely to be of benefit to the bulk of the people, in spite of claims that they are not only necessary and inevitable, but also in the national interest. The impact of the reforms on the lives of sections of the people beyond this narrow minority has already begun to be seen. On the basis of an examination of the relevant figures, one estimate shows that in the first year of reforms, "nearly 6 to 7 million people went below the 'poverty line' in contrast to an annual improvement of nearly 10 to 15 million moving above the poverty line over the last decade." Therefore, in overall terms "it makes a difference in terms of a setback in poverty alleviation pace by nearly 20 millions."[7]

Kurien and other economists are not saying that the Indian economy does not need reform, but they point out that the "thrust of any alternative reform measures must be towards the welfare of the largest segments of our society."[8] At present these segments are excluded from the process of decision making that affects their lives, and their condition is deteriorating. These sectors include the marginalized working class—unorganized laborers, and the landless—the dalits and tribals.

Increasing marginalization of dalits, women, and other sectors continues to be a problem. Our hope that their lot would improve is now shattered. No doubt the movement of the marginalized for justice and participation will be stronger, but resistance to them will be on the increase.

As we have seen, marginalization is linked with globalization. The advanced sectors have achieved considerably more expansion, leading to the improvement of the traditional sector. As one report correctly observes, "much of rural development has simply been extension of urban development." There is an urgent need for an alternate form of development that meets the basic needs of the rural people.

Among the marginalized groups struggling for justice, women are the largest. They are fighting many issues: cultural prejudices, structures of patriarchy, economic exploitation, and unjust laws and traditions. Organized movements of women are beginning to make some impact, but they need to be strengthened. The church is also a male-dominated structure. The rich resources and contribution that women can bring to the life and ministry of the church are seldom made use of. Unfortunately, prejudice against women is nurtured in our families. We tend to foster double standards in sexual morals. Female fetocide, dowry deaths, and other glaring incidents are symptoms of deep-seated prejudices and discriminatory practices and customs.

GLOBALIZATION AS THE VEHICLE OF CULTURAL INVASION

The idea of progress is decisively shaped by western life-style and its structures. Air travel, color TV, super computers, and space technology all are the symbols of progress. When a nation opts for TV, not just the technology but all the cultural and social life that nurture it come with it.

Technology is power, and that power is never neutral. It becomes the carrier of those systems and ideologies (values and cultures) within which it has been nurtured. The tendency is to create a monoculture. Professor Koyama, in his inimitable style, provides a sharp critique to this in all his writings. By monoculture we mean the undermining of economic, cultural, and ecological diversity, the nearly universal acceptance of technological culture as developed in the West, and its values. The indigenous culture and its potential for human development is vastly ignored. The tendency is to accept efficiency and productivity without any concern for compassion or justice, ruthless exploitation of nature without any reverence for nature, which is an integral value of the traditional culture.

M. M. Thomas recently reflected on the impact of modernization on the traditional culture. He writes,

> The modernizing forces of technology, human rights and secularism are today directed by a too mechanical view of nature and humanity which ignores the natural organic and the transcendental spiritual dimensions of reality. No doubt, traditional societies emphasize the organic and the religious aspects of life in a manner that enslaves human beings to natural forces and human individuality to the group dicta. But modernization based on a mechanical world-view atomizes society to permit the emergence of the individual who soon becomes rootless and a law unto itself; and since rootlessness is unbearable for long, the pendulum swings to a collectivism which is a mechanical bundling together of atomised individuals into an equally rootless mass under mechanical State control.[9]

There are groups that strive toward a critical approach to Western values and technology. They want to retain the humane values of tradition. They see the need for holistic development. They are for pluralism and diversity in cultures. They are for science and technology, but not for a neutral kind of scientism that willingly allows itself to be used by the elite. They are for industry, but not industry that destroys the ecological balance and causes pollution. In short, they are asking for an alternate form of development that takes the interest of the poor as central and allows room for their culture and religion.

GLOBALIZATION AND ECOLOGICAL CRISIS

Capital-intensive development and the life-style propagated by the media together create a situation where ecological balance and the sustaining power of the earth for nurturing life are being destroyed. The problem is further aggravated by the process of globalization. In fact, ecological crisis is not merely a Third World problem. The whole planet is affected, and perhaps this issue brings together concerned people of the South and North.[10] Perspectives on this question differ.

The Third World perspective on ecological crisis raises the question of justice as an overriding concern. The life of the poor and the marginalized is further impoverished by the crisis. The shortage of fuel and water add particular burdens to the life of women. It is said that tribals are made environmental prisoners in their own land. Dalits, whose life has been subjected to social and cultural oppression for generations, are facing new threats from the wanton destruction of the natural environment.

On a global level, this concern about the gap in the control over and use of natural resources should be raised to gain a correct perspective on globalization. The modern European person is the most expensive human species in this world. Americans, who represent about 6 percent of the earth's population, melt, burn, or eat over 50 percent of the world's consumable resources each year. Every twenty-four hours, citizens of the United States consume 2,250 head of cattle in the form of MacDonald hamburgers. Extend this style to the entire world and what will be the consequences? These hard questions about the nature of development, life-style, and justice have to be raised. In order to pursue this kind of life-style, we need easy access to mineral resources and energy. Many a political conflict arises out of this need. We try to put an ideological garb over such conflicts; East/West conflict is now replaced by North/South conflict. What is at stake is the sphere of political dominance linked with control of resources. Global peace is possible only if we can diffuse this by the establishment of a world order.

A NEW LOOK AT THE GLOBAL VILLAGE

What is the paradigm of the miracle of the global village we have in mind? People who write and talk about the global village have never lived in a village, so their image of the global village is born out of their references to a technological, industrial culture. One of the prevailing tendencies in such a culture is to put everything into a manageable, organized system. There is very little room for diversity. The clearly defined center exercises control over the periphery, which is why the "melting pot" becomes a favorite image in the United States. But what we see in the village is not a neatly organized, uniform structure. A village is a small, separate unit connected to other units of different shapes and diverse character. It is a mosaic, not a neat, uniform system. The global is very much present in the local. Diversity, not uniformity, is its hallmark.

We simply assume that to gain an experience of the global we need to travel to foreign countries. This is not true. We may travel and see things but still miss the essential values that keep our life human. The consciousness that our local life is bound up with realities and relationships that go beyond the given time and space is what makes us truly global. It is the basic openness to the other—it is affirming the other who is different but integral to our life. It is necessary to affirm the local as unique but exist in the wider network of relationships. In other words, plurality is an essential aspect of the global. It provides the space for different identities to grow in dialogue. When that space is denied, the marginal suffer most. The struggle of the marginal for identity is to be seen as a necessary process to realize the global.

Within each nation there are laws that regulate economic activity and distribution through taxation, minimum wages, and so on. But in international relations, there is no regulative mechanism. The United Nations is powerless. It has talked about a new economic order. Demands include reduction of trade barriers, more stable commodity prices for raw materials, easier access to foreign technologies, better terms of aid, and rapid expansion of industrialization. Some of these demands are legitimate, although there is very little hope anything will be changed. These demands, however, do not challenge the existing international system and its assumptions; they simply want a greater share of the global economic pie. This is usually the demand of the bureaucrats and elites. What the poor people are asking and telling us is that unless we rethink the basic questions of life-style, the use of natural resources, and the reaction between environment and development, we cannot address the question of a new economic order.

Globalization is not a neutral process. An alliance forged by the forces of domination for profit becomes the driving force of much of globalization. The poor and the marginal do not find protection and security under it. But this process is inevitable, therefore a blind rejection of it seems to be realistic. How do we orient the forces of globalization for the furtherance of justice? Can we seek a new global solidarity of the victims of the present system to build a just global order?

THE SEARCH FOR ALTERNATIVES

The Third World perspective on global unity is clear. The present global order—controlled by the MNCs, neocolonial forces, and elites of the countries—does not ensure the values of justice and plurality. The ecological crisis has further accentuated the problem of global injustice. The search is for a global order where life-affirming values are preserved and strengthened. This would mean an economic system that is free of oppression. Kurien, in the above study, points out that today the powerful and all-pervasive market has become a tool of oppression. "What they (people) need, therefore, is not greater market friendliness but 'people friendly markets'." A people-friendly market, he further states, is a social institution deliberately under human direction and control. "The dictum 'leave it to the market' has no place here."[11]

Speaking in cultural terms, M. M. Thomas argues that a "post-modern humanism which recognizes the integration of mechanical, organic and spiritual dimensions can develop creative reinterpretation of traditions battling against fundamentalist traditionalism and actualize the potential modernity to create a dynamic fraternity of responsible persons and people."[12]

An alternative developmental paradigm should be supported by an alternative vision of the human bond to one another and to the earth. It is important that this new vision emerges from the experiences of the poor and the marginalized. "It is our conviction that a new paradigm for just development must emerge from the experiences of the poor and the marginalized."[13]

It is not our intention to give a blueprint for alternative development. That can be evolved only by economists, political leaders, and scientists who are committed to the values necessary for human development. In this task we should learn from the experiences of the poor, for they are close to the earth, and their techniques of preserving the ecosystem should be taken seriously. Those who live close to the land and the sea have developed a way of using earthly resources without destroying them. We cannot develop by polluting our water and destroying our forests. More important is the conviction that a set of values integral to human survival can be learned from the life-style and the worldview of marginal groups. They have lived in solidarity with one another and with the earth. Their communitarian value system is necessary for evolving a just and sustainable form of development. This is the global solidarity that we propose for the future, giving a new direction to the process of globalization. "People-friendly markets," "enabling social changes," and "postmodern humanism" are all attempts to give this orientation to globalization.

TOWARD BUILDING A JUST GLOBAL ORDER: THEOLOGICAL CONSIDERATIONS

Can theology be pressed into service toward building a just global order? Does theology deepen our commitment to a new global solidarity based on justice and peace? The vision for theologizing should emerge from the people's experiences and traditions of faith. Sometimes theologians turn such visions into rigid systems and absolute ideals, but the emphasis on contextual theology is an effort to ground theology in the immediate experiences of people's oppression and suffering.[14]

The faith articulation of women and indigenous groups struggling for their dignity and freedom has helped us in our search for a relevant theology. They are important for our task of building a global solidarity. A holistic view of reality and nonhierarchical form of community are integral to their vision of life. This vision has to be recaptured in our theology. Some of our feminist writers and theologians who are committed to developing ecological theology are beginning to articulate this new vision of doing theology.

HOLISTIC VIEW OF REALITY

Our perception of the structure of reality changes as we become aware of new areas of human experience and knowledge. The dualistic model of classical understanding—spirit/matter, mind/body—is not adequate to interpret our contemporary experience. Moreover, our feminist thinkers rightly point out that such a dualist view of reality is largely responsible for maintaining a patriarchical and hierarchical model of society. A holistic model is closer to our life experiences, including our relation with nature. In fact, theologians who write about ecological concerns are united in their opinion that a holistic view of reality is basic to a responsible relationship between humans and nature. An organic model of reality should replace a mechanistic model in our times. An organic model can interpret "the relation between God and world in ways commensurate with an ecological context."[15] Sallie McFague, taking into consideration the insights from contemporary cosmologists, has described the organic model in the following words:

> The organic model we are suggesting pictures reality as composed of multitudes of embodied beings who presently inhabit a planet that has evolved over billions of years through a process of dynamic change marked by law and novelty into an intricate, diverse, complex, multilevelled reality, all radically interrelated and interdependent. This organic whole that began from an initial high bang and eventuated into the present universe is distinguished by a form of unity and diversity radical beyond all imagining: infinite differences, and diversity that is marked not by isolation but by shared atoms over millennia as well as minute-by-minute exchanges of oxygen and carbon dioxide between plants and animals. All of us, living and non-living, are one phenomenon, a phenomenon stretching over billions of years and containing untold numbers of strange, diverse, and marvelous forms of matter—including our own. The universe is a body, to use a poor analogy from our own experience, but it is not a human body; rather, it is matter bodied forth seemingly infinitely, diversely, endlessly, yet internally as one.[16]

The radical interrelatedness and interdependence of all creation is of paramount significance as we perceive reality. "By reality," writes Samuel Rayan, "is meant everything; the earth and all that it contains, with all the surprises it holds for the future; people and their creations; the conditions in which they live, their experience of life as gift, their celebration of it, no less than their experience of oppression and death, and their struggles and hopes and wounds and songs."[17]

Leonardo Boff goes further and affirms that "Ecology constitutes a complex set of relationships. It includes everything, neglects nothing, values everything, everything is linked together. Based on this we can recover Christianity's most early perception; its conception of God."[18] For him "world is a mirror of Trinity."

This provides a new perspective on Christology. Our tendency in modern theology to subsume all the new questions of theology under a framework that may be described as "Christocentric Universalism" is perhaps not the most helpful paradigm. Too much weight is put on this. Christ-in-relation seems to be a better way of affirming the trinitarian concern of the process of transformation and renewal. A spirit-filled theology that responds to the pathos of people and their liberative stirrings should be evolved. The characteristic posture of the spirit is openness and an ability to transcend limits. The affirmation of the solidarity of the poor is the spirit's creative activity. To discern the spirit's working, we need "Christic" sensitivity, but it can never be wholly interpreted by Christological formulations.

If radical interrelatedness is the characteristic of reality and therefore of the divine, then openness to the other is the essential mode of response to God. The openness becomes the seed for creating new relationships and a new order.

The struggle today is for open communities. This awareness of the need for communities is not new, but today the identity struggle of different groups is projecting the shape of communities as classed. Each group defines its boundaries over against the other. The question is, how can we build a global solidarity of open communities? A community of communities that accepts a plurality of identities in a non-threatening, mutually affirming way is the core of our vision.[19] In fact, the Church is meant to be this solidarity. Leonardo Boff writes: "The ecclesial community must consider itself part of the human community which in turn must consider itself part of the cosmic community. And all together part of the Trinitarian Community of the Father, the Son and the Holy Spirit."[20]

We have a long way to go if we take this vision seriously. The churches are so introvert that they are incapable of becoming a sacrament of this community of open communities in this world. Mission has to take seriously this task of recreating communities. It means a critical awareness of the process and structures that are inimical to an open community—forces that threaten life, practices that seldom promote justice and love, and above all an attitude of apathy toward change.

LIBERATIVE SOLIDARITY: A FORM OF GLOBAL MISSION

A holistic vision of reality is the basis for nonhierarchical open communities. But this vision of wholeness should have a concrete direction. In the prophetic vision of a community, compassion is the concrete dimension of it (Mi 6:5). It is solidarity that is liberative and life-affirming.[21] Justice and loving mercy are the words used by the prophet. Together they may be translated into liberative solidarity. The logic of justice as developed in the West emphasizes rights and rules and respect for the other. It is a balancing of duties and rights. But in the prophets, justice includes caring. Justice expressing compassion is the biblical emphasis. The prophets were not talking about balancing interests and rights, but about caring, the defending of the poor by the righteous God. This emphasis comes with poignancy when we consider our responsibility to the earth, a defenseless and weak partner of humans in creation. Caring love comes from compassion through standing with the poor and being in solidarity with them. It is this solidarity that makes us raise questions about the dominant models of globalization.

It also points to a new direction for global community that celebrated sharing and hope. Jesus rejected the imperial model of unity, which in his time was represented by the Roman empire and the power wielders of the Jerusalem temple. He turned to Galilee, to the poor and the outcasts, women, and the marginalized. He identified with them. His own uncompromising commitment to the values of the kingdom and his solidarity with the victims of society made him an enemy of the powers that be. Conflict was very much part of his ministry. It resulted in death. On the cross, he cried aloud, "My God, my God, why have you forgotten me?" This is a cry of desperation, a cry of loneliness, but it is a moment of solidarity—a moment when he identified with the cries of all humanity.

In solidarity with the suffering, Jesus gave expression to his hope in the liberating God who has his preference in defending the poor and the dispossessed. It is in this combination of total identification with the depth of suffering and the hope that surpassed all experiences that we see the clue to Jesus' presence in our midst and the future he offers us. New wine, a new logic of community that comes from a solidarity culture, was projected against the old wine, the old culture.

> The promise of God's future in such a solidarity culture is an invitation to struggle, advocacy for the victims, and compassion. People who are drawn to the side of the poor come into contact with the foundation of all life. The Bible declares that God encounters them in the poor. With this step from unconsciousness to consciousness, from apathetic hopelessness regarding one's fate to faith in the liberating God of the poor, the quality of poverty also changes because one's relationship to it changes.[22]

The solidarity culture is sustained by spirituality, not the spirituality that is elitist and other-worldly, but that which is dynamic and open.

In our struggle for a new global order, we need to mobilize the spiritual resources of all religious traditions, not only the classical religions, but the primal religious traditions as well. In fact, the classical religions tend to project a type of spirituality that is devoid of a commitment to social justice. There are, however, notable exceptions. We begin to see a new search for the liberational form of spirituality in these religions. See, for example, the writings of Swami Agnivesh and Asghar Ali Engineer.[23] Tagore's words express this kind of spirituality:

> Here is thy footstool and there rest thy feet
> where live the poorest, lowliest, and the lost.
> When I try to bow to thee, my obeisance cannot reach
> down to the depth where thy feet rest among the poorest,
> the lowliest and the lost (*Gitanjali*).

But a distinct challenge comes from the Indian spirituality tradition. Its focus upon inferiority is to be considered important when we talk about a commitment for action. Amalorpavadoss emphasized this in all his writings. Freedom also means liberation from pursuit, acquisition, accumulation, and hoarding of wealth (*arta*), unbridled enjoyment of pleasure's comfort (*kama*), without being regulated and governed by righteousness and justice (*dharma*), without orientation to the ultimate goal (*moksha*).[24]

Mention has already been made of the spirituality of indigenous groups. Their holistic vision and communitarian value systems are essential for the emergence of a new global order. They are signs of freedom we long for. As Paul said, "Where the Spirit of the Lord is, there is freedom." Our longing for a free and open order is a spiritual longing. Only when communities live with mutual respect, when they together eliminate all caste, atrocities, when they together remove poverty and hunger, when all their religions sing the song of harmony, when they together celebrate God-given unity—then the spirit is free. Let us commit ourselves to that global solidarity.

This reflection on liberative solidarity can be concluded by mentioning two concrete expressions of it. One is the emergence of dalit theology in India. Dalits are the oppressed groups, marginalized for centuries by the social and cultural systems. Today dalit consciousness based on a newfound identity has provided the impetus for a dalit theology. Professor A. P. Nirmal describes the methodology as follows:

> Dalit theology wants to assert that at the heart of the dalit people's experience is pathos or suffering. This pathos or suffering or pain is prior to their involvement in any activist struggle for liberation. Even before a praxis of theory and practice happens, even before a praxis of thought and action happens, they (the dalits) know God—in and through their suffering. For a dalit theology "Pain or Pathos is the beginning of knowledge." For the sufferer more certain than any principle, more certain than any proposition, more certain than any thought and more certain than any action is his/her pain-pathos. Even before he/she thinks about pathos; even before he/she acts to remove or redress or overcome this pathos, pain-pathos is simply there. It is in and through this pain-pathos that the sufferer knows God. This is because the sufferer in and through his/her pain-pathos knows that God participates in human pain. This participation of God in human pain is characterized by the New Testament as the passion of Jesus symbolized in his crucifixion.[25]

A few months ago, I visited a Buddhist monk in the southern provinces of Sri Lanka. I had heard about his intense involvement in the struggles of people for freedom and justice. Three of us, theologians, sat at his feet listening in rapt attention to the stories of his involvement—how at the risk of his own life he had to defend young activists. He was constantly clashing with the powers that be. At the end, one of the group asked him, "Sir, how do you explain the motivating power that sustains you in all these?" He thought for a moment and then said, "I do not know, perhaps I am inspired by the compassionate love of Buddha." And then, looking intently at us, he asked, "Don't you think Jesus also teaches us about compassion?" I ventured to say, "Yes, but there is a big difference between the response of some of us Christians to our Christ and your response to your Buddha." I do not see the same intensity of commitment to the passion of Jesus in our churches. That is the crux of the problem. Can compassion—another name for liberative solidarity—unite us?

NOTES

1. Mahatma Gandhi's famous strategy for creating an awareness of the evil of the colonial rule was the call to boycott foreign-made clothes and wear clothes made from homespun materials.

2. Frantz Fanon, *The Wretched of the Earth* (New York: Penguin Books, 1988), p. 250.

3. Numerous writings are available from scientists and ecologists, but it is important to note that the churches have taken this up as an area of concern. World Council of Churches materials are made available to the churches for study and reflection. See David Hallman, ed., *Ecotheology: Voices from South and North* (Maryknoll, NY: Orbis Books and Geneva: WCC, 1994).

4. C. T. Kurien, *Global Capitalism and the Indian Economy, Tracts for the Times 6* (New Delhi: Orient Longman, 1994), pp. 57-58.

5. It is recognized that the tropics hold a rich reserve of the planet's biological diversity. Varieties of species that exist here are being eliminated by the destruction of tropical forests. The United Nations has expressed concern over this, and efforts are underway to preserve them through the World Wildlife Fund, the World Bank, and other agencies. But many Third World leaders argue that these efforts are neglecting the point of view of the South. Biodiversity, it is pointed out, is destroyed by the pattern of development adopted by MNCs and others in the North. They further observe that the farmers' wisdom and techniques of preserving the diversity should be recognized and taken seriously. See Vandana Shiva, et al., *Biodiversity—Social and Ecological Perspectives* (Penang, Malaysia: World Rain Forest Movement, 1991).

6. Ibid., p. 11.

7. Kurien, p. 120.

8. Ibid., p. 123.

9. M. M. Thomas, *The Nagas Towards A.D. 2000 and other Selected Addresses and Writings* (Madras: Centre for Research on New International Economic Order, 1992), p. 27.

10. See Hallman, *Ecotheology.*

11. Kurien, p. 123. See also Amartya Sen, *Beyond Liberalization: Social Opportunity and Human Capability* (New Delhi: Institute of Social Science, 1994). This eminent economist compares India's policy for liberalization with that of China and observes that "The force of China's market economy rests on solid foundations of social changes that had occurred earlier, and India cannot simply jump on to that bandwagon without paying attention to the enabling social changes—in education, health care and land reforms—that made the market function in the way it has in China" (pp. 26-27).

12. Thomas, p. 27.

13. K. C. Abraham, ed., *Spirituality of the Third World* (Maryknoll, NY: Orbis Books, 1994), p. 1.

14. Speaking to a group of German pastors recently, I remarked that all theologies were contextual theologies and Karl Barth was a contextual theologian. Predictably my comment about Barth was received with some hesitation. It was pointed out that Barth had rejected a kind of contextual theology found in the liberal tradition. But they had to agree that Barth was concerned about the Word in the European situation obtaining after the World War and the crisis of liberalism. Further, it was pointed out that his own experience in his parish made a big difference in the manner in which he theologized. Kosuke Koyama's contribution in developing contextual theology in Asia should be acknowledged.

15. Sallie McFague, *The Body of God* (Minneapolis: Fortress Press, 1993), p. 39.

16. Ibid., p. 96. Special mention should also be made of Sallie McFague, *Models of God* (Philadelphia: Fortress, 1987); Jürgen Moltmann, *God in Creation: A New Theology of Creation and the Spirit of God* (San Francisco: Harper and Row, 1985); Elisabeth Schüssler Fiorenza, *In Memory of Her: A Feminist Theological Reconstruction of Christian Origins* (New York: Crossroads, 1984); and Felix Wilfred, *From the Dusty Soil* (Madras: University of Madras Department of Christian Studies, 1995), pp. 258f.

17. J. R. Chandran, ed., *Third World Theologies in Dialogue* (Bangalore: EATWOT-India, 1991), p. 47.

18. Leonardo Boff, "Ecology and Theology: Christian Pan-In-Theism," *Voices from the Third World* 16:1 (June 1993), p. 115.

19. S. J. Samartha has expressed this concern in his discussion on pluralism: "In the new global context, the church has to define its identity and role in history in *relation* to, rather than over *against*, other communities. What, for example, is the relationship between the Buddhist *sangha*, the Christian *ecclesia* and the Muslim *ummah* in the global community? When every religion has within it a dimension of universality is it to be understood as the extension of one's universality overcoming other particularities? In what sense can the community we seek become 'a community or communities' that can hold together unity and diversity in creative tension rather than in debilitating conflict?" Samartha, *One Christ— Many Religions: Toward a Revised Christianity* (Maryknoll, NY: Orbis Books, 1991).

20. Boff, "Ecology and Theology," p. 115.

21. Preferential option for the poor is the characteristic mode of response in liberation theology. In some situations it may be misconstrued as a patronizing attitude. Liberative solidarity has the advantage of entering into a different relation with the poor. Their experiences and their spirituality hold the key for a future order. To acknowledge our indebtedness to the poor is to seek a new future.

22. Dorothee Soelle, *On Earth as in Heaven: A Liberation Spirituality of Sharing* (Louisville: Westminster/John Knox Press, 1993), p. 16.

23. *See especially* Asghar Ali Engineer, *Islam and Liberation Theology: Essays on Liberative Elements in Islam* (New Delhi: Sterling Publishers, 1990). Here the influence of liberation theology cannot be ignored. All the religions are challenged to take seriously the emphasis on liberation. One may quote the stirring words of Deane William Fern at the close of his essay, "Third World Liberation Theology: Challenge to World Religions," in Dan Cohn-Sherbok, ed., *World Religions and Human Liberation* (Maryknoll, NY: Orbis Books, 1992), p. 19: "Liberation theology issues a call not only to Christianity, but to the other religions of the world as well. Are these religions willing to show 'a preferential option for the poor'? Can the communities of the poor which are irrupting throughout the Third World be the basis for a new 'people's theology' which seeks to liberate humanity from all forms of oppression: poverty, servitude, racism, sexism, and the like? Can justice and spirituality become partners in a world embracing enterprise? Can the struggle for justice and belief in God come to mean one and the same thing? Herein lies the stirring challenge of Third World Christian liberation theology."

24. D. S. Amalorpavadass, *Theology of Development* (Bangalore: NBCLC, 1979), p. 15.

25. A. P. Nirmal, ed., *A Reader in Dalit Theology* (Madras: U.E.L.C.I., 1990).

2

Let God Be God

An Asian Reflection

TISSA BALASURIYA, O.M.I.

AN ASIAN SEARCH

The Asian continent has not responded positively to, and has even resisted, the efforts of the churches in modern times to convert it to Christianity interpreted in Western perspectives. The Philippines, where there was no organized world religion, is the only country in which Western missionaries have had widespread success. Perhaps we in Asia need to go further and deeper than elsewhere in order to understand the challenges of the world religions, the peoples' religiosity, and the injustices within our Asian societies and in the world system today. For this we can seek in many directions, such as the understanding among the religions, meeting them in their core values, and relating to Asian poverty and religiosity as shown by Aloysius Pieris in his writings.[1]

Here I wish, first, to go back to the early church's understanding of the identity, message, and work of Jesus, prior to the dogmatic definitions of the Councils. Reflecting on the thinking of the early church, one sees that Christianity would have been more open to the Asian religions and social issues if it came to Asia with the theology and practice of the early church, rather than in modern European colonial times. We have a legitimate right to relate ourselves to the more pristine Christianity that was closer to Jesus and purer in its presentation of teaching and of life.

Second, I seek to address the need for a change in the present world order of local and global injustice. Modern Asian theology needs to go beyond mere contextual theologies and relate to the challenges of the one-world situation and rapid globalization that are taking place in almost all aspects of economic, political, social, and religio-cultural life. Asian problems are global; hence the solutions too have to be global, while being rooted in the local realities.

Christian theology is a faith reflection on the Word of God revealed by Jesus Christ and in the Bible. There is a relationship between Christian theology and the contacts that Christians have had with the cultures and civilizations of the world over time. These contacts present the background environment in which the message of Jesus is expressed. Over time the different languages, philosophies, and myths in which people express their worldviews pose challenges to the evolution of Christian theology.

The understanding of the core message of Jesus has been expressed in widely differing ways throughout history. The church has thought out the basic message according to the situation, context, and idiom of the peoples to whom it was presented. Thus the New Testament has several Christologies, or ways of presenting the life and message of Jesus. John writes of the birth and life of Jesus from a longer term perspective of the divine "logos" than do the Synoptics. The Acts of the Apostles bear witness to Jesus and his life work in several different ways. How Paul introduced Jesus to the Athenians in Acts 17:23 is quite different from the apostolic preaching to the Jews. In Athens he began with "the Unknown God that they worshipped and did not know," and then spoke of Jesus and his death and resurrection. He did not speak, according to the text, of the Old Testament prophecies that were so important for the Jews.

In a similar way, we must think through the basic message of Christian faith in a new way in Asia today. The way Christianity came back to Asia in modern times has caused grave problems for our peoples and for interreligious understanding. In fact, Asians as a whole have been allergic to this message mainly due to its attitude toward other religions and cultures and to issues of justice. In this context we offer some thoughts for rethinking the basic message of Jesus and the presentation of God in our societies. These may have validity for other areas too, especially in the context of the widespread secularization among modern peoples.

TEMPTATIONS FOR OUR THEOLOGY ON GOD

Religions themselves become enslaving when they distort the image of God and interpret the divine in their own favor and exclude others. Every religion is tempted to do so. A religion may tend to absolutize its own community, institution, sacred book(s), clergy, rituals, or rules. This is often the cause of interreligious conflicts.

Theology is tempted to interpret God to suit the interests of a dominant group that may try to define God, as if it could fix the Absolute into its finite words and definitions; second, when it creates God according to its image and likeness; and, third, when it tries to limit and control God. Other ways in which the doctrine of God can be fatally weakened is by attempting to monopolize God-talk, appearing to seek to placate God, and by compromising God's sovereignty.

GRECO-ROMAN THEOLOGICAL DEFINITIONS

Issues concerning human salvation and the identity and function of Jesus Christ were openly debated in earlier times when the church was not the dominant religion and ideology of the empire. Interestingly, there was more freedom in the theology of the church in the first few centuries, when the church was under persecution and sided with the oppressed rather than with the rulers. With the conversion of the Roman Empire to Christianity, there was a corresponding conversion of the church to the values of the empire; these included a compromise with Caesar, Mammon, and Mars (the god of power and war). By the fourth century, theology became an instrument of domination, and remained so until the recent church renewal and theologies of liberation motivated Christians to opt for the poor, the oppressed, and justice.

With the ecumenical councils such as those of Nicene, Ephesus, and Chalcedon, authority became the determinant and criterion of Christian orthodoxy. It was this attitude that impeded the church rulers from appreciating human freedom and the right of legitimate dissent in the church, especially in things over which we do not have absolute certainty. Over the centuries the church authorities were instrumental or involved in the suppression of science (Galileo) or numerous reformers of the church (Savanarola and Joan of Arc) who were burned at the stake.

When such decisions became the ruling orthodoxy, when they legitimized political power, social inequality, male domination, cultural imperialism, and religious exclusivity, there was a serious distortion of the message of Jesus himself. It was worse when they were enforced by the political and ecclesiastical authorities with moral and physical sanctions, as if these dogmas were directly revealed by God to the popes, patriarchs, bishops, and emperors and empresses and their respective theologians. In fact, these dogmatic elaborations have led to divisions among the churches for centuries; divisions which are yet unresolved, as between the Greek Orthodox and Roman Catholic Churches.

A NARROW PERCEPTION OF GOD

Prior to recent decades, both Catholic and Protestant theology had many inadequate representations of God and the relationship between God and humanity.

These doctrines led to even worse consequences in interreligious relations. With such interpretations of the Trinity and of the Incarnation, there could be no understanding between Christianity and Judaism, between Christianity and Islam, and between Christianity and other religions such as Hinduism and Buddhism, as well as the cosmic religions of the peoples of the future colonial empires of Europeans in Asia, Africa, the Americas, and Oceania.

The centuries of Christian-Islamic wars were buttressed, if not motivated, by theological claims that gave each side the conviction it was engaged in a holy war for the cause of God. The interreligious history of the human race during the past 1,500 years has been written in blood, in some measure due to the intolerant exclusivity of dogmas which were deeply (and proudly) held and vigorously propagated by the dominant political, commercial, economic, and military powers from Europe.

Thus when European Christians contacted the Amer-Indian, African, and Asian peoples in the sixteenth century, their dominant, exclusive theology considered membership in the Church as essential for eternal salvation. This led to a Christian practice that was intolerant of all others.

Humanity has paid a very high price in terms of prejudice, hatred, war, and the extermination of peoples and civilizations due to the religious and military power of those who claimed to be the only legitimate disciples and interpreters of Jesus, the prophet of justice and the prince of peace whose message is God's love. The millennial consequences of this theology indicate the nature and extent of the derouting of Christian theology.

The modern renewal of Christian theology in Europe and North America took place during this century due to the impact of trends such as the revival in biblical studies, existentialist philosophy, a better understanding of human psychology, the growth of dialogue within the churches, inter-Christian ecumenism, and respect for religious freedom. Vatican Council II of the Catholic Church was basically a reform of the Catholic Church undertaken by Western bishops according to their convictions of the needs of the churches in their situations. It was, as it were, in passing that a short document on interreligious relations that acknowledged the spiritual values in the other religions was put out by Vatican II. This has all the same turned out to be a very important turning point in the Catholic attitude toward other religions.

In the late 1960s and 1970s, there was a better appreciation of the humanity of Jesus in Western Europe and North America. The bitter experience of World War II and the terrible Holocaust of the Jews made theologians question the traditional theology and church practices that supported the dominant European political and economic system.

The liberation theologies of Latin America and of North American Blacks also brought to the fore the human Jesus and his commitment to human liberation from the conditions of exploitation in the society of his day. The liberation theologies of the Americas did not, at this stage, question the deeper issues concerning Christian anthropology of original sin as defined by the Council of Trent, and the consequent need of redemption by Jesus Christ as the unique savior. They were concerned mainly with issues of class and race. For the Latin Americans, the principal evil was Western capitalism, while for North American Blacks, it was White racist domination. For both these groups, it was sufficient to affirm the socially liberative role of Jesus and his disciples. They made a valuable contribution to the understanding of the social dimension of Christian spirituality. They were engaged in the struggles of their people in Latin America, as in Nicaragua, and in the Civil Rights and Black Power movements in the United States. They did not have to go into the questions of the identity of Jesus in relation to God and hence as savior with reference to persons of other religions, as their environment, as then seen by them, did not demand such a reflection.

The churches have, at the world level, moved during the past two decades to engage themselves in issues of social liberation, as in the struggle against apartheid in South Africa. The World Council of Churches took significant steps in this direction. Yet even today some Christian fundamentalists, who claim to interpret the Bible authentically, propose a very narrow and socially conservative perspective of the salvific message of Jesus.

Feminist theologians, first from North America and later from Europe and the rest of the world, raised deeper questions from about the 1980s onward. They question the use of the Scriptures for marginalizing females in the economy of salvation. They reject the interpretation of the Genesis story of creation and the fall that presented woman as the seductress and the cause of the fall of humanity. The thesis concerning the divine inspiration of the Bible is questioned by showing how the male authors discriminate against females in writing the texts.

Some feminist theologians raise questions as to the nature of the salvific role of Jesus. They posit this function is not due to his biological nature as masculine in gender or his metaphysical reality as the Son of God, but his liberative actions and in the witness of his life for the values of the kingdom of God. Feminists thus go further than other Western liberation theologians in asking questions concerning the human predicament of original sin, the nature of the salvation in Jesus, and even the personality of Jesus Christ as the unique Son of God. Some even ask whether a male Jesus can be a savior of women.

EARLY CHURCH CONTACT WITH ASIA

Before Western Europe was Christianized, Christianity advanced eastward to Asia Minor. Christians were in communication with the Asian schools of thought in the early centuries. Christian thinkers had contact with India and even China, since the routes of communication were open between what is now known as the Middle East and the Far East.

Thus we find that the early church fathers had an opening toward the other Asian religions. Strict exclusive dogmas were not evolved and defined until the fourth century, when Christianity became the religion of the Roman Empire. In the early writings there is no idea of a state of universal human sin as taught in the later doctrine of original sin. Baptism was delayed until late in life. There was no generally accepted concept of atonement by Jesus for such an original sin of humankind. Thus Ignatius of Antioch, writing in the first decades of the second century, "offers no doctrine of atonement. Yet he does have some interesting statements with a soteriological bearing. He refers twice to the blood of Christ (or God), although it should be observed that what he has in view here is subjective response rather than objective achievement."[2]

The divinity of Jesus was not thought of as so exclusive as to prevent other divine manifestations in different times and places. Justin Martyr (100/110-163/167 CE) is keen to prove that Jesus is the one who fulfills the promises and expectations of the Jews from the Old Testament. Jesus is "a God and Lord other than, and less than, the Maker of the universe, who is also called Angel (or Messenger), because he announces, to men whatever the maker of the universe, above whom there is no other God, desires to announce to them."[3] Justin teaches that although the Logos appeared in his fullness only in Christ, "a seed of the Logos" was scattered among the whole of mankind long before Christ. Thus not only the prophets of the Old Testament, but even the pagan philosophers carried a germinating seed of the Logos in their souls, as for instance Heraclitus, Socrates, and the Stoic philosopher Musonious, who lived according to the directions of the Logos, the Divine Word. In fact, they were truly Christians, even though they have been thought atheists.[4]

Clement of Alexandria (c. 150-211/216 CE), a native of Athens who traveled widely in Italy, Syria, and Palestine, knew well the traditions of the various schools of Asia Minor. In his teaching mission, Clement was deeply interested in the search among the philosophers. He was a pioneer in the understanding of the relationship between philosophy and Christianity, of reason and faith. The important official School of Alexandria was influenced by his approach. He too emphasized the term *Logos*. For Clement, all personal manifestations of the Father take place through the Logos. "It is through the Word who proceeds from him that the unknown can be known. . . . The authentic guides of mankind are the ancient philosophers who, truly inspired by God, acted upon by the Logos, have taught the nations divine truth" (*Strom.*, V.12).[5]

Clement mentions along with others: "The Indian gymnosophists, and other non-Greek philosophers, of whom there are two classes, the Sarmanae and the Brahmanas. . . . Some, too, of the Indians obey the precepts of Buddha" (*Strom.*, I.15). This amounts to affirming in so many words, together with the presence of the partial Christian truth in Hindu religion, its positive significance in the history of salvation.[6] Jacques Dupuis quotes Augustine's *Retractiones* I.13.3 in the same direction:

> The very thing which is called the Christian religion existed among the ancients, nor was it absent from the beginning of the human race, until the coming of Christ in the flesh, when the true religion which had already existed began to be called Christian. Therefore, if I have written: "this is the religion which exists in our days, the Christian religion" the meaning is not that it had not existed previously, but that it took the name Christian only later.[7]

The different formulations concerning the Trinity and the nature of the relationship of the human and divine in Jesus show how complex the issues were. Jesus, as reported in the scriptures, was not at all clear on these intricate philosophical and theological issues. The New Testament is capable of different interpretations, as these centuries of debate indicate. The debates were concerning the Trinity (the origin and interrelations of persons within the Trinity; their generation, procession, or eternal begetting) and Christology (how Jesus is God and human, or Word and flesh; the body-soul relationship in Jesus; his intellect and will). To these and many more subtle and indeed truly mysterious questions, the church Councils from the fourth century onward evolved responses based on the scriptures, the prevailing philosophies, anthropology, theological reflection, authority patterns, and popular religiosity. These became part and parcel of the accepted faith of Christians. They were enshrined in the liturgy and recited by the faithful regularly every Sunday throughout the Christian world, and, until recently, in the Catholic Church in mysterious Latin.

IF THE DIALOGUE WITH ASIAN
RELIGIONS REMAINED OPEN

For many centuries Western European theology remained closed to the other religions and to the Asian realities of culture and social forces such as population and land. Christian theology at least implicitly legitimized colonial exploitation and benefited from it during four and one-half centuries, from 1492/1498 until the end of colonialism after World War II. There was no serious respect for the Asian religions and other realities that could generate a meaningful dialogue of Christianity with them.

The issues on which other perceptions have been excluded or on which religious wars have been waged by Christians are of later origin than Jesus Christ or the early church. In that sense we can claim that the genuine early Christian tradition was much more open, inclusive, and tolerant than what became orthodoxy from the fourth century (after the Councils of Nicaea in 325 and Chalcedon in 451). We advocate a recognition of that tradition and a re-rooting of Christian theology in such an open theology.[8]

The theological issues that arise for Christianity in the Asian—and to some extent African—contexts are related to our multireligious societies. This position is now being realized in many other parts of the world also, e.g., among North American Indian tribes or nations, the tribal and indigenous peoples in many parts of the world, and even in Western countries in which Islam and other religions are often more numerous and active than many Christian denominations.

If Christian theology had been elaborated in terms of the philosophies of other people, as of Arabia, India, or China, the belief of the followers of Jesus would have been expressed differently, perhaps in a more tolerant and open manner. There would have been other ways of understanding the manifestations of the divine as theophanies or *avatars*, and other searches for expressing the relationship between God and the universe. Different expressions of the relationships within the divinity, such as the *trimurthi* of Hinduism, would have been possible. Other soteriologies closer to the perceptions of Origen with an optimistic view of universal salvation through processes of purification would have been possible, as would have different understandings of the problem of evil, of suffering, and of enlightenment such as are found in Buddhism.

RETHINKING GOD FROM THE SOUTH ASIAN CONTEXT

These questions are all the more intriguing as in the Asian (especially Indian) context, God is thought of as ineffable, beyond all and within all, transcendent and immanent. God is the Absolute, the ultimate ground of being, creator, sustainer, the alpha and omega of all things, power, omnipresence, the inner core of being, goodness, truth, understanding, compassion, our hope, father and mother, provider, judge and rewarder, peace, beauty, bliss, and so on. In the Indian way of thinking, manifold ways of conceiving of the divine presence are not contradictory. The Indian mind-set is not built on the principles of contradiction of Western logic, but rather on the possibility of a harmony of apparent oppositions. Of course different cultures and religious traditions emphasize different aspects of the divine. In what follows we will provide a few references from the Hindu and Buddhist traditions that indicate the religious background which Christianity has to appreciate to be in genuine, respectful dialogue with our peoples in South Asia.[9]

Hinduism

Hinduism emphasizes concepts of the Absolute as Supreme Being and Cosmic Energy (*Shakthi*). The Absolute is creator, destroyer and preserver; knowledge, consciousness, and bliss (*sat-chit-ananda*); immanence in all, God within us (*Brahman*).

Indian philosophers and poets such as the Bengali Rabindranath Tagore have insightful and beautiful reflections on God. These can relate to or complement the revelation in the Bible. In *Gitanjali*, Tagore writes touchingly and meaningfully for us, linking poetry and religion, the Absolute and the common soil, the grass and the beggars on the road—to be hummed and sung by common people, the carters, fisher people at sea. God is presented as eternity touching our daily chores of living, engaged and detached, peaceful and inspiring.

> IV. Life of my life, I shall ever try to keep my body pure, knowing that thy living touch is upon all my limbs.
> V. I ask for a moment's indulgence to sit by thy side.
> XI. Leave this chanting and singing and telling of beads! Whom dost thou worship in this dark corner of a temple with all doors shut? Open thy eyes and see thy God is not before thee.
> He is there where the tiller is tilling the hard ground and where the pathmaker is breaking stones.
> He is with them in sun and in shower and his garment is covered with dust. Put off thy holy mantle and even like him come down on the dusty soil.
> 45. Have you not heard his silent steps, he comes, comes, ever comes.

This is a God Asians knew before the Christian tradition, and even in spite of some of the elements of the Christian tradition.

Theravada Buddhism

Buddhist doctrine, as we know it in Sri Lanka, does not claim to know the nature of the divine, of the existence of God, nor of the origins of the universe. Buddhism does not set up an infallible body of doctrine or an infallible teaching authority. The Buddha does not have a concept of divine revelation to humankind. Humans must discover the truth concerning human life. The Buddhist environment is therefore one of a certain silence concerning things which are beyond this world, or even about a soul that is immortal (*anatta*). What we know is impermanence and suffering, expressed through the concepts of *anicca*, *dukka*, and *anatta*.

Buddhism does not teach of a God known to humankind and involved in the process of human salvation. As the Venerable Walpola Rahula writes, "Man's position, according to Buddhism, is supreme. Man is his own master, and there is no higher being or power that sits in judgment over his destiny."[10] Salvation is thus to be self-effected, or auto-salvation (hence the importance of self-reliance in Buddhism). Purity and defilement depend on oneself. There is no need of assistance or grace from an outside being for human action and self-purification; no need of an external redeemer, especially of a divine being above the human level (*ananna sarana bhava*). There is a tendency to rely on one's self for salvation that is realized through knowledge (*gnosis*). The *gnosis* that is salvific leads in turn to concern for others, including nature.

Buddhism points a path (*magga*) to liberation (*nirvana*) from suffering (*dukka*) by detachment from craving (*thanha*). It is a school of spiritual growth through enlightenment, achieved by meditation and self-purification. Correspondingly, Buddhism insists on mental and personal purification by meditation. Mind is very important; thought leads to personal transformation. Worship is meditation on the transitoriness (*anicca*), the substancelessness (*anatta*), and the unsatisfactoriness (*dukka*) of existence. As the Ven. Narada Thera explains:

> According to the teaching of the Buddha anybody can aspire to that supreme state of perfection if he makes the necessary exertion. The Buddha does not condemn men by calling them wretched sinners, but, on the contrary, He gladdens them by saying that they are pure in heart at conception. In His opinion the world is not wicked but is deluded by ignorance. Instead of disheartening His followers and reserving the exalted state only to Himself He encourages and induces them to emulate Him, for Buddhahood is latent in all. In one sense all are potential Buddhas.[11]

Buddhism advocates *metta, karuna* (lovingkindness, compassion) toward all beings as the path to our liberation and social harmony. The Noble Eightfold Path is the Buddhist way of life. Buddhism's critical reflections on the claims of theist religions can help us in our evaluation of our own faith and its theological expression. A religion of *metta, karuna* is very close to a mystical union with the Transcendent—without necessarily saying so. This is implied in the Johannine saying "God is love and love is divine." There is no concept of prayer as such to a supreme divine being. The Buddha is honored as one who achieved liberation and shows the path, rather than as superhuman, eternally existent being. Mere external ritual that is effective by the very fact of its being performed (*ex opere operato*) would therefore be suspect in the Buddha's perspective.

Many of the conflicts in social life and in interreligious relationships have been due to the consequences of Christian teachings and the corresponding pastoral practices of the churches. Christian intolerance of other religions has often been based on its dogmas. It is the interpretation of the divinity of Jesus as exclusive and unique, and of Jesus as being the only son of God and the necessary, universal savior, that brought about the opposition and intolerance. Yet there is a much greater closeness in the ethical teachings of the Buddha and Jesus, the founding teachers of the two religions, than is often acknowledged. These two great spiritual leaders would have been able to accept each other. As the Sri Lankan theologian Aloysius Pieris points out: "The only meeting point of the gnostic and agapeic models of spirituality is the belief that voluntary poverty constitutes a salvific experience. Hence Jesus, as God's own kenosis and as proof and sign of God's eternal enmity with mammon, is an endorsement of the Buddhist ascesis of renunciation."[12]

Buddhist and Christian groups are actually coming together in interreligious fellowship on the basis of common action for human values in the face of the advancing dehumanization brought about by the liberal neocolonialism of these days. Such fellowship and common action are promising signs of a new era of Christian action and theology in Asia. Drawing upon the insights and challenges of Hinduism and Buddhism, Christian theology can begin to rethink the very question of God in this context.

FOR A CHRISTIAN RETHINKING OF GOD

The Abrahamic religions (Judaism, Christianity, and Islam) all stress the transcendence of God, and in this respect they are keen to safeguard monotheism. Jesus presents the transcendent God as love, One whom he called *Abba* or Father. His concern is with the realization of the kingdom of God on earth, which is the conversion Jesus wants.

Let God Be God

Any Christian rethinking must respect the ineffable mystery of God. The human mind cannot comprehend God, the infinite. We cannot fully understand even ourselves or another human person. The Absolute cannot be contained in, or confined to, our theological discourse and definitions. Human understanding, words, and language are limited in their capacity to grasp and communicate divine reality or thought.

It is a deep intuition of the Asian religions and philosophies that the Transcendent God is absolutely beyond human comprehension and cannot be contained in our formulations of theology or philosophy. This perception is very important for our search for the Truth and for meaning in our lives. It can help in the promotion of understanding and dialogue among the religions and ideologies. Christianity erred much in the past by thinking of itself as especially privileged by God, and even persecuting other religions. We must be very careful not to use notions of God, revelation, or redemption in a way that is advantageous to one group against others. We can try to improve our understanding and presentation of God by a return to the teaching and life of Jesus as presented in the Gospel narratives.

The Teaching of Jesus Concerning God: God Is Love

Jesus presented a vision of God as a father who is compassionate, forgiving, just, and caring. A central teaching of Jesus was that God is love. He had a loving trust in the father, or *abba* (papa), as he called him. Jesus claimed that God loves us, understands us, and fulfills us. In return we must love God and all human beings in God. "I give you a new commandment: love one another . . . " said Jesus (Jn 13:34). This is the substance of his message, of the law and the prophets. The specificity of the disciples of Jesus has to be such love in interpersonal and societal relationships. Love gives glory to God and fulfills human persons.

Jesus was God centered. He was not Jesus centered, Christ centered, or church centered. His point of reference and worship was always God. This in turn was intimately linked to a human centeredness. With this central theme Jesus introduced a new understanding of the human person and social institutions. Every human being is important and has to be cared for. This is the criterion for admission to the Kingdom: "I was hungry, and you gave me to eat. . . . Enter into the Kingdom" (Mt 25). Jesus preached a new view of life as the fulfillment of the revelation to the Jews. Where there is genuine love, there is God; where there is no real love, God is not there, whatever one's religious affiliation or form of religious worship.

Jesus spoke of God as bringing about the Kingdom of God of right relationships, in which sin, lovelessness, selfishness, untruth, and injustice are overcome and love, mercy, truth, and justice prevail. It is in *right relationships* between persons, among groups, and to nature that sin is overcome. In this respect God can be considered the source and inspiration for all human relationships. As Mary Grey points out:

> if relationality is a basic category of existence, then it is also the basic dynamism of the divine nature, since all creation participates in the being of God. Christianity has tried to express this through the doctrine of the Trinity—a God in relationship. . . . So God must be the divine ground, the limitless creative source of relationality. Could it not be that creating forms of deeper mutuality within society is also redemptive. . . . If broken mutuality and broken relation underlie all injustices, it is there that the redemptive task must begin.[13]

Jesus taught this in the prayer that states "Our Father . . . Thy Kingdom come, thy will be done on earth as in heaven. Give us this day our daily bread, and forgive us our trespasses as we forgive those who trespass against us." Sharing of food is of the essence of the kingdom. Mercy and forgiveness are primordial conditions of the Reign of God over us. Jesus conditions God's mercy on our forgiveness of others. With an unforgiving hatred of others, we cannot be friends of God, for God loves all. Hence Jesus worked for relationships in which mercy and love would be predominant.

Jesus emphasized the Kingdom or Rule of God and righteousness over us, rather than the rule by any earthly power or organization. The Kingdom of God is primarily within us. He did not stress the power of the religious authority or a church. His mission and gospel were concerning the values of the Kingdom rather than the growth of a religious institution. He began a movement of human understanding, love, and sharing, not a mere organization.

The community he gathered around him was to live the values of this divine dominion. This is a very fruitful perspective now, as humanity is looking for more universal values for human understanding. The kingdom of God is also a criterion for evaluating particular historical churches. His kingdom means that the plan of God for humankind is to be fulfilled in a radically profound way, here on earth. It is a reversal of the usual conditions of society.

—The poor become rich (Lk 6:20)
—The first are last (Mk 10:31)
—The small become great (Mt 18:4)
—Those who lose their lives find it (Mt 23, Lk 4)
—The hungry are filled, the weary find rest
—Those who weep laugh, the mourners are comforted
—The sick are healed, the lame walk,
—The humble inherit the earth, the lowly are exalted
—The blind see, the deaf hear
—The prisoners are freed, the oppressed are liberated
—And the dead live.

These are the strange promises of Jesus to be partly realized in this life by persons and by humanity over the ages. We can discern them through faith and contribute to them by struggling in hope. Love is their fulfillment, joy their fruit. To live the values of this spiritual mastery over our lives is to realize a new power, a joy and a peace that surpass all other joys. It is a pure, selfless, active, creative, and liberating joy. This is the joy of the wedding feast to which liberated humankind is invited. It is for us to respond willingly by a conversion of heart, a reversal of values, and a fundamental option for life—to live in solidarity, friendship, and effective sharing in love. Then heaven would have begun for us here on earth. This is redemption, salvation, liberation, and human fulfillment. Jesus died testifying to this.

The experience of the early church epitomized in Acts 10 and 11 shows that what is important for God, and hence for the early Christians, was that Cornelius was God-fearing and did good. It is the person's deeds that counted, rather than his birth or the letter of the Jewish law. This was a clear indication against the idea of a chosen people whom God favored. It is a smashing of our preconceived ideas of sacred and profane, pure and impure, and good and bad. "All our pre-conceived ideas seem to be shattered. The Holy Spirit is always unpredictable; the least expected thing was that the Holy Spirit should dwell in all those uncircumcised Gentiles, and even more, should command Peter to transgress the Torah."[14] We cannot know what God's relationship is toward another, Panikkar argues.

Nobody knows before hand what God wants, thinks, does or is. If we behave as if we had some criterion regarding the Ultimate Reality which we here call God, we are assigning to ourselves a role which is higher than God's. Then God is not free. He has to submit to what we think He is, and what we expect Him to do because He has always done it so, or He has promised to do it so: *a Deus ex machina*. This, however, is what the text disproves. We have no criterion whatsoever, when we utter the name of God, by which we may say what this God is, thinks or wills—how He is going to act or what He is going to do.[15]

This experience was a primordial event for the early church. It meant a new experience of spiritual community. It clarified what Jesus had been teaching through his parables and the experience of his life. It meant a conversion of the apostles in the sense of transcending their mental beliefs and attitudes. It is noteworthy that, in this story, it is the apostles who needed conversion rather than Cornelius. The church had to be a learning church, with the Spirit guiding them through the experience of being in the world. Sacramental theology can also reach very significant conclusions from this episode. It shows that the *res sacramenti*, the reality of conversion or right relations implied in the sacraments, is far more important than the external ritual that should symbolize the reality.

Though the disciples of Jesus learned this very early, yet it is a lesson they have to learn in an ongoing manner. The claim to limit God's favors to one's religion is what I have called religionism in an early book.[16] Like sexism and racism, religionism is when one religion considers itself superior to others, and that it alone has the key to salvation or has a privileged path to it. Such perceptions are not reconcilable with an all-loving God. A just and perfect God would provide for each person and culture all that is required for the spiritual fulfillment of each one. God would not treat some as stepchildren! We must see that our interpretations of doctrine or the Bible do not render God unjust toward some others. Thus the Bible does not limit God to the Bible; it is our interpretation that tries to do so. We would be exercising power over God if we presumed to prevent God from speaking to other peoples and religious groups. Even all the religions together cannot limit God from self-revelation in any form God desires.

GOD AND GLOBAL JUSTICE

The development of rapid, instantaneous, worldwide communications through computers, fax machines, and E-mail has made the contacts and injustices in and among the peoples of the world ever more intense. Hence also the need to reconsider our theology in the new world situation of globalization and capitalist domination almost everywhere.

A renewal of Christian theology with the Asian context in mind will have to consider that Asia and Africa have been given a raw deal by modern history, due to the carving out of the world system by the Western powers. Asians are more than half the human race. Africa is the poorest continent, and millions are prematurely dying. Some Asian countries are Newly Industrialized Countries (NICs), yet Asia still has the largest number of poor people who live below the margin of subsistence. Today the poor throughout the world are exploited by the same global forces, often in collusion with local elites, and using local rivalries of nationality, race, ethnicity, tribe, and religion.

Global Theology: One God, One Earth-Nature, One Humanity

The God of Jesus' revelation is the creator, lover, and provider of all humanity. See the birds of the air, the lilies in the field? All of us are of one common humanity, live on this limited planet earth, and come from the one God. *God is the God of life*. God alone has the right over life and death. God opposes the idolatries of absolutist rulers and false principals, such as the "free market," which leads to the death of so many through unnecessary starvation in a world of plenty. On the other hand, God alone is the fullness of life, and all who seek God find life (Am 5:4,6,14). All who seek righteousness find God in some way.

The redemption taught by Jesus shows us the path to deliverance from mammon and selfishness through commitment to others in self-giving love. He came that we may have life, and life more abundantly (Jn 10:10). Fullness of life is more than mere existence or mere duration. It includes also health, happiness, and community. Life is a participation of humans in the life of God in such a way that earthly life makes possible and prepares for eternal life (as Mt 25 indicates). Life for others on earth is the condition for eternal salvation. The realization of the kingdom of God is in righteousness, peace, and joy in the Holy Spirit (Rom 14:17). Eternal life is already present here (Eph 2:5f). We must live no longer to ourselves, but to God (Rom 14:7). This perception and value-of-life orientation is altogether different from the intolerant, classical Western European theological position, in which the right to life on earth could be limited by the openness to eternal life through membership in the church.

A Vision

The present, powerful world political system is unjustly structured. It was built by force, especially after the European invasions of the other continents since 1492. It is maintained by force, buttressed by a system of international law that has been developed within its parameters. The international economic system is an accompanying structure of global exploitation of the poor and of nature. This is mainly a male-dominated world order in which physical force is the ultimate determinant of issues. The present distribution of resources among human beings and nations is utterly inequitable.

From these realities and teachings flow several consequences in relation to a global theology. We are the first generation in humanity's long history that has the means to ensure to all an adequate means for a decent human life, and that almost in abundance. A just solution to the problems of the vast and harrowing global imbalances requires a just world order. This needs more than changes within individual countries.

Its objectives should be to insure that every human person has a right to life and should be ensured the basic essentials of life. Consequently each one has a right to the means of livelihood to be obtained from our common planet earth; that each society is able to provide the basic amenities, including educational and health services for the well-being and cultural development of its members; that our planet earth is cared for and is so treated that it would be a suitable home for present and future humanity.

From these objectives would follow the following points. In interhuman relations, there should be no discrimination against any persons or groups on account of gender, color, race, tribe, religion, or caste. Creation is more important than a Christian claim of a special role in salvation. God is concerned about all human persons from all time.

The resources of the earth should be shared equitably among all human beings, both present and future. We have to rethink God and human relationships to relate Christian theology to these challenges. The whole world (dis)order needs to be reshaped for world justice, including justice for Asia. The people without land have a right to the land without people. Asians have a right to a due share of the resources of the earth. Today the Asian peoples (especially the Chinese) have to restrict their families to one child due to their inability to move to any other lands. All the open spaces of the world have been occupied by the European peoples. They neither cultivate the land nor allow others to come into the areas occupied by them, except under racially discriminative immigration laws and practices. There is no free market for land as such.

Nature, God's handiwork, the substratum of all earthly existence, should be cared for by all, for the sake of all. To destroy nature is to destroy human life itself, as human life is possible only within a well-balanced natural environment. Hence human beings who, as intelligent and free persons, are the custodians of nature, should not exhaust or destroy the earth's natural resources, especially those which are nonrenewable. This implies an intergenerational contract by which each generation cares for itself and succeeding generations in the use of natural resources and the stewardship of nature. The dominant capitalist values and life-style of Westerners (now shared by many affluent Asians) uses up an unbearable amount of the earth's resources. They are the principal polluters of the earth and destroyers of nature. This life-style is neither replicable throughout the world nor long sustainable.

We must have a vision of alternative values, relationships, and structures at local, national, regional, and international levels. This vision needs to be articulated regarding specific areas such as transportation, housing, health, education, land use, and land distribution. Thus we can see the limits of the present system of private motor car transportation due to the limits of oil resources, pollution, and the unbearable and growing traffic jams in towns and cities. The need for alternative modes of transportation and care for nature belong together. Though we do not still see how the alternative society will emerge, and an immediate overall change in the whole structure may not be feasible, we can work toward realizing the vision, even in a piecemeal manner, joining other committed groups.

A revaluation of modern history will bring us to the right and needs of compensation of former colonized peoples for centuries of exploitation by the European peoples since 1492. This should lead at least to the cancellation of the present foreign debt of poor countries, which is an unjust and unbearable burden on them. This requires a mission from the poor countries to the rich peoples.

Strategies

Strategies of action for integral human liberation need to be developed. A common query is, What can we to do, given the immensity of the problems? Where can we begin? We seem so helpless and hopeless in this situation. We need to go beyond the position of powerlessness and try to discern the trends and the kinds of solutions that are necessary and feasible in the long term. We need to realize the power of the weak and the exploited of the world. That is a prophetic task and option.

Faith in Jesus is belief in his values, and hope is the confidence that the God of history will see to their realization in some measure on earth in our time. For us faith is belief in those values in relation to our situation, and trust that our lives will be meaningful in working in hope toward such objectives. Such a Christology can be a source of self-empowerment toward liberation for ourselves and for others. One of our theological strategies can be the development of the understanding of the Jesus mission and spirituality in building human community according to the values of the kingdom that Jesus proposed: love, sharing, justice, freedom, truth, and peace. The Cosmic Christ, the Logos universally present and active as in John and Paul's writings, can be understood as operative in the entire human history, leading it to its desired goal, even today. Combating the forces of personal and societal exploitation should be an essential element of Christian spirituality and the mission of the church.

The struggle against the forces of evil in each one and in the world requires a clear *analysis* of the forces that are operative in the world. There has to be an identification of the allies and enemies of human fulfillment, and consequently of God's plan for humanity. We need to evaluate reality carefully, with a consciousness of the impact on the poor and in consultation with expertise that is sympathetic to this cause. Mahatma Gandhi's principle of evaluation of situations and policies was: "How does it help the poorest of the poor?" Theology needs to follow the same principle today.

Today global problems need global responses. Asian-level problems need Asian remedies. A structural problem needs a structural response as well. We must realize the inadequacy of our past methods. We can learn from transnational human rights movements such as Amnesty International (AI), which have evolved global-level strategies in particular areas of concern by using modern means of communication—in the case of AI, challenging governments to respect human rights.

Transformation requires a struggle against all forms of discrimination and exploitation, particularly those of gender, race, ethnicity, color, tribe, caste, class, religion, and nationality. Each of these requires a transcending of one's natural group and its interests and identification with the wider human community and its interests. Developing consciousness and peoples' power across national frontiers is necessary. We need to begin with feasible objectives and felt needs of the oppressed.

An essential element of a strategy of liberation is the self-purification of groups in the process of the struggles, so that the different groups may understand each other and cooperate for the common good and for victory against the overall forces of domination. This is a challenge to each group—workers, women, Third World movements, religions, human rights groups, and apostolic movements in the church. Each group has to see that it is necessary to work toward global objectives while being concerned with one's own particular objectives.

Human beings, however, will not easily change substantially. Change is prevented by ignorance and attachment to one's self-interest, even when this is seen as harmful to others. We must be aware of the obstacles to such transformation. These are both internal to ourselves, our organizations, and our movements and external to them. Religious legitimations and other rationalizations may come between the somewhat-informed conscience and the effective goodwill of persons and groups. The social conditioning of the affluent prevents them from appreciating or seriously sympathizing with the plight of the poor in their countries, and especially in other countries. Hence the resistance to change, even among persons of apparent good will.

In an ideal situation, an equitable sharing of the earth's resources would be brought about peacefully by a common global authority. In any case, there seems to be no power today capable of violently overthrowing the world power of global capital and the trilateral alliance of the United States, Western Europe, and Japan. The first colonialism was successfully contested country by country, due to the conflicts among the colonizers themselves. Their colonial political domination collapsed after World War II. In today's neocolonialist situation, the exploiting forces are linked together globally and include the colluding local rulers and elites. The dominant political system will not permit the capitalist economic system to be violently overthrown in any significant country. Thus developing the spirituality and strategies of nonviolence is a major need at the present. Gandhian spirituality and methodologies of struggle show alternatives that may have at least limited success.

The liberation of the European and North American peoples is one of the most important and necessary, but difficult, tasks in this process of humanization of the world for furthering the values of the kingdom of God in the 1990s. They have set up the present world order, its legal and ideological legitimations, and its military defenses. The world system, led by the transnational corporations, today oppresses the poor among them also. The result is large-scale, long-term structural unemployment leading to much social unrest and the alienation of the poor and the weak from the system, in spite of the limited material social securities that it grants them.

The immense goodwill among ordinary Western Christians needs to be harnessed for the transformation of the world, especially of the so-called Christian countries. Such a conversion of Christians should be the highest priority of the churches. The mission in foreign countries undertaken by Europeans and Americans can serve as an eye- and heart-opener for the affluent Whites. They should not be satisfied with the traditional work of the missions—building the church overseas—or with social work in the poor countries. They can use their awareness of the exploitative system to generate consciousness and action in the seats of powers in their home countries. Hope for the poor in the poor countries depends in good measure on the contestation of the evils of the system from within the centers of power.

Third World elites are often partners of the rich countries in the exploitation of the poor. Many influential Christians in poor countries belong to this category. They seek their self-advantage to the detriment of the poor and of their countries. They too need conversion like the affluent Westerners.

Transformation of the Churches

Such radical transformation of the world order should be a primary objective of Christians and the churches. The goal should be for all humans to live peacefully and justly on this earth, sharing equitably its resources.

In this difficult situation we can reflect on the potential impact of the Christian groups in the world. The churches, at the present moment of human history, can be valuable multinational agencies of integral human liberation and of the care for nature. To do so they must awaken themselves effectively to this historic calling and join with others of good will in joint action for the common cause of each person and all humanity. The conversion of the nations to the core values of humanity and of the religions can be a prime task of the religious communities themselves (including the churches). From the Christian perspective of world history, this could be a way toward the recapitulation of all things in Christ, understood in a cosmic sense.

Christians are in most countries and cities of the world today. We have many "full-timers" who are well motivated to serve the people, though many may still lack the analysis of the global system. The churches have a major responsibility in educating their elite members not to be such exploiters of their own poor, a task which requires a re-education of the clergy and educators themselves. Very often the school systems of the poor countries convey the values of the affluent and exploitative society to the younger generation. Effective re-educational strategies are as necessary in the poor countries as they are among the affluent nations.

Pope John Paul II's apostolic letter on the Third Millennium, *Tertio Adveniente Millenio*, reminds Christians of our deficiencies during the second millennium, especially with the colonial expansion of Europe. He calls for continental Synods in preparation for the jubilee of the year 2000. The World Council of Churches has accepted the concept of jubilee, including reparation for 500 years of colonial exploitation, within its theme for the WCC General Assembly in Harare in 1998.

The development and acceptance of a global theology evolved on the basis indicated here could contribute toward a realization of this jubilee by bringing about a deeper conversion of Christians to God and the Jesus of the gospels. It can help to integrate the positive insights of the theory and practice of different movements such as feminism, secularism, democracy, human rights, modernity, socialism, the religions, pentecostalism, mysticism, popular religiosity, action groups, peoples' movements, cooperatives, co-dependency groups, and others, deepening them and assisting them in realizing their fullest dimensions.

Such a global theology will dramatically reshape the pastoral action of the churches. The life of the parishes, religious congregations, lay movements, and other church groups will consequently have to be rethought. Movements that neglect the social and global dimensions of the demands of the Spirit of God will have to be converted to God as revealed by Jesus. The sacraments must be related to redemption in real life on earth by right relations among persons and nations, and with nature and God.

A reorientation of Christian life and thinking in these directions will lead to conscious Christians contesting the dominant system of power in society at all levels, including in the churches themselves. This will mean that Christianity will become once again a counterculture, opposing the evils of the dominant killer system in the world and in the societies where Christians live. Martyrdom in different forms will be the lot of those who thus opt for the values of the gospel. Christians would then have returned full circle to the basic orientations of the early disciples of Jesus.

The God of history would thus purify theology of its traditional irrelevancies and motivate it to a commitment to present human exigencies. Christians would then be more humble servants of the human cause. They will be glad to suffer, where necessary, for the same causes for which Jesus and the martyrs of all ages, including ours, have given their lives. The cross will have a renewed practical meaning in our times. Christians will at the same time celebrate where truth, justice, love, and life prevail, and thus where the reign of righteousness is being built on earth.

Christian spirituality, meditation, and prayer should bring us to a deeper realization of God's concern for all, especially the poor and the weak. The closer we go to God, the greater will be our participation in the struggle for better relationships at all levels. The spirituality of the cross informs us that if we take such steps we will come under attack from the powers that be, just as Jesus had to face. But in the weakness of the cross is a transforming power. Seeing God in the poorest of the poor is a contemplative union with God leading to commitment to change these evil situations. Through such union we not only meet the God who is God, but we truly find our lives transformed.

NOTES

1. Aloysius Pieris, S.J., *An Asian Theology of Liberation* (Maryknoll: Orbis Books, 1988) and *Love Meets Wisdom: A Christian Experience of Buddhism* (Maryknoll, NY: Orbis Books, 1988).

2. Geoffrey W. Bromiley, *Historical Theology* (Edinburgh: T & T Clark, 1978), p. 5.

3. Justin Martyr, *The Dialogue with Trypho*, trans. A. L. Williams (London: SPCK, 1930), 11 (*Dialogue* 56.4).

4. Johannes Quasten, *Patrology*, vol. 1 (Maryland: Newman Press, 1950), 209 (*Apology* 1.46).

5. *See* Jacques Dupuis, *Jesus Christ and His Spirit: Theological Approaches* (Bangalore: Theological Publications in India, 1977), p. 15.

6. Ibid., p. 17.

7. Ibid., p. 19.

8. Cf. Tissa Balasuriya, *Right Relationships: De-Routeing and Re-Rooting of Christian Theology* (Colombo: Logos CSR, 1991), chapt. 3.

9. Islam also proposes challenges in Asia, from the perspective of a radical monotheism that calls into question the Christian presentation on the Trinity, the Incarnation, and redemption by Jesus Christ. The dialogue with Islam requires a clarification of the Christian teachings on all these issues. We can not go into these here, but rethinking in terms of the theology in the early church would be very helpful in this regard too.

10. Walpola Rahula, *What the Buddha Taught* (Bedford: Gordon Fraser, 1967), p. 1.

11. Narada Thera, *Buddhism in a Nutshell* (Colombo: Vajirarama, 1947), pp. 3-4.

12. Pieris, *Love Meets Wisdom*, pp. 86-7.

13. Mary Grey, *Redeeming the Dream: Feminism, Redemption and Christian Tradition* (London: SPCK, 1989), pp. 86-7. *See also* Isabel Carter Heyward, *The Redemption of God: A Theology of Mutual Relation* (Washington, DC: University Press of America, 1982).

14. Raimundo Panikkar, "Closeness and Universality: Can Christians Claim Both?" *Cross Currents* 38:3 (Fall 1988): 310.

15. Ibid., p. 312.

16. Tissa Balasuriya, *Planetary Theology* (Maryknoll, NY: Orbis Books, 1984), pp. 117-19.

3

Religion, Spirituality, and *Umunthu*

A Perspective from Malawi

AUGUSTINE C. MUSOPOLE

Responding to a suggestion I had made concerning the ancestors as being one of the theological issues that needed to be addressed with urgency in African Christian theology, my western Africanist theologian correspondent wrote, "In my opinion, the 'theological status of the ancestors' is better left as an open question that we are advised to leave in the hands of a gracious God, rather than spend time and ink building elaborate theological sand castles that lack any concrete Scriptural basis."

I was not surprised by the response, for it only confirmed to me how theological questions are culturally determined and what is significant in one cultural context may not be even an issue in another. To be concerned with the question of the ancestors may ultimately be an open question, like all theological questions are, but historically it cannot be an open question when preachers have declared that all those who have died without Christ are under sin and, therefore, are not saved.[1] Immediately it raises the question of the relationship of history and the gospel of salvation. To raise the question is not a matter of building theological sand castles when for many African Christians the matter touches on their past and way of being in the world. It is about what gives meaning to their existence, and to deprive them of that is to rob them of part of their existence.

As to concrete Scriptural basis, there is much in the Scriptures about ancestors. To Moses, the Hebrew God was "the God of our ancestors" (Ex 3:13), and yet John the Baptist turns around and says, "Do not presume to say to yourself, 'We have Abraham for our ancestor' ... " (Mt 3:9). Paul asserts that it is not those who are physically descended from Abraham who are children of Abraham, but rather those who are reckoned righteous on account of their faith, as Abraham was (Rom 4:1-12). There is something happening about ancestorhood in the Bible which might have some implication for African ancestors.

To Africans, the question of ancestors warrants serious theological inquiry because it is at the heart of who they are as persons and cultures. The call to conversion touches directly on this reality and relationship. To leave it as an open question is to leave one's identity, community, spirituality, and history as open questions. It is not to seek one's existential meaning and purpose. No, to us as Africans the question is very significant, indeed, and has to be dealt with if we are to avoid the problems of inappropriate religious syncretism and spiritual schizophrenia. These two problems have to do with the relationship between African religion and spirituality on the one hand, and Christian religion and spirituality on the other. Are the two so diametrically opposed that one has to be rejected in favor of the other, or is the reality of Jesus capable of unifying the two into a higher and richer synthesis by way of recapitulation? It is this relationship and the problems related to it that I intend to explore and critically examine in this chapter.

I am writing as an African and Christian theologian who is committed to doing theology within the cultural context of Malawi. Two elements are critical in my identity: the historico-cultural element and the Christian gospel element. The Christianity that I have received is Western in its ethos. I was raised on the small catechism and a spirituality based on a Scottish Presbyterianism and form of worship. My late father was a Presbyterian minister who seemed to have suppressed much of the traditional practices, because I never heard him say anything much about them. It seemed as if it were taboo to talk about things traditional.

As I was growing up, Christianity meant family prayers in the morning and evening, prayers at school at the beginning of classes, and prayers at church on Wednesdays and Sundays. It also meant going through Sunday school and church membership classes. It was a communal activity in which one got involved. There was nothing personal about it. I was never taught to pray on my own, even though when I was a bit older I could lead in prayers. One thing that seems to have made Christianity personal is when my father asked me to memorize the following scripture verse in English: "The Lord is my helper; I will not be afraid. What can man do to me?" (Heb 13:6). I do not seem to remember much of what I learned in Sunday school. Apart from certain rules relating to proper conduct, the Christianity that was being passed on to me seemed to have little to do with life as lived in the community. It was a matter of certain practices and learning by rote certain statements. That was also the way I felt about my western-type education. It was not until I was about eighteen that I encountered the living reality of Christ and the gospel at a national conference organized by the Student Christian Organization of Malawi. I was greatly helped in this by a testimony to the same reality of another student. I made a very deliberate decision to choose to attach my life to Jesus and make Christianity personal. Up until then, I had done Christian things as part of my upbringing and tradition. This time, it was my choosing. Gradually, I saw my life drastically transformed. Christianity was not simply a matter of being a member of a church, but it meant becoming a disciple of Jesus Christ and, in the light of this membership, became meaningful. The terms *savior* and *Lord* took on a very new and significant meaning for me. I was gripped by an inner joy and peace that I had not known before. My past life, as far as I could see, lay clearly before me and I was able to confess the many awful things that I find to have been disgusting to God and now to me. The Bible became alive to me, and I became alive to the Bible. I loved to read it, reflect on its message, and committed myself to living it out. It was exciting to be a Christian, and I loved it. I began to share my newfound life with others and maintained a vital relationship with God. I wrote to my parents, telling them that they had a new son. It is this transforming experience that led me to seek theological training and which now, among other things, informs the way I theologize.

One day in 1985, as I was walking to a prayer meeting at a friend's house, the question of the meaning of Jesus as savior and Lord to Malawians impressed itself on my mind with great force. I knew there and then that here was a theological issue that needed to be reflected upon. It is now apparent that it is a matter that is giving concern to many African theologians. However, to answer that question one has to deal with the Africanness of Malawians and their history on the one hand, and the reality of Jesus over and beyond, even apart from, western Christianity. To do this, there are many cultural, historical, religious, and intellectual problems to overcome. If this does not happen, Malawians are bound to continue suffering a disruption in their spirituality[2] by being strangers to Christianity as received and alienated from their African spirituality. The appropriation of western ways due to my education is insufficient to make me feel at home in western Christianity. I do not have the cultural content and, in many ways, western education has become a source of life contradictions and identity crisis. It is this experience of a "double consciousness" (cf. DuBois in the *Soul of the Black Folk*) or "double spirituality" that theologically makes the question of my Christian identity within my Africanness an urgent one. The issue at stake is how to be both African and Christian without suffering from a split consciousness or spirituality.

I intend to proceed in the following way in addressing this question. In the first section I will consider my African religio-cultural traditions and spirituality, and then move on in the second section to the advent of Christianity in Malawi. I will end in the third section by considering some theological approaches to resolving the problems arising from the encounter between my African spirituality and the Christian faith as it has been received.

MALAWIAN SPIRITUALITY

Misuku lies on the eastern section of Chitipa District in northern Malawi. It stands at about 5,500 feet above sea level. To its north is the Songwe River, which forms Malawi's northern boundary with Tanzania. The Misuku Area is divided into three major mountain ridges which run in the east-west direction. The middle ridge is slightly lower than the other two. The one to the east is the Mughese. It is covered with equatorial forests, and so is Wilindi ridge that lies to the west. The middle ridge, consisting of a chain of interlocking hills, is the most densely inhabited. On one of these hills called Misuku is the headquarters of Chief Mwenemisuku (meaning the Lord or owner of Misuku). About half a mile from Misuku is Mughoma, where one finds the religious shrine of Mwenemisuku, the territorial shrine of the people of Misuku. It is both a cemetery and a place of worship. There are two round houses that are used by the couple appointed as religious custodians. While the chief exercises political functions, it is the prerogative of the custodians to perform the religious functions for the chiefdom. When I last visited the shrine in December 1993, they had not as yet appointed a custodian since the death of the last one. The chief, who was attempting to extend his influence over the shrine, was told in no uncertain terms that he was stepping beyond the boundaries of his political jurisdiction. While the chief maintains communal peace, the custodian of the shrine is responsible for peace with the land and the ancestors.

It is the responsibility of the custodian of the shrine to perform from time to time certain ritual functions to ensure prosperity, happiness, and harmony in the land. Even though there is no daily community worship at the shrine, the custodian is duty bound to observe and perform rituals that are symbolically linked to certain messages and natural phenomena, and in so doing plays his or her part in maintaining cosmic harmony. For instance, the custodian's head always has to be covered with black cloth to preserve life, since a white or red cloth would invite thunderstorms and thus endanger life. He has the function of a Rain-caller, and as such he or she cannot shave her hair. A shaven head is like a deforested or desert land that cannot attract rain. The hair represents the forest, and the forests of Misuku are very significant in the life of the people, in attracting rain and preserving water. The custodian is the embodiment of mysterious power that he or she wields for the good of the community. There are a number of taboos that must be observed; for instance, not to acknowledge the calls of an approaching person, lest the powers invested in the custodian become of no effect. The shrine is near a forested area because it is thought that forests have mysterious powers. This belief has helped to preserve the equatorial forests. The few surviving at this height are of their only kind in the whole of Malawi.

Once in a while, a crisis of major proportion affects the chiefdom and disrupts the normal running of affairs. It might be an epidemic, drought, famine, frequent landslides during heavy rains, or too many deaths. The custodian summons the leading persons in the land to perform prayers for the land, offer sacrifices, and plead with the ancestors to intercede with God. During the prayer time, they pray that the bad air that is causing the problem should be blown away and new healthful air return. They call upon the ancestors and the spirits of the great mountains, great rivers, and great forests, and the great spirits of the land to aid in the cleansing of polluted air, to reestablish good life, and to restore health and harmonious living again. Two words describe what happens. The word *ukwiputa*, meaning to blow-clean oneself, describes the whole ceremony of worship. This word has been retained within Christianity to describe the same activity. The other word is *shighuluke*, meaning let the bad winds, illnesses, or deaths be blown away. It is a term that comes from the threshing floor where chaff is separated from the grain. The term is used as the congregational response to the petitions made by the shrine custodian during worship. The sacrifices include an animal, flour, seed, and beer, which have been brought from every village in the land. The people's expectations are that God and the ancestors will intervene and bless (*ukusaya*) the community with abundant life again.

The theology behind the religious traditions and spirituality of Misuku revolves around cosmic relationality of a hierarchy of beings and life-power. *Kyala* (God) is acknowledged as the most high being (*Ndungumale*), creator (*umupeli*), the source of all life and sustainer of the whole universe. Then comes the sphere of *abashuka* (literally, the resurrected ones, the ancestors), the leading men and women in their own time who headed their clans, lived noble lives, were leaders and mothers of the people, and lived exemplary lives. Since they cared for their people well by being generous, courageous, and fecund, they are thought to continue to be so predisposed toward the living in their spiritual existence. It is the ancestors who mediate between the living and God, since they are spirits, as God is spirit. While the ancestors are buried in the *masheto* (spirit ground, that is, graveyard) and are said to be sleeping there, they are not limited in their spiritual existence to that spot or area, but rather are free to move around. The term *masheto* comes from the verb *kushetuka* and the noun *umushetu*, that is, having the character of a shadow or an apparition. It applies to situations where something appears as fast as it disappears, without leaving a trace. This is how the nature of spirits is conceived.

The beliefs about the ancestors are clearly seen in the way mortuary rituals are carried out. The common expression to describe one who has just died is *alekani*, meaning that a person has sundered apart or a separation has taken place. It is thought that the body is only a dwelling place for the spirit/breath (*mwoyo*) that animates it, and it remains alive as long as the spirit/breath is in it or as long as the body is able to maintain the spirit/breath. When it can no longer maintain the spirit/breath, the spirit/breath separates and must return to where the clan had its historical origin, to join other spirits. The other word describing when death has occurred is *atuleka*, meaning the person has left us, and it connotes the spiritual journey that the spirit of the dead person has to make to the ancestral home. For the people of Misuku, death does not spell the end of existence. It may be the end of historical existence, but not of spiritual existence. Stories abound of people near death seeing those who are already dead either welcoming them or telling them to return and attend first to some family business.

The grave is constructed with a side chamber called *ifungu* (bedroom) and the grave itself is often referred to as *inyumba* (house). The body is laid in the side chamber with the face turned toward the direction of the person's ancestral origin, and then the chamber is sealed before the grave is filled with dirt. In the olden days, they would bury the dead with utensils and food for use on the journey to the ancestral home, which was often deemed to be a long journey. It was like retracing all the past years of several generations of one's clan's existence. One often hears people bid their farewells and send greetings to those who have already died through the person they are burying. I do remember attending a funeral where, as the body was being laid into the chamber, one called out that the head of the deceased was not lying comfortably, having noticed that it was bent to one side at the neck. It was as if the dead person was going to strain his neck lying in that position. Those taking care of the body responded by making sure the neck was straightened.

When a person dies from a dreaded disease, rituals take place to prevent the spirit of the dead person from acting out its suffering and bitterness on the living or the living suffering from what has killed the person. Usually some medication is provided that all who have touched the body have to take or use to purify themselves. The medication also acts as an inoculation against the disease. In the past, the death of a chief was accompanied by militaristic dancing as a way of mourning, paying respects, and a send-off ritual of defying death as an existential disruption of family and relationships. Among the Tumbuka and the Chewa of Malawi, the corpse is referred to as "chief" and is respected as such. In all cases, it is to the ancestors, remembered or not, that the living relate in their daily living through ritual practices, observations of taboos, and verbal expressions. Oaths are made to the ancestors, or they are called upon to be witnesses to the making of oaths. Therefore, the ancestors are very central to the life of the Sukwa/Ndali people of Misuku.

It was said earlier that in their prayers they call upon the mountains, the rivers, the forests, among other things, to help respond to their needs. A strong bond exists between the people and the land they occupy. They recognize the fact that the land and its major features have a power and resources they have no control over. They therefore acknowledge a mutuality of existence and make a pact of cooperation that no one be harmed by the activities of the other. It is from the land that their food grows; it is in the land that they bury their dead. From the forest they get their firewood, water, building materials, and it is the forests that attract the rain. It is on the mountains that they have established themselves, and mountains are known to undergo landslides from time to time. They live in awe of mystery and power as perceived in the world of nature. They believe that through ritual activity and maintaining harmonious relationships they are able to realize prosperity, health, and happiness, while at the same time preventing disasters from taking place repeatedly. Hence the greeting is *mwaghona, mwaghona ifiwaya*, meaning literally, have you slept and survived from epidemics? People sleep in order to rest or because they are sick. Otherwise they are up and about their various tasks. Sleeping well is a sign of wellness, of abundant life, of involvement in the community of the living. The word *ifiwaya* has connotations of that which leaves one at a loss, desperate, and when guns were introduced, the machine gun was named "ichiwaya," that which kills like an epidemic and overwhelms the victim. So while they sought abundant life, more often than not, survival was the least they could expect in a precarious world.

The individual's role in this cosmic network of relationships is tied to his or her bondedness to the community as a whole. While individuality is encouraged, individualism is scorned, resisted, and even punished through social sanctions, if not by outright ostracism. The individual is understood only in the context of the community, to which he or she is taught to develop a very special feeling through various communal activities. While the individual feels he or she owns the community, the community also feels it owns the individual. There is a mutuality of relationship and commitment. The youth start learning this aspect of their lives from a very early age in their families, but also in the way they see families rallying to each other's aid in home building, gardening, harvesting, sickness, funerals, social activities, cooking, and in the exchange of gifts that takes place the whole year round. Community is a way of life, and programs only supplement it; they do not make it. Community is people caring about each other, not participation in programs. Community happens where there is commitment to other people as members of a community. For the people of Misuku and all Malawians, programs are a creation of a community, but they do not create community. Young people are introduced to this commitment at an early age. The Sukwa/Ndali peoples of Misuku do not have rites of puberty, and so learning from other people how to function in a community is critical for both the young people and their parents. Inappropriate behavior is a bad reflection on the parents, a sign of failure in parenting.

What creates community is *ubundu* (humanness/personhood). The word *ubundu* has its variants in the other languages of Malawi, for instance, *bunthu* in Tumbuka, *umunthu* in Chichewa. It is this that is inculcated in the life of every child. What is the understanding of *ubundu*? There are generally two aspects to it, a moral integrity aspect and an economic productivity aspect. Essentially it has to do with the content of one's character. While the form of the human as a biped *homo erectus* is significant, especially the face, it is inadequate for the quality of *ubundu*. To have the form is to be potentially *mundu* (human/person). To have *ubundu*, one has to combine the two aspects mentioned above by wisdom (*amahala*), wisdom being understood as the choosing of right means for right ends. To simply excel in one aspect would not do. To severely lack any one of the two is to verge on becoming a beast with a human face (*chinyamana*). To lead a life that lacks moral integrity is to reduce oneself to the level of animals, and to be economically unproductive is to feed on the life blood of other people, just as a witch does. It is to be antisocial and antihuman. Character is the index for determining whether one is maintaining and growing toward full and authentic *ubundu*. One's activities are the measure by which character is assessed, and consequently one's *ubundu*. Therefore, *ubundu* is the organizing principle of one's character, community, religiosity, and spirituality—in short, one's life (*ubumi*)—and life the organizing principle of one's existence. To grow toward what is authentically human is to move in the direction of God's purpose and will as manifested in Jesus, the Christ, who had *ubundu* in full.

The theology of the Sukwa/Ndali people of Misuku is based on the actual practice of living aimed at aiding all other lives within the cosmic community and maintaining its harmony. Critical attention is given to how the community lives out its collective and individual life in order to maintain the cosmic relationships and harmony, especially through the maintenance and growth of *ubundu*. While God is acknowledged as creator, the theological focus is on life-in-community-and-communion which is the relationships of all things under God. Therefore, everything is endowed with some unique existential power for its own life and security, but also for the life and security of other elements in the cosmos. It is to this religiosity, spirituality, and theological orientation that the gospel of Jesus Christ was proclaimed. What was the encounter like? Let us look at the advent of Christianity before answering this question.

THE ADVENT OF CHRISTIANITY

Malawi's initial contacts with western Christianity are unknown, but it is probable that the first contacts with the Portuguese in the seventeenth century involved some form of Christianity. Alpers has observed,

The intrusion of the Portuguese into the Indian Ocean after 1498 signalled the beginning of a new era throughout the East. The reasons for their presence there are well
known and are grouped under the contrasting symbols of God and Mammon. Actually, both Portuguese economic expansion and Portuguese missionary activities overseas were but different aspects of the same imperial drive which was and remains one
of the hall marks of western capitalism.[3]

The Portuguese established several trading posts along the Zambezi River, into
which flows the Shire that connects it to Lake Malawi to the north. At one of these
stations, Sena, a seminary was established for the education of Portuguese children
and those of the local chiefs. This seminary did not last long and had very little
impact on the surrounding areas. However, there is evidence that some elements of
Christianity found their way into the interior in the area now under Malawi. One of
these elements was a song in praise of Mary used by fishers as a work song.[4] H. L.
Duff, who arrived in Malawi in 1898, reported that the Tonga mentioned a Jesuit
priest as the source of this song. The other element was the adaptation of the Christ
story to M'bona, the territorial guardian spirit of the Mang'anja people of southern
Malawi. Before the start of any western missionary work among the Mang'anja,
M'bona was described as the black Jesus, Son of God. This adaptation is not an isolated event. The Nyau secret societies have figures resembling a Portuguese cavalry
horse, and many words of Portuguese origin have become part of the vocabulary of
Chichewa, the national language. This indicates that the people of Malawi were
open to foreign religious practices.

The early Portuguese attempts at evangelization in this part of the world failed
to materialize. It was not until 1861 that a missionary team of the Universities Mission to Central Africa, under the leadership of Bishop Mackezie, arrived and established a mission station at Magomero, in southern Malawi, and the evangelization
of the country began in earnest. However, even this attempt was not to be. Within
five years, due to the early death of some members and the hostility of the Arab
slavers and their African cohorts, the mission was abandoned, only to return almost
thirty years later. In 1875, a mission of the Free Church of Scotland called Livingstonia Mission arrived to start missionary work in response to and in honor of
David Livingstone (hence the name Livingstonia Mission). It was followed a year
later by another mission of the United Church of Scotland called Blantyre Mission.
While these two missions resulted from the death of David Livingstone in 1873, they
started within a year or so of the Berlin Conference that partitioned Africa among
European countries. Imperialism and colonialism came immediately at the heels of
missionary activity, making both mixed blessings, as far as the African people of
Malawi were concerned.

Christianity did not come into a religious vacuum, but to a people whose very
way of life was their religion and their universe a religious universe. Even though
the intensity of this religiosity and its institutions varied from people to people, all
of them shared a worldview that had much in common, especially in its major features. Although John Mbiti's statement to this effect has been quoted *ad nauseum*,
it has to be repeated. Mbiti stated, "Africans are notoriously religious. Religion per-
meates into all the departments of life so fully that it is not easy or possible always

to isolate it. A study of these religious systems is, therefore, ultimately a study of the peoples themselves in all the complexities of both traditional and modern life."[5]

African religious sensibilities are to an African culture what the nervous system is to the body, and it is only as a living phenomenon that it can be properly studied. It is to this religious world that Christianity came, supposedly to be a light of salvation to the Malawian peoples. The missionaries' perception was probably greatly informed by the perception of the prophet Isaiah because, like him, they had responded to the call of God by saying, "Here I am, send Me." But unlike Isaiah, they may not have confessed their own personal sin and those of their race, nor do they seem to have seen God's own glory, otherwise the glory might not have been so much focused on European enlightenment.[6] Like Isaiah, they had seen the people of Malawi as an anguished people walking in darkness.[7] Furthermore, they saw themselves as having the spirit of God upon them to proclaim the good news to the oppressed.[8] The radical monotheism of Isaiah, which saw other religious expressions as idolatrous, informed their theology, and they were ready to tolerate no compromises. On top of all this was added the cultural arrogance that was used as the standard for defining other people's humanity.

In 1881 Livingstonia Mission moved from Cape Maclear, near the end of the lake, where it had established itself, to Bandawe in the north. In 1894, the headquarters were moved again, to Khondowe plateau, where the famous Overtoun Institution was established under the visionary leadership of the Rev. Dr. Robert Laws. By this time, Livingstonia Mission had already established several stations from which the gospel of Jesus Christ spread to various areas through its educational, medical, and technical training and the evangelistic endeavors of Malawian converts. One station was established in 1882 close to Misuku Hills at Ncherenje under Dr. David Kerr-Cross. For various reasons, the mission was abandoned.[9] However, missionary outreach continued, and the first school to be established in Misuku was Mughofi in 1903. It was established by Malawians who had been trained by the Livingstonia Mission. What was it that the Malawian people found attractive in western education, culture, and religion that made them become its active agents? What insights does this provide in interreligious relationship then and now? We cannot consider these questions without assessing the attitude of the missionaries to African traditional religion. To this end we will look at the work of Donald Frazer, one missionary of the Livingstonia Mission who was somewhat sympthetic to African traditional religions.

DONALD FRAZER

Donald Frazer arrived in Malawi in 1896 after serving with the Student Volunteer Missionary Union as Traveling Secretary in Britain at the same time that John R. Mott was serving in America. The work of the Livingstonia Mission had pretty much been established and was bearing fruit in terms of evangelistic outreach, education, industrial training, transportation, trade, and medical services. It was a time that another missionary, Walter Elmslie, described as reaping time.[10] However, Donald Frazer was assigned to an unexplored territory, and he proved very adept. He quickly learned Ngoni and Tumbuka, the two local languages, which he used in his preaching from the very beginning. His amicable personality, which was marked by constant smiling, endeared him to the local people. He went into their villages, ate with them, swam with the boys, and preached to them. A companion of Frazer had this to recall: "I have vivid recollections of the abandon with which Frazer threw himself into the work, and the great facility he had of attracting the people. He always managed to make the fullest use of the material he had at hand, and drew the best out of the native teachers. Very soon our little school was all too small and had to be enlarged, and the whole country soon lay open to his evangelizing zeal."[11]

Of the Livingstonia missionaries, it was Frazer who seemed most sympathetic to African religiosity and spirituality, seeing in it a possibility of some mutual inter-action.

Like Robert Laws, Frazer was of the opinion that western education was a pre-requisite for the general enlightenment of the Africans and this had to take the form of training for commerce, industry, and agriculture. However, this was not the main goal of their missionary work, which was the planting of Christianity. Frazer was proving very successful in reaching the people with the gospel. He was preaching to thousands of people and baptizing hundreds. He once remarked, "It is glorious to be allowed to live here. The sense of God so near, so strong, so triumphant, does not allow one moment's depression. All that one may lose here of health, of home luxuries, of mental development and inspiration, is made up a hundredfold in such partnerships."[12] When Frazer saw the emotional response that accompanied repen-tance, he tolerated it thinking that the expressionless Scottish character need not be imposed on the Africans.

While Frazer was open to the work of the Holy Spirit to cause conviction of sin accompanied by heightened emotions, contrary to the prophet Joel and the endorsement of Peter on the Day of Pentecost, he did not approve of visions. When he began to get reports of some having visions, he used sedatives on those who had such experiences, in order to counteract the vision's effects on their faith. Some of the missionaries were concerned that his evangelistic mass meetings would produce a superficial Christianity which they had avoided by delaying baptism until people had been thoroughly prepared. The fear of the other missionaries, especially Elm-slie and Laws, was that Christianity would be mixed with traditional beliefs that they considered, if not evil, then as part of a pagan culture that had to be redeemed by western education and Christianity.

Frazer had a different view. He wanted to seek out the similarities that Ngoni and Tumbuka religion had with Christianity. As Michael Stuart has observed, "For him, polygamy, beer drinking, dancing, and other prohibitions were not the major criteria in becoming a Christian."[13] In this, he was supported by Miller Patrick, the Vice-Moderator of the Foreign Mission Committee, who wrote to Frazer, "The new faith, he realized, would not hold them unless it were translated into the idiom of their own thought and linked up with the best of their traditional practices. So dance and game and song were not tabooed; they were to be purified, born anew, and baptized into the cultus of Christ."[14] Donald Frazer took this to heart and made it a policy of his missionary work. He encouraged the composition of hymns based on local rhythms and dances. The result was one of the richest legacies enshrining African spirituality in a Christian form produced by African Christians and a veritable source for a Malawian theology. In addition to having hymns composed following local rhythms and dances, Frazer incorporated some local marriage customs in the marriage ceremony. At one point he tried to persuade the Presbytery to legalize the custom of widows remarrying their deceased husband's brother. Elmslie, supported by other missionaries, continued to oppose Frazer's seemingly syncretic innovations.

Concerning the African way of thinking, Frazer described it in this way: "For circles and curves are more like the flowing moods of Africa. She thinks and acts without sharp and sudden angles. She rounds her corners, for space is unlimited; she never leaps her obstacles on the path, but turns aside and encircles them, for time seldom presses."[15] This observation is based on practices rooted in the African worldview. In this worldview, God was acknowledged as the creator, and so at this point there was not a major difference, except in the details of conception of this deity. Frazer wrote,

> The difference between the AbaNgoni and the Christian missionaries was not one of faith, but of ethics. All the news the white men brought of God and immortality was good and welcomed for Africa never doubted God. They knew him as the author of life and of death, and that in some dim way he was mixed up with their doings. They never doubted that the spirit of man only inhabits his body and when death comes to the body the spirit still lives and goes to the world of the spirits. But all that was now being told to them of the character of God and what conduct God demanded from those who worship him was new, and much of it unacceptable.[16]

What was unacceptable was not teaching about the character of God, but rather certain ethical demands that were being made of them. These demands centered around beer drinking, polygamy, certain forms of dancing, and waging wars. The Ngoni people were militaristic and invaded their neighbors constantly for food.

On education, Frazer espoused a different philosophy from that of Robert Laws. Laws was for the creation of an elite educated class that could meet the needs of the colonial administration, while Frazer was for mass education that could be a catalyst in creating a richer personality and nationality rooted in the life of the people. Frazer saw Law's idea as creating a class that would be rooted in western life-styles to suit Europeans who were settling in Malawi and that such a development would be harmful, as it was bound to result in the destruction of village communities. Already the imposition of taxes by the colonial administration was forcing many men to leave their communities and look for work at plantations owned by European settlers. Family life was being disrupted for the sake of providing cheap labor for European estates. Frazer's views prevailed over those of Laws when Laws' plan to build a university were abandoned and he himself relieved of his leadership of the mission.

Frazer wanted the Livingstonia Mission to prepare the Africans of Malawi to exercise the right to manage their own affairs. In this he saw Christ as the key. He wrote, "It is not a cry of Africa for the Africans, or Africa for the Europeans, that will hew out the open path, but Africa for Christ, when Africa through Christ will find her fullest life."[17] However, for Frazer, it was the Europeans who, in spite of their many acknowledged mistakes, had the responsibility of Christianizing Africa. African religiosity could be assimilated into Christianity only under European supervision. It was not a task that Africans could be left to carry out on their own. He once stated:

> The duty that lies before Europe is twofold: that of reparation for havoc in the past, that of preparation for right development in the future. . . . European character, capacity and experience can lead Africa to the strength and maturity of nationhood. A momentous stage has been reached in the vast growth of the "Dark Continent." Europe must bring all her treasures of influence, insight, and experience to bear on the development of this great country. Europe has received her summons, and for weal or woe the trend of Africa's future will be decided by Europe.[18]

Against his better judgment and knowledge of white colonialists, Frazer trusted them unrealistically. It was for woe that European presence continued and that the future of Africa was not to be decided by Europe, as he thought, but by Africa itself. Frazer's optimism rested on the fact that Europe had the Christianity, the commercial know-how, and the civilization. What he forgot was that Europe was still pagan, governed by exploitative capitalism that would eventually re-enslave Africa. Since European civilization was technologically, not ethically, defined, it proved to be very inhumane to the Africans. Frazer understood the disadvantages of European commerce and civilization without Christianity, but he excused bad whites. He maintained, "On the other hand she had her 'Oil River Ruffians' spreading an influence around them (Africans) utterly deleterious to the country and its inhabitants, and tending to exploitation of the basest kind. Yet they too were pioneers of civilization."[19] To the African sense of being human (*umunthu*), these would not be considered the bearers of civilization, but rather beasts with a human face.

As for African religion, he saw in it what he called "many broken lights of God."[20] He interpreted it as animistic, in which the objects of worship were souls or spirits. He comments, "Animism, like all other phases of human development, has its lights as well as its shades. The terrible darkness of Paganism is revealed here and there by qualities and virtues not unworthy of Christianity."[21] To Frazer, paganism was almost seen as a religious system. What he forgot was that by the same token there were as many pagans in Europe as well, but these he excused. Social Darwinism and racist attitudes had taken a better hold of Frazer at this point. His ambivalent attitude is seen when he warned against overzealous governments banishing African social practices. He said, "Anything that tends to more humane behavior must have its germs of secret good, even animism cannot be regarded from every point as altogether and absolutely evil."[22] In the mind of many missionaries, then and today, the veneer of Christianity over European cultures exempted them from being called pagan. To Frazer, Europeans were a superior race.[23] Pagan Europe was more preferable to pagan Africa and Christendom preferable to European paganism, that is, European civilization without Christianity.

While Frazer saw a role for the African church in mitigating both the evils of traditional society and those of European civilization, it could only be done under the supervision and guidance of Europeans. He asserted, "But the character of the African, at his best, is still subject to so many limitations that, as we have seen, it is not safe or wise to send him forth beyond the supervision and guidance of Europeans."[24] St. Paul was more trusting in the guidance of the Holy Spirit and the gentile Christians than Frazer was of African Christians. He could not trust them to the care of the Holy Spirit. He then went on to justify his position by saying,

> We must remember that if paganism has a sadly downward pull on the European, in spite of the comparative isolation which surrounds him as a foreigner, and in spite of his inheritance of traditions and tastes which have grown through the centuries of Christian life, the pull on the native, only recently drawn out of the mire of paganism, and living, as he does, amid sights and sounds which are for him a very active temptation, must be much more insidious.[25]

Convinced of this control, the missionaries remained in charge of the church in Malawi until the mid-fifties, when the rumblings of decolonization started to grow louder all over Africa.

The missionaries may no longer be physically in charge of the churches in Africa, but ideologically and theologically what they put in place controls the way churches behave. Their external paraphernalia, the gown and cassock, silver communion vessels, and the liturgy are all evidence of their continued presence and influence. Theologically, European confessions are authoritative in explaining the life and mission of the churches, regardless of the fact that they belong to different historical contexts. In spite of the changing times, there have been not any attempts at formulating new confessions for the Church of Central African Presbyterian. Such a state of affairs continues because the missionary church developed and encouraged a maintenance leadership and not a creative and innovative leadership. A maintenance leadership is unable to meet the challenges of changing situations and new questions, but is excellent at maintaining traditions and practices. The result has been that in many cases theological reflection has been taking place outside the churches and without the involvement of the church leadership. The church leadership has been very suspicious of these developments. Theological reflection as part of the churches' ongoing mission is imperative for the success of that mission today in Malawi. Theological reflection is called for if the churches are going to avoid fostering spiritual schizophrenia among the members. On what basis should the churches carry out the theological reflection so as to come up with a unified spirituality between the traditional African spirituality and the Christian?

THEOLOGICAL FOUNDATION
FOR A MALAWIAN SPIRITUALITY

The Culture of God and Human Culture

One name-attribute that is used for God among the Chewa people of Malawi is *Namalenga*. The name-attribute is derived from the verb-stem *-lenga*, meaning create. The name-attribute is feminine by virtue of the prefix *Na-*, but has the same meaning as the more masculine designation of *Mulengi* (Creator) and the connotation is that creation, like giving birth, is a feminine task. In the same way that a woman is the source of new human life, so too God is the source of all life. How that creation takes place is not the issue, but rather life is the issue here. To talk of creation is to talk about the vitalistic, life-affirming, life-sustaining, life-renewing, life-transforming, and life-redeeming culture of God in all its variety and manifestations. The culture of God is a gracious one in that it "richly provides for us with everything for our enjoyment" (1 Tm 6:17). Human culture is not primary, but rather it is secondary and a consequent of a living and creative God. The vitalistic culture of God is characterized by unity-in-diversity and diversity-in-unity as two sides of the same coin. Each aspect of God's cultural creativity is related to other aspects, and all point to God as their *Namalenga*. God is a God of varieties even though God may not vary essentially. It is upon this vitalistic culture of God that we, as human beings, and all other creatures try to create our own cultures. However, they are not independent of God's vitalistic culture, but are founded on it. Our cultures are to a large extent a variation on a common human theme. It follows that while spirituality may be varied, it has a common origin. Therefore, African spirituality and biblical spirituality can find their common origin and can mutually enrich each other. They are meant to be a gift to each other as each enshrines within itself some authentic developments as shaped by its particular history.

The Cultural and Religious Mosaic

Since our God is a God who delights in variety even within a single species, it would be unthinkable if the cultural and religious expression rooted in such a God were monolithic. The problem is not with the variety of cultural and religious expressions, but rather it centers around fallacious thinking that fosters the exclusion and demonizing of the different. In the story of the woman at the well (Jn 4:1-24), we see Jesus dealing with this problem. To begin with, the wrong thinking involved the localization of God in Jerusalem and Mount Gerezim by Jews and Samaritans respectively and mutual exclusion. The practical result was that Jesus was asked how he dared ask water of a Samaritan woman. Jesus delocalizes God by defining worship in terms of spirit and truth, not in terms of places and ethnic identities. What matters for Jesus is the worshiper living in integrity and truth. While the Jews had discriminated against the Samaritans, such discrimination is dispensed with where worship is according to what is true and spiritual. Jesus removes the barriers of cultural and religious exclusion. He did not come to abolish cultures and religious expressions, but rather to fulfill them. It is a gross mistake to try to limit Jesus to one relationship to human culture. Jesus is neither in, nor above, nor against, nor anything else, but as Paul points out, he is all in all.[26]

Subject to the truth and the guidance of the Spirit, Jesus challenges any cultural and religious expression to strive toward the truth and integrity, that is, to conform to the vitalistic culture of God, and not to be satisfied with its narrow and petty status quo. This story seems to say to me that each culture must strive to establish values that bring human growth to its fulfillment befitting the vitalistic culture of God by being open to its own theological flaws resulting from ethnic thinking and exclusiveness and embracing the liberation that comes with God's truth. God's culture unites, while human cultures exclude. For Malawi, one element that accords with truth and spiritual worship is the quest for *umunthu*.

Cultural Gifts for the Common Good

Each culture emerges as a gift to other cultures for the Common Good. The Common Good is that which contributes toward abundant life for all. It is marked by a sense of love and justice. There are no people who are so devoid of insight, beauty, and dignity that they cannot be considered a testimony to God's creative vitalistic culture, even to God's sense of humor. Not all cultures are gifted in the same way, nor have they all equally developed their gifts. Since all cultures are a gift for the Common Good, they need to be accepted on their own terms and learned as such, not as anthropological specimen, but as cultural neighbor and friend. We have to learn to immerse ourselves with them so as to learn from them about themselves and they from us about ourselves. This is what incarnational learning is all about. Jesus was the word that became flesh and dwelt among us, and without becoming flesh there is no way in which John could have testified to having seen his glory as full of grace and truth (Jn 1:14), nor could Jesus have spoken of needing no testimony of the human since he knew what was in the human (Jn 2:25). It is by learning other cultures from within their context that we are able to critically appreciate what they are all about and then truly share with them our own. It is when the gospel takes on the cultural context of the people with whom it is being shared that it can truly manifest its own character. The gospel is God's gift for the Common Good, and the idea of *umunthu* is one of Malawi's cultural contributions for the Common Good. John 10:10 may be culturally rendered that Jesus came that they might have *umunthu* and have it in all its fullness. This is the dynamic equivalent of abundant life.

Critical Openness to and Appreciation of All Cultures

The reality of personal and societal sin and evil in the world which, among other things, induce self-deception, forces us to be critically open to all cultures even though they exist as gifts for the Common Good. Mutual criticism involving appreciation of positive and profitable elements while pointing out that which is life-denying and dehumanizing is most welcome in view of the Common Good. Cultural aggrandizement and self-interest that does not contribute to the Common Good is theologically sinful because it is counterproductive to the abundant life promised in the gospel.

Jesus denounced the Pharisees and teachers of the law for letting their cultural chauvinism get in God's way. He said, "You have a fine way of setting aside the commands of God in order to observe your own traditions" (Mk 7:9). Cultural traditions get in the way of the gospel. Ethnocentricism, regionalism, religious conflict, sexism, racism, and classism are all injustices that are rooted in our narrow cultural identity. All cultures have a 24 and Tutsi in them.[27] The tragedy of Rwanda raises serious theological problems concerning the mission and role of the church in Africa today.

I have lived in Britain and America. One thing that strikes a visitor to New York City is the number of ethnic restaurants and foods. There is Italian pizza, Mexican burritos or fajitas, a variety of Chinese dishes, American apple pie and hamburger, yogurt, Middle Eastern pita bread and shish kebab, Ethiopian njela, and Ghanaian Kenke. All these make for some very good eating for anyone who is open to new foods. It also provides a good lesson in cultural openness, good living, and mutual enrichment. The different is your other alternative. By being critically open to all cultures and, therefore, to all peoples, one is able to appropriate from other cultures all those insights and practices that foster the Common Good, truth, and integrity, and to be suspicious of those elements that promote divisions, selfishness, and injustice among peoples. In this way, all cultures move toward the culture of God, a culture of abundant life and responsible living.

Jesus and Religious Pluralism

The question of the place of Jesus in a religiously pluralistic world is theologically a controversial one. I do not expect to venture into it at present for lack of space. All I want to do is to raise some questions. Are we asking the right question, and are the assumptions that lie behind the question adequate for the answer we are looking for? Has Jesus (not Christianity) anything to contribute to all cultures and religions? Have these cultures and religions anything to offer to Jesus? How did Jesus deal with religious pluralism? Can Jesus be confined simply to his Jewish context? I am raising these questions to distance ourselves from our own historical conditioning. Volumes of books have been written on these questions, but the matter of religious pluralism is more our problem than that of Jesus. He seemed to have had no problem with it. It is a problem for us because it carries with it a lot of historical baggage.

Two stories come close to this matter, both involving women. The first is that of the woman at the well. The second is that of the Syro-Phoenician woman (Mk 7:24-30). In the first story, while Jesus makes some culturally particular statement, he resolves the issue by delocalizing God from sacred sites. In the second story, its exegetical and linguistic difficulties notwithstanding, he resolves the matter by pointing to faith as opposed to ethnicity as the common denominator for divine action. If Jesus, according to Paul, is the one who unifies all things in the cosmos, then pluralism is not an issue. It is being trapped in our particularity that is the problem. This does not mean that our particularity should be jettisoned, but rather that while rejoicing in its positive aspects, its own limitations and flaws be acknowledged and that it is not the be-all and end-all of our existence. The problem of pluralism also results from adopting a narrow view of God and revelation. This was the problem of the Sadducees and Pharisees.[28] Just as cultures are gifts to each other for the Common Good, so too are religious expressions in their differing insights.

Jesus has to be presented within the context of each religious expression and the consequences left to the Holy Spirit. Here too, a critical openness is called for.

Love, Freedom, and Religious Particularity

To the great shame of Christianity, too many wars have been fought in the name of God and truth. Christianity has not lived up to its own creed of loving even the enemy. More often than not, it has allowed that creed to be cast aside in favor of the sword, ethnicity, gender, class, political ideology. Often I have been asked this question: Why continue to be a Christian in view of what Western Christian nations have done to you and your race as an African? It is an embarrassing question arising out of a history of shame. Western Christendom and institutional Christianity cannot be morally defended for their betrayal of the gospel. I continue to be a Christian because of who Jesus is to me—Savior and Lord. It is my experience of Jesus as redeemer that persuades me to continue pursuing the living vision that Christianity has often betrayed and subverted. It is a living vision of life, love, and freedom (*umunthu* in all its fullness). There is nothing wrong with being particular, as long as one is not captive to it, that God is not made captive to it, and so also the rest of humanity. Only love of God and humanity can free us from this danger. The freedom to which we are called by God is responsible and constructive. Christianity, as a religion of love even of the enemy, is called to a responsible encounter with other faiths. When it is true to its calling, Christianity fosters responsible particularity in view of what God is doing in the whole world. Hence John the Evangelist says, "For God so loved the world that God gave the only child God had that whoever puts one's trust in that child should not self-destruct, but rather have life with an eternal dimension" (my rendering).

Religion in the Global Village

The age of religious cultural monopolies is quickly coming to an end with the emergence of the global village. The village square (called *bwalo* in Malawi) belongs to all, and all participate in the village market. Using the description of the open market in talking about religion does not make religion a commodity but points to the choice that buyers have to make among various merchandise. Is it possible to conceive of our global village, with its multicultural and multireligious expression, as an open market in the village square where the currency used is love? Love is the essence of life, and without it life is impossible. The point is that if religions are going to indeed be means for the creation of communities of abundant life, peace, justice and integrity, then they have to allow freedom of expression and be tolerant. Human growth demands freedom to make choices, to question tradition, and to seek its improvement. Human growth has to do with commitment to truth and being responsible for the truth that one acknowledges. It is not the function of the gospel to put people into a straitjacket of legalism and traditions, but rather to liberate them. Jesus pointed this out when he said, "If you hold my teaching, you are really my disciples. Then you will know the truth, and the truth will set you free" (Jn 8:31). St. Paul reiterated this when he said, "You, my brothers and sisters, were called to be free. But do not use your freedom to indulge the sinful nature, rather serve one another in love. The entire law is summed up in a single command, 'love your neighbor as yourself' " (Gal 5:13). If love is not the mode of operation, Paul warns that mutual destruction is inevitable. History's testimony is loud and clear on this score. The market is as just as the people who operate in it. Here I can only speak for Christianity and say that in an unjust market, the best that Christianity can do is to begin to learn in earnest and practice what it means to love even the enemy and to make it its mode of operation. It is in this kind of love that the gospel power lies, and it is the only path to the experience of abundant life that defies even suffering (Rom 5:1-8). If the theology of the cross means anything at all, it is primarily that the cross is an expression of this kind of love. Love is the cross-cultural language.

NOTES

1. Cf. John 3:16, 14:6; Acts 4:12.

2. P. A. Kalilombe, "Spirituality in an African Perspective," in Rosino Gibellini, ed., *Paths of African Theology* (Maryknoll, NY: Orbis Books, 1994), pp. 115-35.

3. E. A. Alpers, *Ivory and Slaves* (Berkeley: University of California Press, 1975), p. 39.

4. Ian Linden, *Catholic, Peasants and the Chewa Resistance in Nyasaland 1889-1939* (London: Heinneman, 1974), p. 5.

5. J. S. Mbiti, *African Religions and Philosophy* (London: Heinemann, 1969), p. 1.

6. Isaiah 6:8.

7. Isaiah 9:1,2.

8. Isaiah 61:1. This verse and those following were used both by David Livingstone and Joseph Booth to explain their presence in Africa. *See* George Shepperson and Thomas Price, *Independent African* (Edinburgh: University Press, 1987), p. 51.

9. Owen Kalinga, *A History of the Ngonde Kingdom of Malawi* (Berlin, New York, and Amsterdam: Mouton Publishers, 1985), pp. 131-33.

10. Walter Elmslie, *Among the Wild Ngoni* (Edinburgh: Oliphants, Anderson, and Farrier, 1899), p. 127.

11. Quoted in Agnes Frazer, *Donald Frazer of Livingstonia* (London: Seeley and Service, 1923), p. 4.

12. Ibid., p. 55.

13. Michael Stuart, *Ngoni Elites, the Southern Tumbuka, and Livingstonia Missionaries in Ngoniland: A Critical Assessment of the Work and Thought of Donald Frazer (1870-1933)*, unpublished M.Div. Thesis, Union Theological Seminary, New York, 1985, p. 43.

14. Millar Patrick, "Donald Frazer: Knight-Errant of Christ," *Life and Work* (October 1935): 393.

15. Donald Frazer, *African Idylls* (London: Seely, 1923), p. 138.

16. Donald Frazer, *The Autobiography of an African* (London: Seely and Service, 1925), p. 55.

17. Donald Frazer, *The New Africa* (New York: Negro Universities, 1927), p. 30. In 1915 there occurred in the then Nyasaland, now Malawi, what has been called The Chilembwe Rising. It was an armed insurrection in protest of the way the White-dominated administration treated Africans. Before that Joseph Booth had popularized Marcus Garvey's slogan, "Africa for the Africans."

18. Donald Frazer, *The Future of Africa* (London: Student Volunteer Missionary Union, 1911), p. 104.

19. Ibid., pp. 244-45.

20. Ibid., p. 116.

21. Ibid., p. 130.

22. Ibid., p. 132.

23. Ibid., p. 246.

24. Ibid., p. 266.

25. Ibid., p. 267.

26. Richard Niebuhr, *Christ and Culture* (New York: Harper and Row, 1951). *See also* Colossians 3:11.

27. Reference to the Hutu and Tutsi ethnic conflict and the Tutsi genocide which resulted in 1994. The two World Wars were caused by the same cultural forces.

28. While many incidences in the life of Jesus could be cited to illustrate this point, however, the encounter between Jesus and the Pharisees over taxes to Caesar and that with the Sadducees over the question of the resurrection in Mark 12:13-27 are good examples.

4

Syncretism and *Kenosis*

Hermeneutical Reflections in the Indian Context

MICHAEL AMALADOSS, S.J.

The increasing interest and involvement in inculturation and interreligious dialogue in missiological practice and theory frequently give rise to the discussion of the problem of syncretism in the context of cultural and religious pluralism. While most people tend to use the term in a pejorative sense, some people try to give it a positive meaning.[1] Due to this confusion some people suggest that the term *syncretism* be abandoned and a more neutral substitute be found.[2] The problem, of course, is not with the term but with the process that the term refers to. The process is not going to disappear because we abandon the term.[3]

SYNCRETISM AND THE *THEOLOGIA CRUCIS*

In a recent article on a stranger-centered missiology, Professor Kosuke Koyama suggests that our approach to believers of other religions must be based on the scriptural injunction of showing hospitality to strangers.[4] He refers in passing to the problem of syncretism,[5] but seems to sidestep it by focusing on the *theologia crucis*. When we are with the other believers, we must not focus on the religious systems that divide us but on the human persons and their idols of greed and self-righteousness. God calls everyone to flee from the worship of these idols. Koyama concludes: "Repentance (metanoia) is a creative moment in which missiology of *theologia crucis* begins. In repentance, we can truly 'extend hospitality to strangers.' This is the spirit of the stranger-centered missiology."[6]

I quite agree with Professor Koyama that in interreligious situations it is better to focus on persons and moral behavior rather than on religious systems and beliefs. But human persons are believers, and it is in the name of their beliefs that they often

fight each other. Therefore we cannot ignore their religious identity. In another article, however, Professor Koyama speaks of "strangers" as people belonging to other
cultures and religions. The *theologia crucis* would persuade us not to dominate or
eliminate them, but to welcome them and serve them.

> The peripherized Christ is the boundary breaking Christ.... When does Buddhism
> become an "other" faith to Christianity? Is the Buddhist critique against human greed
> "outside" the teaching of Jesus?... Self-giving is Christ's fundamental attitude
> towards "outsiders". The Self-giving Christ, the one who is radically open and vulner-
> able, is related to every one. Hence, for him there is no outsider.[7]

Professor Koyama then is led to ask: Is not our discussion on syncretism often distorted by a Christian center-complex?[8]

In the following pages I would like to look at the process of syncretism a little
more closely and elaborately and suggest that the kenotic attitude of Christ is indeed
the proper starting point in our approach to people of other cultures and religions.
Our talk about syncretism will certainly be different when we have the same mind
that was in Christ Jesus (Phil 2:5).

In countries like India, in which believers of different religions are trying to live
together as one community and in which Christians are trying to reach out to others in dialogue, not only as "strangers," but as friends and collaborators in the promotion of freedom, fellowship, and justice for all, we feel the need of going beyond
extending hospitality to strangers.[9] The fear of syncretism, however, is always a
block that hinders creative efforts. It may therefore be useful to look at this problem of syncretism from an experiential point of view. This is what I propose to do
in the following pages. I shall do so in the context of our experience in India.

THE EXPERIENCE OF SYNCRETISM

It is not necessary for us to go into the history of the term *syncretism*. At a recent
meeting of scholars, syncretism was described as "contested inter-penetration of
religions."[10] While "inter-penetration of religions" describes the process of syncretism, the adjective "contested," though it tries to be neutral, seems to add a negative note. One could very well ask: Contested by whom? For what reason? We shall
come back to the description and the questions after we have looked a little at the
experience. In order to simplify our reflection and help clarify the issues involved,
I shall limit myself to the experience of Roman Catholic Christians in India. Hinduism and Buddhism have spread across India and Asia respectively through a
process which we Christians would consider syncretistic. Therefore, taking their
experience into account may confuse our discussion.

Looking at the experience of Roman Catholic Christians in India, one can notice
the interpenetration of religions in four different ways. Christians at a popular level
continue to indulge in practices that others at an official level would consider pagan
and superstitious. One notices such popular religiosity everywhere, including
Europe and the United States. Here I am not referring to the so-called Sects, but to

sections of the Christian community itself. Secondly, in India we also have some people, whom one would consider elite and theologically well-informed, who claim to integrate in themselves their double roots as Hindu and Christian. They would even call themselves Hindu-Christians. Thirdly, we have the process of inculturation, particularly after the Second Vatican Council, which often moves from an intercultural to an interreligious process, given the difficulty of a clear distinction between religion and culture with regard to rituals and symbols in a religious context. Finally, interreligious dialogue leads to common praying and mutual presence, even participation, in each other's ritual. Let us briefly look at these four kinds of experiences.

SYNCRETISM: POPULAR AND ELITE

Catholic popular religiosity is very much alive in India. The people enthusiastically participate in the official liturgy of the Church. But besides that, people have their own practices that accompany the change of seasons, rites of passage, and times of special needs such as sickness or other misfortune.[11] These are traditional rites that have been "christianized" by the addition of a Christian symbol or prayer or by being linked to a Christian mediator such as an angel or a saint. In one place, during the festival of the local patron, the people sacrifice cocks and goats. Occasionally, some may even cross boundaries to seek the support of other religious mediators. The official Church, while discouraging the crossing of boundaries, tolerates some of the practices and encourages others. The Church has its own popular devotions, intercession of saints, and blessings for various occasions. It acknowledges ritually the role of spirits, good and evil, in life.

Some of the elite may consider the people superstitious. But no one, neither the elite nor the people themselves, would doubt their identity as Christians. This situation is different from what may happen in some other cases like the Afro-American Cults, in which some Christian elements are integrated in what is basically an African religious tradition.[12] It is not a question of two parallel religious traditions practiced side by side, either. It is also different from the phenomenon of groups breaking off from the main body to set up Independent Churches or New Religious Movements.[13] Some theologians explain this as the grafting of the metacosmic religiosity of official Christianity onto the cosmic religiosity of the people.[14] They integrate well and do not clash, because they cater to different needs of the people. An anthropologist has characterized them as the pragmatic and transcendental aspects of religion.[15] At the level of meaning, also, an integration seems possible between a supreme divinity and a multitude of mediators, which may include even living people recognized as having special powers—of healing, for example.[16] Questions and doubts arise only when the mediators belong to other religious systems.

A second kind of religious interpenetration takes place in people who claim to consciously integrate in themselves their double religious roots, though Christianity remains the basic tradition. Brahmabandab Upadhyaya called himself a Hindu-Christian, claiming to remain a Hindu culturally though he had become a Christian religiously. He became a *sannyasi* or renouncer, got involved in the national free-dom movement, and reflected on the possibility of grafting the thought of Thomas Aquinas to the philosophies of India. When he died, people disagreed about whether he died a Christian or a Hindu.[17] Raimondo Panikkar speaks of passing through Hinduism and Buddhism while remaining Christian all the time.[18] Aloy-sius Pieris speaks of passing through Buddhist experience.[19] Swami Abhishik-tananda lived through Hindu spiritual experience, under the guidance of Hindu Gurus, while remaining a Christian *sannyasi*.[20] These passages normally involve use of the other religious Scriptures, methods of prayer and spiritual experience, and a dialogue with the theological reflection of the other believers. What distin-guishes this process is that this is very personal. These people remain Christian, but feel enriched by their passage through the other religious experiences and seek a conscious integration.

SYNCRETISM AND INCULTURATION

What is popularly known today as inculturation is also looked upon by some as a syncretistic process. If inculturation is no more than an encounter between a reli-gion (Christianity) and a culture, then one can hardly speak about syncretism in relation to that. The actual situation, however, is different. The Gospel comes already inculturated in a historical tradition. Any culture that the Gospel encoun-ters is already animated by a religion. The Gospel-Culture encounter is really an intercultural and interreligious encounter.[21] Culture and religion are not the same, but are closely related. Though the description given above implies that the rela-tionship is incarnational, I would prefer to see it as dialogical.[22] The great religions claim to relate to different cultures. On the other hand, most contemporary cultures are animated by a plurality of religions. One of the major reasons to posit a differ-ence between religion and culture is that, at least in the case of the great religions, the root experience from which the religion arises is claimed to be beyond culture, either as revelation (Judaism, Christianity, and Islam) or as an insightful experience that transcends the normal conditionings of culture so as to be properly inexpress-ible (Buddhism).

In practice the dialogue between Christianity and culture takes various forms according to the attitudes and convictions of the people involved in the dialogue. Some think that the first culture(s) in which the Gospel is revealed is normative in such a way that other cultures can only add to it, not replace it. Cardinal Poupard in the African Synod (1994) went even further to say that every Christian must be a little Semitic, a little Greek, fully Roman, and authentically African. Others, how-ever, think that in dialoguing with various cultures (and religions) Christianity becomes catholic or universal precisely by integrating other cultural and religious symbols and experiences.[23] Here there is a great variety of attitudes, and accusa-tions of syncretism are common. Let us look at some typical ones without attempt-ing to be exhaustive.

Some start with the supposition that Christianity is the true religion. Every other religion is false, if not evil. These will see inculturation as the translation in various cultures of the revealed truth of Christianity. Even at this level, some would privilege the Judeo-Greco-Roman cultural complex as providentially chosen by God.[24] Even the pioneers of inculturation like Matteo Ricci and Roberto de Nobili argued for the integration of Chinese and Indian symbols and practices, saying that they had only a cultural and social, not a religious significance. Others think that while Christianity is the fullness of God's self-revelations, other religions are partial or preparatory revelations containing the "seeds of the Word." They have good and holy elements which can be integrated, even though they do not add anything substantial. There can, however, be differences of opinion in judging what these elements are. In the process of liturgical inculturation, for example, while some elements like the Indian oil lamp and some gestures like the waving of lights as a sign of honor were taken up, some people thought it syncretistic because these elements are found also in the context of Hindu worship. Some others think even a symbol that normally appears in a religious context can be reinterpreted in a Christian context. Such, for example, is the symbol *OM*, which is variously interpreted in Hinduism and Buddhism, but which is interpreted as a symbol of the Trinity in a Christian context, since it is made up of the three syllables A + U + M. In the same way, Indian theologians were favorable to the use of other religious scriptures even in the liturgy, suggesting that they can be read and interpreted as cosmic revelation preparatory to the Old and the New Testament. Still others adopt a more pluralistic approach, seeing other religions as complementary, but pointing to the same divine mystery. Christian experience of the Mystery is limited by history and culture, so other religious scriptures and symbols can be positively enriching.[25]

In this discussion of inculturation I have focused rather on recent efforts made by the elite after the Second Vatican Council. Popular religion is often the people's own way of inculturating the Christian faith in their life and experience. What is opposed at the elite level is often tolerated or ignored at the popular level, especially when the symbols emerge from cosmic religiosity and do not belong to another great religion.

SYNCRETISM AND INTERRELIGIOUS DIALOGUE

A fourth kind of interpenetration takes place in situations of formal or informal interreligious dialogue. When believers of different religions are living together as members of the same society and culture, interreligious relationship can take various forms. One could keep religious belief and practice separate but seek to base common life and relationships on common moral principles such as freedom, justice, and truth.[26] Another level is when people come together as believers in the defense and promotion of common human and spiritual values. When Pope John Paul II invited various religious leaders to come to Assisi to pray for peace in 1986, it was carefully explained, in order to avoid any impression of syncretism, that they did not come to pray together, but came together to pray, each one in his or her own way. But even being merely present with respect when another is praying supposes that one acknowledges that the other is praying and that the other's prayer is valuable and not just superstitious. Praying together with the members of other religions is not uncommon in India. The *Guidelines* published by the Bishops' Commission for Dialogue, while discouraging active participation in the official rituals of other religious communities, recommends "a religious presence, flowing from the respect and sympathy which we owe to what is sacred and to the religious conviction of the other persons."[27] Only active participation in what is "specific and exclusive to other religions" is qualified as "false syncretism."[28]

A group of theologians examining the possibility of sharing worship do not exclude participation even in the official worship of other religions. "As the deity is a manifestation of the divine Mystery, we may participate as Christians as long as our Christian identity is not jeopardized or compromised."[29] The same group goes on to say: "Eucharistic hospitality to followers of other religions could be our expression of a common bond that exists *de facto* within the universal economy of salvation."[30] Such an openness to believers of other religions is based on a double principle. The first is: All symbols and rituals are related to the ONE Sacrament of humanity, Jesus Christ."[31] The second is that everyone, through an experience which is necessarily "limited, partial and culturally influenced," expressed through symbols and myths, is reaching out to the Transcendent Reality.[32] According to these theologians, then, in an interreligious setting, "three kinds of interactions are possible: total rejection, total acceptance and creative interaction. The last one should be our concern in the multi-religious experience of India."[33] One could rephrase "creative interaction" as "dynamic syncretism," but seen in a positive way in the context of an acknowledged common journey of the whole of humanity toward the Ultimate.

SYNCRETISM: LEGITIMATE AND ILLEGITIMATE

After this rapid survey of situations in which some accuse others of being syncretistic, I would like to reflect on the questions that these phenomena raise. People who talk about syncretism distinguish between objective and subjective syncretism. A religion could be considered objectively syncretistic when it contains elements from one or more other religions. Syncretism would be subjective when a person integrates in his or her own religious practices elements from various religions. This distinction is not really very meaningful, because a religion becomes significant only when some people practice it.

If syncretism is described as religious interpenetration, it can be considered legitimate or indiscriminate. One can think of three experiential situations. Here I am not taking into account parallel or dual religious practices in which people use two different religious systems without any intermingling.[34] It is a situation of religio-cultural and political domination in which the dominated feel obliged to conform to a foreign system, but without really feeling at home in it and without abandoning their own system. Leaving this situation aside, one can still see three different situations.

VARIETY OF SITUATIONS

It is not unknown for some people to indulge in religious practices, black magic for example, intended to harm someone, which they themselves would consider foreign to their own legitimate religious practice. This is illegitimate syncretism. Another situation is when a religion, particularly a great religion, has grown and spread through integration of various elements in the context of historical and cultural pluralism. This would be considered legitimate syncretism.

Between these situations we have a third, in which people who follow a particular religious practice that contains elements from different religious and cultural traditions do not consider such syncretism illegitimate or indiscriminate. But others around them accuse them of being illegitimately syncretistic. Here again one can think of three situations. In the case of religious movements like the Voodoo in Haiti or the AfroBrazilian Cults, it is always the outsiders who accuse them of being illegitimately syncretistic, often with the implied understanding that all these people are supposed to be Christian. This may be more a social problem of belongingness than a religious one; that is to say, they are probably "social" Christians, who have not made an option for Christian commitment. The second situation is that of the "popular" or cosmic pole in every great religion. The elite in every religion variously condemn, tolerate, or selectively encourage what they consider superstitious or illegitimate among the common people. The people themselves do not see it as a problem. They may even know to how justify it, if their attention is called to it. A third situation is of those people who are trying consciously to inculturate their religion in a new religio-cultural context and in the process are exploring, experimenting, searching, and growing. Such pioneers are often accused by others more "traditional" of being illegitimately syncretistic. At this level, differences in religious practices are supported by differing theological views on other religions and on religious interpenetration.

FACTORS IN THE PROCESS OF SYNCRETISM

The real question is not whether there is religious interpenetration or not, but whether it is considered legitimate or illegitimate. Three factors seem important in considering this question: the intention of those who practice religion, how a religious symbol is interpreted, and how the legitimacy of other religions is evaluated. These three factors are obviously interconnected, but let us look at them one by one.

Religion can be looked at either as a body of truths or a creed in which one is called to have faith, or as a way in which one is called to live. If religion is seen as a way of life or spirituality, then it cannot ignore the problems of life that people face every day: material, physical, and psychic needs; difficulties of relationships with others; questions of meaning in life. A religion that attends to these problems will have to be one that is incarnate in the life and the world of people. This incarnation takes place in terms of symbols, rituals, and mediators that relate to the immediate problems of the people. Starting from these basic experiences, one could rise to more abstract levels of reflection. But rootless reflection or speculation will be perceived as irrelevant. The God of the Bible reveals not abstract truths. God is present and active in the history of the people. God becomes incarnate in Jesus, catering to their needs of health and freedom, fellowship and justice.

Great religions, in becoming universal and transcending a particular culture, may tend to lose their roots in reality and culture. While this may satisfy some, the people need a God who is close to their lives through symbols and rituals accessible to them. The elite may consider the people superstitious, but people need a religion that is relevant. Besides, the elite too have their own superstitions. People therefore tend to integrate in their praxis symbols and rituals that relate to their life in the world. They are often cosmic in nature: sacred places and times, personification of natural forces and spirits. But in the context of a great religion, people know how to relate the symbols and rituals of their little tradition to the great tradition, seeing them as local, historic, or symbolic manifestations of more universal principles. What is basic and makes the whole praxis meaningful is the intention of the people to live and order their lives in relation to the Ultimate. Religion is a relationship. The concrete symbols and rituals in which this relationship is experienced and lived are mediations. They have no difficulty in borrowing them if necessary from various sources available to them in their experience. It is the basic relationship to the Ultimate and the intention or purpose of achieving or maintaining it that integrate the various symbols and rituals that the people feel comfortable in using.

INTERPRETING THE SYMBOL

This leads us to the second reflection. People make a clear distinction between symbol and the reality symbolized. In the past one used to speak too easily of idolatry. Today one is more careful. People can move easily in the realm of meaning and interpretation. Some Christian traditions are accustomed to making a radical distinction between faith and religion, between revelation and experience. Today there is a growing realization that faith is not human if it does not find expression in symbol and ritual. And these symbols and rituals do not come from nowhere. They emerge out of the cosmic, social, and personal experience of the people. As such they are culturally conditioned and pluralistic. Revelation itself, even if it is divine, has to be mediated in terms of the historical experience of a human community and find expression in its cultural symbols and rituals.

This articulation between reality and its expression in experience and symbol makes possible a pluralism of symbols of the same reality. It also points to the limited nature of every symbolic expression, which is never adequate to the reality it is symbolizing. Since symbols belong to a particular historical and cultural context, the reality they refer to can only be reached through interpretation that takes this mediation and context into account. Religion, creed, and ritual are basically symbolic. This symbolic world is a continuum that goes from the cosmic to the metacosmic. People who live these symbols are aware of the Reality they symbolize, though they may spell it out only when they are made to reflect on their experience. Surveys among Hindu believers in India, who may be more easily accused of improper syncretism than the Christians, have shown that the people do reach out to the Absolute beyond the symbols and mediators, distinguishing between, but also relating, the divine power and its many manifestations. Speaking of peasants in South India, Gabriele Dietrich says: "They may worship God in a certain form, but their understanding of God also transcends this form."[35]

People who come from an intellectual tradition that dichotomizes religion from faith and who have a very conceptual approach to revelation where truth is the adequation of reality and intellect do not feel comfortable in the world of symbols. But the world is what it is, and if they do not feel comfortable in it, it is their problem. They should not sit in judgment over those who carry on their lives and their relationships with others and with the Ultimate in the normal way. Truth and its absoluteness are often an issue in discussions on syncretism. Whereas a rational-conceptual perspective tends to equate truth with its conceptual expressions and attribute to the concepts the absoluteness of the truth, the symbolic perspective accepts the symbols as the relative and pluralistic expressions of the absolute truth. The Absolute is not denied, but remains the horizon which makes the plurality of its symbolic expressions meaningful.

One might object that such an affirmation of pluralism does not make place for revelation. Today an emerging theology of religions does not distinguish between revealed religions and others that are merely human, but starts with the affirmation that all religions mediate divine-human encounter in some way and involve some revelation as divine self-manifestation. This does not, however, mean that all religions are the same. Some religions may claim a special revelation and a special call. But in the perspective of the universal salvific will of God, this special call has to be considered in dialogue with other religions, not in opposition to them. From our point of view, however we may define the special place of Christianity in the history of salvation, we affirm that Christians have to meet other believers in a dialogue of life in their common journey toward the Reign of God.[36] The other religions are then seen in some way as providing complementary perspectives. In such a dialogical situation, religious interpenetration would seem to be a normal phenomenon, even if each religion keeps its identity and organizes the material it borrows from other religions around its own basic structure. The perspective is not that of either-or, but of both-and.

ILLEGITIMATE SYNCRETISM

The practice of syncretism as religious interpenetration is therefore legitimate. This does not mean that it cannot be done sometimes in an improper manner. While we say generally that religious symbols are mediations of mystery, we do not pretend that there is no admixture of human imperfection, error, and even sin. Secondly, in the process of bringing symbols together there may be a lack of integration.

Thirdly, superstitious or magical motivations in particular cases are not excluded. This means that phenomena of religious interpenetration may need to be judged. But the criterion of negative judgment is not that some elements belong to another religion or culture. We have rather to point out in particular cases the magical motivation, the lack of integration, or the influence of human limitation or sin. In other words, the causes of improper syncretism are subjective. While we should constantly examine ourselves, since all of us are capable of improper syncretism, we should be careful in condemning others.

SOME CRITERIA

We can also formulate certain other criteria that can help us in discernment. I am formulating them in a positive way. Their absence will indicate improper syncretism. But I must begin with a caveat. Just as we should not rush to judge others, we are not called to pronounce judgment on what we consider syncretistic in other religions. Religious symbols and rituals are normally found in a social context. Every religious group has a right to determine the symbols and rituals that are expressive of its own current identity. But it has no right to judge other groups. On the contrary, if it wishes to be relevant in an ongoing way, it has to be ready to dialogue dynamically with other cultures and religions.

Within this caveat, I can think of three broad criteria. The first criterion is that in and through the symbolic practices of a community one can discern true religiosity, a basic turning to God, a sense of dependence, an attitude of surrender, an openness to transcendence. But where there is an attitude of magic, symbols lose their transparency and are instrumentalized. In such a situation, improper syncretism can arise.

Another criterion is openness to the other. Normally religious practice must try to promote basic human and spiritual values—the values of the Reign of God, such as freedom, fellowship, justice, and love—both at a personal and a communitarian level. Where people are closed up in their own personal needs, they tend to live in their own symbolic world. Popular religion is also need-based, but it acts in a social context and its needs are related to values. There is more danger of improper syncretism in contemporary secularized societies, where religion has become privatized and individuals feel free to pick and choose their beliefs and symbols. When they focus on purely personal needs, they may tend to improper syncretism.

The third criterion supposes that in an intercultural and interreligious situation we are open to engage in dynamic dialogue. In this case the symbols and elements that we borrow from another religion or share with them in a common ritual bring something new: a new dimension, a new perspective, a new way of saying something, a new expressive symbol, and so forth. But these new elements should not contradict any values that we hold dear. Noncontradiction in such circumstances is not identity, but compatibility and community. The compatibility can be convergent or even dialectical, but it contributes to growth. A certain tension need not be excluded, but it must be creative.

SYNCRETISM AND *KENOSIS*

Such an open attitude to other religions supposes that our attitude to our own religion as a system of symbols and rituals is humble. This humility does not doubt God's self-revelation to us through the Word and the Spirit, but it is aware that this revelation is received and transmitted by people who are historically and culturally limited and conditioned. God is absolute, but our own experience of and relationship to God are relative. It is here that the *kenosis* of the Word is a paradigm for us. When the Word chose to become human, it emptied itself. We can see as part of this emptying its self-conditioning in history and culture. This need not be a problem if we understand, first of all, that the Word has also had other manifestations, however limited, in different circumstances of culture and history (Heb 1:1); and secondly, that the purpose of God's self-manifestation is to lead all things to their fullness (1 Cor 15:28; Rom 8:21-22). This fullness is not given, but to be achieved (Eph 1:3-14). In this perspective, we are aware of our own limitedness on the one hand, which makes us open to and receptive of others. On the other hand, we are impelled to dialogue with others so that through mutual interpenetration we can converge toward unity and reconciliation, purifying in the process what is merely human as limitation and sin, in ourselves and others. Kenosis, then, refers not merely to a personal attitude, but also to the Word's self-manifestation in Jesus.

Accusation of syncretism is often made in the context of a relationship of power. It is made against the people's religious praxis by the official and elite groups of a religion. It is often made also in an atmosphere of exclusivism, in which one group feels that it has access to the whole truth. It can also be a self-defensive search for security that might eventually lead to fundamentalism in religion. In all these cases, kenosis, with reference both to God and to the others, is a useful and necessary antidote.

Syncretism is not something to be afraid of if we set it in the context of the eschatological movement of people, with their cultures and religions, toward fullness in the Reign of God. Discernment, of course, is needed—even judgment, perhaps. But the special vocation of the Christian can be seen as a mission to cross the frontiers of cultures and religions, "extending hospitality to strangers," not allowing anything of value to be lost, but reconciling all things in Christ so that God will be all in all.

NOTES

1. Cf. Andre Droogers, "Syncretism: The Problem of Definition, the Definition of the Problem," in Jerald D. Gort, et al., eds., *Dialogue and Syncretism: An Interdisciplinary Approach* (Grand Rapids, MI: William B. Eerdmans, 1989), pp. 7-25.

2. Peter Schineller, "Inculturation and Syncretism: What Is the Real Issue?" *International Bulletin of Missionary Research* 16 (1992): 50.

3. Cf. Robert J. Schreiter, "Defining Syncretism: An Interim Report," *International Bulletin of Missionary Research* 17 (1993): 50-53.

4. Kosuke Koyama, " 'Extend Hospitality to Strangers'—A Missiology of Theologia Crucis," *International Review of Mission* 82:327 (1993): 283-95.

5. Ibid., p. 292.

6. Ibid., p. 294.

7. Kosuke Koyama, "New World, New Creation: Mission in Power and Faith," *Mission Studies* 10 (1993): 74, 75, 77.

8. Ibid., p. 76.

9. Michael Amaladoss, "Liberation as an Inter-religious Project," in *Leave the Temple: Indian Paths to Human Liberation*, Felix Wilfred, ed. (Maryknoll, NY: Orbis Books, 1992), pp. 158-74.

10. Droogers, "Syncretism," p. 20.

11. *See* Paul Puthanangady, ed., *Popular Devotions* (Bangalore: NBCLC, 1986).

12. Cf. Robert J. Schreiter, *Constructing Local Theologies* (Maryknoll, NY: Orbis Books, 1985), pp. 146-47.

13. Cf. Allan R. Brockway and J. Paul Rajashekar, eds., *New Religious Movements and the Churches* (Geneva: WCC Publications, 1987).

14. Aloysius Pieris, *An Asian Theology of Liberation* (Maryknoll, NY: Orbis Books, 1988), pp. 71-73.

15. David G. Madelbaum, "Transcendental and Pragmatic Aspects of Religion," *American Anthropologist* 68 (1966): 1174-91.

16. Cf. Eric de Rosny, *L'Afrique des Guerisons* (Paris: Karthala, 1992).

17. Cf. B. Animananda, *The Blade* (Calcutta: Roy and Son, 1947).

18. R. Panikkar, *The Cosmotheandric Experience* (Maryknoll, NY: Orbis Books, 1993).

19. *See* the title (and also the contents) of Aloysius Pieris, *Love Meets Wisdom: A Christian Experience of Buddhism* (Maryknoll, NY: Orbis Books, 1988).

20. Swami Abhishiktananda, *La montee au fond du coeur* (Paris: O.E.I.L., 1986).

21. Cf. Michael Amaladoss, *Becoming Indian: The Process of Inculturation* (Rome: Centre for Indian and International Studies, 1992).

22. Cf. Michael Amaladoss, "Inculturation and Internationality," *USG Bulletin* 94 (1994): 28-37.

23. Cf. Leonardo Boff, *Church: Charism and Power* (New York: Crossroad; and London: SCM, 1985), pp. 89-107; and Carl F. Starkloff, "The Problem of Syncretism in the Search for Inculturation," *Mission* 1 (1994): 75-94.

24. Cf. Joseph Ratzinger, "Christ, Faith and the Challenge of Cultures" (mss. 1993).

25. Cf. D. S. Amalorpavadass, ed., *Research Seminar on Non-Biblical Scriptures* (Bangalore: NBCLC, 1974); M. Amaladoss, "Other Scriptures and the Christian," *God's Prophetic People*, R. J. Delaney, ed. (Stuttgart: World Catholic Biblical Federation, 1985), pp. 281-94; and Catholic Bishops' Conference of India (CBCI), Commission for Dialogue and Ecumenism, *Guidelines for Inter-religious Dialogue* (New Delhi: CBCI, 1989), pp. 55-56.

26. Cf. Hans Kung, *Global Responsibilities: In Search of a New Global Ethic* (London: SCM, 1991).

27. CBCI Commission for Dialogue, *Guidelines*, pp. 81-82.

28. Ibid.

29. Paul Puthanangady, ed., *Sharing Worship* (Bangalore: NBCLC, 1988), p. 796.

30. Ibid., p. 800.

31. Ibid., p. 790.

32. Ibid., p. 793.

33. Ibid.

34. Cf. Schreiter, *Constructing Local Theologies*, p. 148.

SYNCRETISM AND KENOSIS 69

35. Gabriele Dietrich, *Religion and People's Organization in East Thanjavur* (Madras: Christian Literature Society, 1976), p. 137. *See also* A. M. Abraham Ayrookuzhiel, "Religion, Spirituality and Aspirations of the People," *Religion and Society* 25:1 (1978): 29; idem., "A Study of the Religion of the Hindu People of Chirakkal (Kerala)," *Religion and Society* 24:1 (1977): 5-54.

36. Cf. Theology Advisory Committee of the Federation of Asian Bishops' Conferences, "Theses on Inter-religious Dialogue," FABC Papers, No. 48 (Hong Kong: FABC, 1988); M. Amaladoss, *Walking Together: The Practice of Inter-religious Dialogue* (Anand: Gujarat Sahitya Prakash, 1992).

PART TWO

THE CRUCIFIED MIND

5

In the Image of the Crucified God

A Missiological Interpretation of Francis of Assisi

MARY MOTTE, F.M.M.

INTRODUCTION

The image of God who suffers undermines mission if it starts from a position of strength and power. Recent theological studies have opened this perspective of God who enters into humanness, inserted in and engaging with the life of people. Different missiological approaches, starting from the image of the suffering God, have emerged.[1] In this paper I wish to explore such a missiology following criteria derived from Francis of Assisi through his witness to Gospel life. Francis did not consider himself a missiologist or a theologian; his lived experience, however, suggests a hermeneutic that can be helpful in attempting to discern a missiological opening for communicating the Gospel message in the present time.

Starting from Francis' understanding of his relationship to God and others, one discovers the centrality of his intuition about the Incarnation. From this intuition two other concepts follow: the vulnerability and powerlessness of God, who chose to be clothed in human form.[2] Incarnation and the related concepts of vulnerability and powerlessness constitute a framework for mission—communicating the Gospel message—which implies radicality in relationships and witness. This is borne out in the consistency of Francis' life and his conviction about "following in the footsteps of Jesus."[3]

Francis stands on the horizon of history, a strange figure, poorly clothed and different. Yet, many people think of him as a caring and compassionate person. He had a breadth of compassion that, even at the distance of more than eight centuries, still characterizes him. Such a wide embrace transformed this simple man into a person who can be considered in a variety of ways: Francis preaching to the birds, Francis embracing the leper, Francis visiting the Sultan of Egypt, and Francis on Mount

Alvernia, experiencing in his own body the pain of crucifixion.[4] He is the patron of ecology, and one recalls his familiarity with "Sir Brother Sun, Sister Moon and the Stars, Brother Wind, Sister Water, Brother Fire, and Sister, Mother Earth."[5] These are more than romantic names; Francis actually entered into a relationship with all of nature.[6]

Undoubtedly, the most popular images of Francis are those of a happy man, one who cared and lived compassionately among his brothers and sisters. And yet, is the image of happiness sufficient to explain why this little poor man from thirteenth-century Assisi, a world so different from the world at the end of the twentieth century, can still evoke interest among people, even people diverse in their religious beliefs? Was his personality so contagious as to survive eight centuries, or was there another dynamic operative in the person of Francis?

Louis Dupré credits Francis with shifting human understanding from the universal to the particular. He captures the paradox that has teased the minds of so many scholars in describing Francis as a "barely educated religious genius" who "upset an intellectual tradition which he hardly understood and which he certainly had no intention of challenging." The core of this paradox is Francis' "devotion to Jesus of Nazareth, the individual," and this "opened a new perspective on the unique particularity of the person."[7] Later Franciscan scholars developed this line of thinking in philosophy and theology.[8] However, the insight of Francis himself was a dynamic impulse that brought about an existential change in the way of understanding God in relation to creation.[9] It is this powerful insight that transformed his relationships and explains why Francis continues to speak in a relevant way to people in the late twentieth century.

INTUITING THE ENFLESHMENT
OF GOD IN JESUS OF NAZARETH

The core of Francis' insight centered in a grasp of the significance of the Incarnation, the meaning of God-with-us, the enfleshment of God in Jesus of Nazareth. To help people enter into this nearness of God, Francis reenacted the Bethlehem scene at Grecchio, a small village in Umbria, Italy.[10] He was seized with the tremendous truth that God transcended whatever "boundaries" could exist between the majesty and power of the Creator in relation to creation, and entered into creation. The powerful contrast present in the insertion of the Creator into creation is evident in the letter Francis wrote to the religious order that he began:

> O admirable heights and sublime lowliness!
> O sublime humility!
> O humble sublimity!
> That the Lord of the universe, God and the Son of God,
> so humbles Himself
> that for our salvation
> He hides Himself under the little form of bread![11]

This tremendous truth, encompassing the majesty and total otherness of God with the touchable humility of God-enfleshed-in-humanness, consumed Francis' insight. For him, the Eucharist (e.g. "the little form of bread"), exemplified the joining together of "sublime humility and humble sublimity."[12] This truth became a driving force in Francis' life and influenced his way of understanding the Gospel.

In the early days of his conversion, Francis met a leper on the road.[13] We know of this meeting from Francis himself who, at the end of his life, wrote at the beginning of his Testament which he left to his followers, "While I was in sin, it seemed very bitter to me to see lepers. And the Lord Himself led me among them and I had mercy upon them. And when I left them that which seemed bitter to me was changed into sweetness of soul and body. . . . "[14]

Even after several years, one can *feel* the initial repugnance Francis experienced in this encounter. The fact that he remembers the event in his Testament for his followers indicates how significant this encounter proved to be in shaping his life and understanding. Celano, companion and biographer of Francis, speaks of Francis overcoming himself when he met the leper, in order to approach him and kiss him.[15] Bonaventure, also a disciple of Francis and theologian, in describing the event, comments that Francis saw in the lepers to whom he continued to minister, the image of Christ crucified. Both Celano and Bonaventure stress the repulsion Francis experienced toward the sight or smell of a leper. Both note that he overcame that repulsion and kissed the leper.[16]

In the embrace of the leper, Francis went beyond venerating the memory of the crucified Christ and experienced something that reached into his consciousness and touched him deeply. Since he would remember this moment at the end of his life, recalling it at the very beginning of his Testament, associating it with the beginning of his new way of life, Francis indicates that this image was formative in shaping his comprehension of God's mystery. Throughout his life, he sees this encounter "willed and directed by God."[17] As he continually deepens his experience of what it means to "follow the teaching and the footprints of our Lord Jesus Christ,"[18] Francis came to understand that God, the "all-powerful, most holy, most high and supreme God,"[19] became human in Jesus Christ. In that humanness, God became inserted in human history, participating in the joys and sorrows, the happiness and tragedies from within. By this insertion, God opens possibilities through the events that come about in the context of human freedom, the gift of the Creator to the creature, which, in the consistency of God's action, is not denied when misdirected in sinfulness.

David Bosch begins his reflection on "The Vulnerability of Mission" by recalling the novel *Silence* by Shusaku Endo.[20] In this story based on the actual experience of Jesuits in Japan in the sixteenth century, Endo considers the dilemma so many have experienced, the silent God who does not respond to suffering and torture. There is no answer to prayer that pleads for alleviation, even alleviation for the others. The central character, Father Rodriquez, sometime after his ordeal in which he found no help from God, argues with Christ, telling him about the resentment he feels because of God's silence. Christ's response, "I was not silent, I suffered beside you," provides an insight similar to that of Francis. It is one that is often missed. Bosch comments,

> Can we ever "explain" the shattered limbs and broken skulls of the innocent; can we ever in our theologies, account for houses being reduced to rubble, forced removals, and emaciated children staring at cameras with hollow eyes? There remains an unfathomable mystery here, and at the same time something so repugnant that we can never find peace with it, never supply it with a tag and file it away into our theological systems.[21]

Francis understood that in the embrace of the leper, God embraced him and made him coparticipant in the reality of human experience, in that space where such participation is most vitally experienced, at the outer limits of humanness, at the periphery of life. "Only those who have experienced the inhuman misery of human beings will be permitted membership in his community."[22] Francis insisted that those who wished to join him mingle with the lepers. Why this insistence, and why this requirement for membership in the community? In order to respond, one needs to look at the vision Francis had for himself and his followers, namely to walk "in the footsteps of Jesus of Nazareth."[23] He realized the Gospel opened the way for human persons to understand the depth of God's love that reached beyond the communitarian fullness of the Trinitarian God and embraced every human person and all of creation. God, for Francis, was the God of infinite majesty—Father, Son, and Spirit—who, in becoming incarnate in Jesus of Nazareth, entered into all aspects of humanness, except sinfulness. This is a God of infinite compassion, who stands beside and suffers with; a God who chooses to be clothed in the cloth of humanness,[24] enabling women and men to enter into the process of salvation. If Francis of Assisi presents us with an image of God that is both captivating and engaging, it is his capacity to grasp the mystery of God through the Incarnation.

MINORITY: VULNERABILITY AND POWERLESSNESS

Francis' grasp of the meaning of the Incarnation led him to live a way of relationship predicated on profound respect. God, in assuming humanness, became accessible to the other, even to the Son's giving himself up to death. In giving instructions to his brothers on how they were to conduct themselves as they went about in the world, Francis indicates a framework of powerlessness:

> they should carry *nothing* for the journey *neither* (Lk 9:3) *a knapsack* (cf. Lk 10:4), *nor a purse, nor bread, nor money* (Lk 9:3), *nor a staff* (cf. Mt 10:10). And *into whatever house they enter,* let them *first say: Peace to this house* (cf. Lk 10:5). And, remaining in that house, they may eat and drink *whatever* [their hosts] *have offered* (cf. Lk 10:7). They should not offer resistance *to evil* (cf. Mt. 5:39), but if someone should strike them on one cheek, let them *offer him the other* as well (cf. Mt 5:39; Lk 6:29). And if someone *should take away their clothes,* they should not deny him also their tunic (cf. Lk 6:29). They should give *to all who ask; and if anyone takes what is theirs,* they should not demand that it be returned (cf. Lk 6:30).[25]

Francis spoke of his community as the Frates Minores, the lesser brothers.[26] The expression carried much meaning in thirteenth-century Assisi, derived from the clear distinction of classes in that society.[27] For one who understood the paradox of "sublime humility and humble sublimity" in God, there could be no other designation for those who would "follow in the footsteps of Jesus Christ." Minority is not just a way of speaking; it was and is a choice to live in a specific way and to look at the world from a specific position—namely to live poorly and to regard the world from the place of the poor. It is vulnerability.

> The brotherhood of Francis is to be a place free of every desire for power and dominion; only listeners and servants abide there, and there is no room for potentates and lords. This basic stance of the brothers is defined by the word *minoritas*, a word that is so important that the name of the community is derived from it: *Fratres minores*, Lesser Brothers. . . . [28]

The space of the poor is space marked by vulnerability, and in entering that space one becomes vulnerable. In the Incarnation, the Son of God took on human form and inhabited the space of the poor; he accepted the conditions of vulnerability. Francis of Assisi intuitively grasped that he had to enter into the space of the poor of his day, because only in this space could he approach the condition God assumed in the Incarnation.[29] The embrace of the leper opened the way for his understanding.[30] The most genuine expression of the Good News comes when one is embraced by those who stand at the periphery, the excluded. To arrive at this condition of vulnerability, one needs to be committed to just relationships which are defined by "respect for the dignity of every human person, loving acknowledgment of each one's fundamental right to freedom of conscience, respect for the integrity of creation."[31]

These are the constitutive elements of just relationships. "The truth that we hold as Christians is that God's Son has come among us with the gift of saving love. A corollary to this truth is the dignity, freedom and integrity of those among whom God's Son has come with unconditional love."[32] In other words, relationships that are just pose no conditions. In situations where conditions are posed from external forces, then an essential expression of mission is to strive to overcome such limitations. But the basis lies in a person-to-person encounter. Following Francis' insight, the one who consciously desires to communicate the Gospel message must be vulnerable. As a missiological concept, minority relates to the current "preferential option for the poor," and the journey toward solidarity and accompaniment that option has opened up for many who are seized with an urgency to communicate the Gospel message.

Francis illustrates this attitude of minority in numerous situations during his life. Perhaps one that is most helpful to our present discussion is his way of relating to Islam and the Crusades. The medieval Church fostered the Crusades, and many well-known preachers at the time preached in favor of the Crusades and encouraged men to join the army of the Pope and fight the Saracens. Francis refused to preach for the Crusades, a service he would have been expected to carry out; nor did he allow any of his brothers to do so.[33] Yet Francis had a very profound sense of loyalty to the Church. He traveled from Assisi to Rome to have his new brotherhood approved by the Pope. His Testament is full of references to the Church which indicate that his loyalty and fidelity extend beyond persecution from within the Church, as well as beyond the ignorance of some of its ministers.[34]

His genius for radicality is seen in the way he chose to emphasize his position and make his protest. The Pope granted a plenary indulgence[35] to all those who participated in the Crusades. Francis petitioned the Pope to grant the same indulgence to all those who visited the little Church, called the Portiuncula, in Assisi on the second of August. So, instead of fighting in the Crusades, one could go and pray in the little church on the plains of Assisi and receive the same reward.[36]

Francis did not see himself in competition with anyone, even those who seemed so alien to and feared by medieval Christian society. A person who is poor, from whom nothing can be taken away, who has nothing to lose, can be embraced by someone who is different. This is how minority, experienced in the space of the poor, can open a way to communicate Good News. God's love is from within; it does not set conditions but reaches out in a free embrace toward the other. Any attempt to control, to crush, to dominate is wrong, and any reason that would prompt such attempts is too limited to communicate the mystery of God incarnate. Francis, imbued with this conviction, having lived it and allowed minority to shape his whole way of life, was able to look at the Saracens as people who had a right to hear the Gospel message. This was a unique insight in his time. Francis was the first medieval founder of a religious community to direct his energies and those of his followers toward people who had not heard the Gospel message.[37]

TRANSFORMATION IN THE LIFE
EXPERIENCE OF FRANCIS

Filled with such a sense of vulnerability and powerlessness, Francis was free and could approach even those most distant, namely the Saracens. He desired to preach the Gospel to the Saracens at a moment when hatred of the Saracens appeared quite divorced from the command to love one's neighbor.[38]

In 1219 he set out for a third time to go to the Saracens. On two previous occasions, he had to turn back before reaching his destination.[39] He went to Damietta, where the Christians and Saracens were engaged in a raging and bloody battle. Sultan Al-Malik al-Kalim had proposed peace to Cardinal Pelagius, the papal legate and leader of the Fifth Crusade, in February 1219. If the Christians would leave Egypt, Jerusalem would be returned to them. The Cardinal, in spite of the advice of some of his military officers, refused the offer. Francis arrived at the scene of battle in August 1219.[40] It is not so difficult to imagine the sight that must have greeted Francis upon his arrival, given the sight of human slaughter transmitted instantly by communications media in our contemporary wars. And Francis' reaction? As one biographer notes, "Unless we have completely misunderstood Francis' character, the piles of corpses must have been a memory that haunted him all his days."[41]

Having arrived at the scene of battle, Francis took care of the wounded, and tried to persuade the soldiers to stop fighting, but they laughed him to scorn.[42] Then he went to visit the Sultan, taking along another brother, Illuminatus. Soldiers from the Sultan's army captured them and treated them cruelly before bringing them to the Sultan. Al-Malik al-Kalim was the nephew of Saladin, who had taken Jerusalem in 1187. He was a good and wise man, about the same age as Francis, had received a good education, and was especially fond of the mystical poetry of the Sufis. The Sufis were Islamic ascetics who dressed in coarse wool—not unlike Francis.[43]

Bonaventure, in his life of Francis, describes the meeting between Sultan Al-Malik al-Kalim and Francis:

> The Sultan asked them by whom and why and in what capacity they had been sent, and how they got there; but Francis replied intrepidly that they had been sent by God, not by man, to show him and his subjects the way of salvation and proclaim the truth of the Gospel message. He proclaimed the triune God and Jesus Christ, the Savior of all, with such steadfastness, with such courage and spirit, that it was clear the promise of the Gospel had been fulfilled in him, "I will give you such eloquence and such wisdom as all your adversaries shall not be able to withstand or to confute (Lk 21:15)." When the Sultan saw his enthusiasm and courage, he listened to him willingly and pressed him to stay with him. . . . [44]

Francis' primary motive in visiting the Sultan was to announce the mystery of God's love. The motive of martyrdom was also present. The spirituality of the Middle Ages, as in earlier ages, valued martyrdom, so Francis, a man of his times, viewed martyrdom as the perfect union with Jesus, who died for us. However, in Francis this desire was secondary; it was consequent to proclaiming the love of God for every person. It was "a returning of love to Christ through a willingness to die like him for those who persecute us and who remain always worthy of love because they are loved by God."[45]

A MISSIOLOGICAL HERMENEUTIC
DRAWN FROM LIFE EXPERIENCE

Francis returned to Assisi. He had not succeeded in converting the Sultan. He was physically weakened. While in the east, he contracted the eye disease that would cause him so much suffering and in a few years would deprive him of his sight.[46] Yet as we consider what Francis did after meeting the Sultan, it becomes clear that he learned a great deal through this experience.

He returned with a new insight about prayer. He was deeply impressed by the Islamic custom of announcing the hours of prayer.[47] Having no need to exert power over the other, Francis was able to learn more about prayer from the followers of Islam. In two different letters he gives instruction about announcing times of prayer and calling people to praise God at those times. One of these letters is written to the leaders of the peoples; the other is written to the guardians (superiors) of the brothers' communities:

And you should manifest such honor to the Lord among the people entrusted to you that every evening an announcement be made by a town crier or some other signal that praise and thanks may be given by all people to the all-powerful Lord God.[48]

And you must announce and preach His praise to all peoples in such a manner that at every hour and whenever the bells are rung, praise, glory and honor are given to the all-powerful God throughout all the earth.[49]

Another insight gained from meeting the Sultan that changed Francis is seen in the missionary orientation included in The Earlier Rule of 1221.[50] This chapter in the Rule is entitled "Those who are going among the Saracens and other nonbelievers," and it begins with the text from Matthew 10:16: "The Lord says: 'Behold, I am sending you as lambs in the midst of wolves.' Therefore, be 'prudent as serpents and simple as doves'." Then follows an instruction to the minister and servant, who is, in the language of today's canon law, the superior,[51]

any brother who, by divine inspiration, desires to go among the Saracens and other nonbelievers should go with the permission of his minister and servant. And the minister should give [these brothers] permission and not oppose them, if he shall see that they are fit to be sent; for he shall be bound to give an account to the Lord (cf. Lk 16:2) if he has proceeded without discretion in this or other matters.

From these texts we can see that Francis was aware of the danger inherent in going among the Saracens; he had also endured some difficulties when he and Brother Illuminatus were taken by the soldiers before they reached the Sultan. The emphasis in the lines that follow is on the source of such a specific calling within the Order—it is by divine inspiration. And while the minister has a role, he must fulfill it with a discerning attitude that is open to recognize God's action.

Francis next addresses how the brothers who go among the Saracens and nonbelievers are to live. He indicates they are to "live spiritually" and then offers two ways of doing so:

One way is not to engage in arguments or disputes, but to be subject "to every human creature for God's sake" (1 Pet 2:13) and to acknowledge that they are Christian. Another way is to proclaim the word of God when they see that it pleases the Lord, so that they believe in the all-powerful God—Father, Son and Holy Spirit—the Creator of all, in the Son who is the Redeemer and Savior, and that they are baptized and become Christians. . . .

Francis went to the Sultan fired with enthusiasm and a sense of urgency to proclaim the Gospel. And he did so. In his encounter with Islam, he entered even more deeply into the mystery of Jesus, who "became obedient, even to death on a cross" (Ph 2:8). Transformed by this understanding, he stood before the Sultan confident in his belief, and a vulnerable, powerless person. In this moment, Francis' understanding of how the Gospel was to be proclaimed was transformed. To proclaim the Gospel required first of all "to be subject to every human creature for God's sake, 1 Pet.

2:13"[52]—to be vulnerable and without power. The Gospel is about God's totally unconditional love for every person, expressed in the sending of the Son. To proclaim the Gospel, one must be capable of being embraced by the other unconditionally. That is how God loves every person, and one who is the messenger about the good news of God's love cannot limit the gift of God. The embrace itself becomes the message. The one who stands before the mystery of God with a discerning mind and heart will know when it will please God "to proclaim the word of God. . . . so that they believe in the all-powerful God—Father, Son and Holy Spirit—the Creator of all, in the Son who is the Redeemer and Savior, and that they be baptized and become Christians."[53]

Francis also went to the Sultan desiring martyrdom. He came away with a deeper and more pervasive understanding about the meaning of martyrdom. In the same mission chapter of The Earlier Rule of 1221, after describing how the brothers may go among the Saracens, he then addresses "all the brothers, wherever they may be . . . should remember that they gave themselves and abandoned their bodies to the Lord Jesus Christ. And for love of Him, they must make themselves vulnerable to their enemies, both visible and invisible, because the Lord says, 'Whoever loses his life for my sake will save it (cf. Lk 9:24) in eternal life (Mt 25:46).' "

It was the offering in the midst of daily events that gave everything into the Father's hands for the salvation of the world. In his letter to the Friars Minor, he says, "hold back nothing of yourselves for yourselves so that He Who gives Himself totally to you may receive you totally."[54] Francis now related obedience—the brothers are to remember they gave themselves, with a liability—"they must make themselves vulnerable to their enemies, both visible and invisible." The one who lives the Gospel and proclaims it to others takes on the obedience of the Son expressed in the Incarnation. It is a concept of service in humility, of obedience that extends as far as the offering of one's life—powerlessness.

> The missionary situation is a situation of obedience to which one should submit oneself in analysis and in life. Simultaneously it involves the radical renunciation of violence and the exercise of power; it involves a decision to choose those social ranks in society where one has no right of command; it involves an undermining of social hierarchies through obedience.[55]

CONCLUSION

I stated at the beginning of this paper that the life experience of Francis of Assisi suggests a hermeneutic that can be helpful in delineating a missiological approach to communicating the Gospel message in our time. The context in which this encounter takes place, at least in the western world, is one marked by lack of meaning, loss of identity, and a lack of the sense of the sacred. The global context, largely influenced in a negative way by the west, is one marked by ethnic divisions, racism, and war.[56] If we encounter the Gospel only from a naive traditional understanding of our particular culture, we cannot experience the transformation intended by the Gospel message, nor can we effectively communicate its message to others.

Bosch has stated that only too frequently the Church, when confronted with crises such as the present one in western culture, digs trenches and waits for the crises to pass.[57] The hermeneutic suggested by Francis' life offers another way, a model proposed by the Incarnation. The image of God taking on the cloth of humanness seized Francis' imagination and transformed his understanding of himself in relation to God and to all creation. He approached the leper and was changed when the leper embraced him. In a person consumed with one of the worst diseases of the time, and a disease that was particularly repugnant for him, Francis discovered the embrace of the suffering God. Following this experience, Francis became increasingly more insightful about his calling "to follow in the footsteps of Our Lord Jesus Christ."[58] This led him to the Sultan and eventually led him to learn more about prayer and communicating the Gospel message from this meeting with Islam.

Near the end of his life, Francis went to Mount Alvernia to fast and pray. While there he experienced the wounds of the crucifixion in his flesh. This deeply mystical encounter, attested to by his first biographer, Celano, as well as his early companions, indicates how completely Francis identified with God in the Incarnation.[59] The "sublime humility and the humble sublimity" came to Francis in this moment when he beheld "a man having the appearance of a seraph with six wings," a seraph of "unspeakable beauty," who gazed upon him lovingly. After this experience, which he was unable to understand intellectually but which totally captivated his heart, Francis perceived in his hands, feet, and side the wounds of the crucifixion.[60]

The fruit of this experience is expressed in the "Canticle of Brother Sun," which Francis composed shortly before his death.[61] His body was racked by pain. Through the imagery of sun, moon, stars, wind, water, fire, and earth, he proclaims the mystery of God, the God who took on the cloth of humanness and embraced all the elements of creation to transform them beyond all limitation.

> Praised be You, my Lord, through those who give pardon
>   for Your Love and bear infirmity and tribulation.
> Blessed are those who endure in peace
>   for by You, Most High, they shall be crowned.
> Praised be You, my Lord, through our Sister Bodily Death,
>   from whom no living man can escape. . . .
> Blessed are those whom death will find in Your most holy will,
>   for the second death shall do them no harm.
> Praise and bless my Lord and give Him thanks
>   and serve Him with great humility.[62]

In such a context, the image of the God who suffers challenges a deeper probing of the meaning of the Incarnation and Redemption in today's world. The hermeneutic suggested by the life of Francis focuses on the mystery of the Incarnation:

> God enters the alienated human world in Jesus of Nazareth. God restores the beginning again in the act of self-emptying: God expropriates the divine nature, renounces all power and privilege, becomes a slave among humankind and dies the death of a criminal on the cross. In its total nakedness and for this reason must Jesus be stripped

of his garments—the cross restores the original human innocence: because Jesus has nothing but his own naked existence as his own, he belongs exclusively to God, he is the Son of God.[63]

Francis perceived his relationship to God, to the Church, to every person, and to all creation as a way of relationship rooted in the mystery of God as revealed in the Incarnation. Francis chose for himself and for his followers "to follow the teaching and footprints"[64] of Jesus, "to live according to the form of the Holy Gospel."[65] Walking in the footprints of the Gospel, his life became a continually deeper giving over to God, allowing the Spirit of God to work in him in imitation of Jesus of Nazareth. Francis became thoroughly imbued with the Spirit of God, so that it is not so much "Saint Francis of Assisi the medieval Italian mystic who appeals to the world . . . as it is the Holy Spirit of the Lord, which penetrated his personality so totally."[66]

Retrieving his vision for our way of mission engages us in a deeper contemplation of the mystery of the Incarnation, through which God first embraces us in unconditional love. Francis desired to proclaim the Gospel to "all men and women" from the beginning of his conversion. That desire led him to absorb the words of the Gospel, as Celano tells us "he was not a deaf hearer of the Gospel, but committing all that he had heard to praiseworthy memory, he tried diligently to carry it out to the letter."[67] His life was a journey that led to an ever more profound understanding of what it means to walk in the footprints of the Gospel, which unveiled for him the significance of God's embrace of all creation in the person of Jesus of Nazareth. That is why Francis, contrary to attitudes and actions prevalent in his world, was able to learn from the Sultan. That is why he came to understand that all proclamation of the Gospel among those who have not heard this Good News must be prefaced by "living spiritually, not in arguments or disputes," but by "being subject to every human creature for God's sake," acknowledging "they are Christian."[68] This is how one communicates the embrace of the Trinitarian God, which is the good news of a love that is totally unconditional and always present.

A missiological approach to communicating the Gospel message in modern western society would approach persons within the context of the present crisis, not in judgment, but in openness. However, the messengers of the Good News must be clearly identifiable as those who claim to walk in the footprints of Jesus of Nazareth. They will be different, perhaps strange, and standing at the periphery. But their stance toward others will be open to be embraced by others who also stand at the edge of society—the excluded. It is not an image of a denouncing prophet that Francis offers us, but the image of a crucified God that describes his way of mission. It is marked by vulnerability and powerlessness—minority. This is not the only way, nor is it necessarily the best way, but it is an important way to radically live relationships and witness toward transforming modern society with the Gospel sign of God's Reign.

Today, more and more people are being pushed to the edge. There is increasingly less space for those who are limited physically, mentally, or morally or for those who are different ethnically, racially, or religiously. An ingenuous prophetic voice that would bring the Gospel message into this context is urgently needed. The mystery of God present in the Incarnation indicates the Cross as the framework for mission—a way of communicating the Gospel message marked by vulnerability and powerlessness. As it did in the life of Francis, this way of mission implies radicality in relationships and witness lived with consistency and conviction.

NOTES

1. Cf. Moltmann, 1995; Gutierrez, 1973; Koyama, 1974, 1976, 1984; Bosch, 1994.
2. Cf. Rotzetter 1994a: 124.
3. Rule 1221:1; cf. also Esser 1994: 19.
4. Cf. Celano I: 57, 58, 94.
5. Canticle, 3, 5-9.
6. Cf. Leclerc 1982: 131-34.
7. Dupre 1993: 38.
8. Ibid.
9. Cf. Leclerc 1982, 135-43.
10. Celano, I: 84-87; cf. also Rotzetter 1994a:124.
11. Letter to the Entire Order: 27.
12. Cf. Rotzetter 1994a: 124.
13. Cf. Celano, I:17; Celano, II: 9; Bonaventure, I:5; II, 6.
14. Testament 1-3.
15. Celano I:17.
16. Celano I:17; Bonaventure LM I:6.
17. Rotzetter, 1994a: 19.
18. Rule 1221: 1.
19. Rule 1221: 23.
20. Bosch,1994: 73-75.
21. Bosch 1994: 77.
22. Rotzetter 1994a: 19.
23. Rule, 1221: 1.
24. Cf. Salutation, 5.
25. Rule 1221: Chapter XIV.
26. Rule 1221: 5-7; Letter to the Faithful II: 4-15; Admonitions 1; Letter to the Order, 23-29.
27. Cf. Rotzetter 1994a: 9-11; 62-63.
28. Ibid.
29. Cf. Rotzetter 1994a: 77.
30. Cf. Rotzetter 1994a: 18.
31. Cf. Motte 1995:1.
32. Ibid., 2.
33. Cf. de Beers 1981: 29-30.
34. Testament 4-9.
35. Indulgences are a practice of the Roman Catholic Church that has been in force for many centuries. Granting of indulgences is a way in which the Church recognizes that sin damages relationships between God and humans and among humans. These relationships are not automatically restored in the acknowledgment of sin; they need to be restored through a process of reconciliation. The Church encourages individuals to perform works of piety as

a means of bringing about this healing. It also draws upon the treasury of the Communion of Saints, whereby the prayers of all its members redound to the good of all. At times the practice of indulgences has been abused and misunderstood; the case of offering a plenary indulgence for the Crusades may well be a case in point (cf. Paul VI, 1967).

36. Cf. de Beers 1981: 30.
37. Cf. Buhlmann 1994: 87, 90-91; Lehmann 1994: 35.
38. Cf. de Beers, 1981: 27-28.
39. Cf. Buhlmann 1994: 89-91; de Beers 1981: 30.
40. Cf. Celano I: 57; Bonaventure I: 9.
41. Holl 1980: 38.
42. Cf. Buhlmann 1994: 91-92.
43. Ibid., 91; Holl, 1980: 139.
44. Bonaventure 1968, 9:8.
45. de Beers 1981: 30-31.
46. Cf. Bulhmann 1994: 94.
47. Cf. Buhlmann 1994: 95; de Beers 1981: 36; Lehmann 1994: 43.
48. Letter to the Rulers of the Peoples, 7.
49. First Letter to the Custodians, 8.
50. Cf. Buhlmann 1994: 97.
51. This title of minister, which is still in use among the Friars Minor, indicates how deeply Francis had grasped the idea expressed by Jesus about leadership as service (cf. Mt 20:28; Mk 10:45).
52. Rule 1221: 16.
53. Ibid.
54. Letter to the Entire Order, 29.
55. Rotzetter 1994b: 52.
56. Cf. Bosch 1995: 1-4.
57. Bosch 1995: 4.
58. Rule 1221, 1.
59. Cf. Celano I:91; Bonaventure I:13-1.
60. I Cel. 94.
61. Cf. Lerclerc 1983: 127-34.
62. Canticle of Brother Sun, 10-14.
63. Rotzetter 1994a: 77.
64. Rule 1221: 1.
65. Testament, 14.
66. Armstrong, Brady 1982: 21.
67. 1 Cel., IX:22.
68. Rule 1221, 16.

BIBLIOGRAPHY

Armstrong, Regis, ofm. cap., and Ignatius Brady, ofm., eds., *Francis and Clare: The Complete Works.* New York, Ramsey, Toronto: Paulist Press, 1982.

Bonaventure. "Legenda Major," in *Saint François d'Assise: Documents—Ecrits et Premières Biographies*. Edited by Théophile Desbonnets, ofm, and Damien Vorreux, ofm. Paris: Editions Franciscaines, 1968, pp. 579-722.

Bosch, David. "The Vulnerability of Mission," in *New Directions in Mission and Evangeliza-*

tion 2: Theological Foundations. Edited by James A. Scherer and Stephen B. Bevans. Maryknoll, NY: Orbis Books, 1994, pp. 73-86.

————. *Believing in the Future: Toward a Missiology of Western Culture.* Valley Forge, PA: Trinity Press International, 1995.

Buhlmann, Walbert, ofm, cap. "Francis and mission according to the Earlier Rule of 1221," in *Spirit and Life: Mission in the Franciscan Tradition,* Vol. 6, 1994, pp. 87-108.

Celano, Thomas de. "Vita Prima," in *Saint François d'Assise: Documents—Ecrits et Premières Biographies.* Edited by Théophile Desbonnets, ofm, and Damien Vorreux, ofm. Paris: Editions Franciscaines, 1968, pp. 211-339.

de Beer, Francis. "St. Francois et l'Islam," *Concilium: Spiritualite—Francois d'Assise: Un Exemple?* vol. 169, 1981, pp. 23-36.

Dupré, Louis. *Passages to Modernity.* New Haven, CT: Yale University Press, 1993.

Esser, Cajetan, ofm. "Saint Francis and the Missionary Church," in *Spirit and Life: Mission in the Franciscan Tradition,* Vol. 6, 1994, pp. 17-26.

Francis of Assisi. "Canticle of Brother Sun," "Letter to the Rulers of the Peoples," "Letter to the Entire Order," "First Letter to the Custodians," "The Earlier Rule of 1221," "Salutation of the Blessed Virgin Mary," "The Testament," "Second Version of the Letter to the Faithful," "Admonitia," in *Francis and Clare: The Complete Works.* Edited by Regis Armstrong, ofm. cap. and Ignatius Brady, ofm. New York, Ramsey, Toronto: Paulist Press, 1982.

Gutierrez, Gustavo. *A Theology of Liberation.* Maryknoll, NY: Orbis Books, 1973.

Holl, Adolf. *The Last Christian: A Biography of Francis of Assisi.* Garden City, NY: Doubleday, 1980.

Koyama, Kosuke. "What Makes a Missionary? Toward Crucified Mind not Crusading Mind," in *Mission Trends No. 1* (ed. G. H. Anderson and T. F. Stransky). Grand Rapids, MI: Eerdmans, 1974, pp. 117-32.

————. *No Handle on the Cross: An Asian Meditation on the Crucified Mind.* Maryknoll, NY: Orbis Books, 1977.

————. *Mount Fuji and Mount Sinai: A Critique of Idols.* Maryknoll, NY: Orbis Books, 1985.

Leclerc, Eloi, ofm. *Francis of Assisi: Return to the Gospel.* Chicago: Franciscan Herald Press, 1982.

Lehmann, Leonard, ofm, cap. "Essential Aspects of Mission according to Chapter 16 in the RegNB," in *Spirit and Life: Mission in the Franciscan Tradition,* Vol. 6, 1994, pp. 35-46.

Moltmann, Jürgen. "The Crucified God," in *Faith and the Future: Essays on Theology, Solidarity and Modernity,* by Johann-Baptist Metz and Jürgen Moltmann. Maryknoll, NY: Orbis Books, 1995, pp. 89-99.

Motte, Mary, fmm. "The Purpose of Mission: At the Service of the Reign of God," in *Mission Update, USCMA,* 4:2 (1995).

Paul VI. "Apostolic Constitution on the Revision of Indulgences—1 January, 1967," in Flannery, Austin, op. (ed.), *Vatican Council II: The Counciliar and Post Conciliar Documents.* Northport, NY: Costello Publishing Company, 1975.

Rotzetter, Anton, ofm. cap. "Francis of Assisi," in *Gospel Living: Francis of Assisi Yesterday and Today* (A. Rotzetter, ofm. cap., W-C Van Dijk, ofm. cap., T. Matura, ofm.). St. Bonaventure, NY: The Franciscan Institute, 1994a, 3-148.

_____. "The Missionary Dimension of the Franciscan Charism," in *Spirit and Life: Mission in the Franciscan Tradition,* Vol. 6, 1994b, pp. 47-58.

6

Koyama, the Cross,
and Sweden in Dialogue

LARS LINDBERG

Christians throughout the *oikoumene* in the worldwide Church today are involved in theological dialogue on many levels. In biblical, dogmatic, and ethical matters, churches and denominations in all countries and continents have much to learn from each other. In order to learn from one another the churches need teachers, however, a new kind of teacher who is part missionary and part pilgrim. The teacher who is needed for learning in the *oikoumene* must also be one who can facilitate dialogue.

Kosuke Koyama is a Japanese theologian who is just such a pilgrim and missionary. Throughout his long career he has traveled from country to country and moved from old theological positions to new ones. In the Swedish churches we are prepared to listen to him as one of the prophetic voices in the worldwide Church today. In the pages that follow I would like to reflect upon Koyama's message in dialogue with modern, secularized Sweden.

JAPANESE THEOLOGY: KITAMORI, KAGAWA, AND KOYAMA

The Christian Church in Japan is rather small in size, but we have heard important messages from there through the years. I recall as a teenager being impressed by reading and listening to the Japanese theologian Toyohiko Kagawa. Kagawa inspired many in Sweden with his ability to see the Kingdom of God at hand not only in church life but in efforts for peace, in social work institutions, and in trade unionism. Some found it strange that Kagawa was invited to our country jointly by the Mission Covenant Church *and* the Cooperative Movement, but to me it looked quite natural. At home and in church I was encouraged to see this Christian social reformer as an ideal. Later I came to recognize that in his deep understanding of the universal importance of Christ's death on the cross, Kagawa was more than a social activist.

Kagawa and Koyama both stand in a Japanese tradition of "the theology of the cross." The central thinker in this tradition is the Lutheran theologian Kazo Kitamori. His book, *Theology of the Pain of God*, sought to bring about a reorientation in Protestant theological reflection in the wake of the second World War and the Japanese catastrophe at Hiroshima and Nagasaki. Kitamori was partly influenced by Karl Barth, evident for instance in the manner in which God's revelation in Christ and in the Holy Scriptures was central in his theology. But unlike Barth he allowed himself to be influenced by world religions, especially by Neo-Buddhist negative theology. Kitamori sought to understand the mystery of the atonement in terms of the Father's suffering on the cross. During the fifties and sixties he was very influential in Japan, and Kosuke Koyama was his most famous student.

In August 1983, Koyama visited Sweden to deliver the main address at the Swedish "Kirchentag" in Jönköping organized by the Swedish Ecumenical Council. The theme of the address was "Jesus Christ, the hope of the world," delivered in the large Pentecostal church of Jönköping. Koyama's message to the Swedish ecumenical rally was based on the theology of the cross. The true God, he stated, is the God revealed in Christ who is helping others, not himself (Mark 15:31). "False gods help themselves. They don't help others." The true God is seen in the Crucified One, who establishes his centrality by going to the periphery, to the marginalized people, the poor and the oppressed. The Lord is a jealous God, a hot God, a loving God.

In January 1994, Swedes had an opportunity to meet Koyama again, this time together with the faculty and students of the Stockholm School of Theology. His message was still centered on the cross and the crucified Jesus. His theme for his lectures this visit was "Missiology of Theologia Crucis." Koyama told us about his background in a Christian family in a Confucian-Buddhist culture, his encounter with the biblical God, and his baptism at the age of twelve. He told us of his experience of God during the second World War, recalling the atomic bombs being dropped over Hiroshima and Nagasaki and the unconditional surrender of the almighty Japanese Emperor to the allied military forces. In all this, the young Kosuke Koyama found a personal interpretation of the self-denial of Christ to be the very center of the Christian faith. He developed in these lectures what can also be found throughout his books: a missiology of *theologia crucis*, which is an understanding of the Christian mission from the event of the cross.

Koyama rejects emphatically the crusading mentality of the Christian mission, from the medieval crusaders to the colonial and triumphalistic Western mission of the last centuries. He wants to replace "the crusading mind" with "the crucified mind." I hear a similar message and critique of the Western mission in the well-known Japanese novelist Shusaku Endo's book *Silence*, a story about the Jesuit mission in Japan during the seventeenth century. I hear it as well when Endo is writing *A Life of Jesus* to his fellow countrymen. Endo tells us in a preface to the American edition: "I wrote this book for the benefit of Japanese readers who have no Christian tradition of their own and who know almost nothing about Jesus."[1]

Sweden, on the other hand, is an example of a post-Christian country. The sociologists say, with regard to the figures of church attendance, that Sweden, together with Denmark, is the most secularized country in Europe. With that background I want to enter into a dialogue about mission and evangelism with the missionary theologian Kosuke Koyama. What can we in northern Europe learn from Koyama's theological thinking, with its background in Japanese culture and religion, and in his experience of the dialogue between East and West, South and North? What does Koyama's theology of the cross mean to the Swedish situation? What does it imply when he is talking about "the agitated mind of God," "the crucified mind of God," "the mind of God that loves"?

A QUESTION OF CREDIBILITY

In a few short words I would like to describe the situation of the Christian faith in Sweden today, using it as a case study of secularization in Western Europe. The situation of the churches in Sweden seems strange to most foreigners. More than 90 percent of the population belongs to the Church of Sweden, the Lutheran State Church. All Swedish citizens are members of the State Church, unless they have withdrawn their membership (permitted by law only since 1951) or were born to parents who don't belong to the State Church. If you ask a man in the street, "What church do you belong to?" he very often doesn't understand your question. What is more, most members of the Free Churches of Sweden (approximately 300,000 communicants) have not withdrawn their membership in the State Church. Consequently, an ecumenical secretary in Geneva pointed out, you get the impression from the figures reported from Sweden that this country is about 105 percent Christian!

The Free Churches are stronger in Sweden than they are in the other Scandinavian countries. In Denmark, Norway, and Finland, the revivals of the nineteenth century stayed within the State Church, whereas the revival movement in Sweden came into conflict with the Lutheran Church and had to leave it, leading to the formation of new church bodies. The largest of the Free Churches are in the Pentecostal Movement (in Sweden a stronger and more mature movement than in most other countries) and the Mission Covenant Church (a congregational body belonging to the World Alliance of Reformed Churches). In addition to these two bodies there are also Baptists, Methodists, the Salvation Army, and other Protestant denominational groups. The Roman Catholic Church and the Eastern Orthodox Churches are growing in Sweden, due mainly to immigration. The Roman Catholic Church is about the same size as the Pentecostal Church and the Mission Covenant Church, and has a growing influence on Swedish society and Swedish church life. Orthodox influence remains less noticeable.

Some years ago, a World Council of Churches ecumenical team consisting of seven members representing various Christian denominations, cultures, and nationalities visited Sweden for three weeks. The team was invited by the Swedish Ecumenical and Missionary Councils and was asked to help the churches see their mission to the Swedish people more clearly. The report of the team included questions, observations, and statements about evangelism in Sweden, and has proved to be quite helpful for the churches in understanding their task and their situation.

It came as a surprise to many church leaders that the report's analysis found no clear distinction between the State Church and the classical Free Churches in Sweden. The report talked about "a church, which is part of the system" not only in reference to the established Church, but in reference to the so-called Free Churches as well. In fact, I think the team was right in its observation that both traditional Swedish churches (State and Free) can be looked upon as established. We in the churches are very much part of the social system. Perhaps the most important problem facing evangelism in Sweden today is thus the loss of a Church which is "salt" and "a prophetic voice" in society.

One of the members of the international team, a Pentecostal journalist from Kenya, stayed on in Sweden for theological studies. After a year in Sweden she said, "If I had known one year ago what I know today, I would have been more critical in my comments. The Swedish churches have lost their contact with the working class population. Swedish church people are well educated, well established and well isolated." In time we might find the close ties between the Swedish state and the Lutheran Church loosening, which we who are in the Free Churches would of course favor. But the fact will probably remain that Swedish churches are in many respects an integral part of the established social system. As in many countries, church people in Sweden belong to a high degree to the middle classes, and partly to the upper classes. This isolation poses a crucial problem for evangelism. A Baptist minister said recently, "In our church we didn't learn how to *live* in solidarity with the working classes in order to change their situation, but we learned how to get successful and thereby how to *leave* the working classes."

Public participation in church life in Sweden is relatively low. The average Swede doesn't call herself an atheist, but her faith is often hidden and anonymous. Sweden is known as a country with a tradition of strong emancipation and deep secularization. It is a characteristic feature of Swedish life that you don't show your interest in Christian faith openly by taking part in church activities or talking about religious issues and your own religion with friends. But those anonymous Christians, according to the sociologists, are often active in their private prayer and may listen to church services and other religious programs on radio and TV. The religion of the Swede is often anonymous, not very public, presenting a challenge to anyone who would seek to strengthen the public witness of the church in this country.

Despite these new challenges posed by the situation the churches find themselves in today, the work of evangelism in Sweden often continues to follow a traditional pattern. In the Lutheran Church, the minister in her sermon often starts from the assumption that her listeners all already belong to the church, as they were born in Sweden, baptized as children, and confirmed as youth. The high church movement in the Church of Sweden has begun to question this traditional pattern, but for the most part the State Church takes the issue of membership for granted. Questioning such assumptions has been more characteristic of the Free Churches. The traditional pattern of evangelism in the Free Churches consists of Sunday school, youth activities, public worship, as well as more concentrated efforts through different types of evangelical campaigns and revivalist meetings on the local church level (although the evangelical campaigns are now being questioned by a growing number of Free Church people). The traditional pattern of evangelism in the Roman Catholic Church, the Orthodox Churches, and other bodies with many immigrants is of religious work limited to those who already belong to the Church.[2]

The international team mentioned above provided a deep and searching criticism of the Swedish churches and their work of evangelism. But the report of the team also helped the churches see "signs of the future church," which was encouraging. The ecumenical group found in Swedish church life "a holy impatience," especially among young people. "This widespread holy impatience, this yearning to be more faithful to Christ, is itself one of the most important of the signs we have found of the future church of Jesus Christ in Sweden!" it exclaimed.

And indeed the report has proven to be true. A new atmosphere has come to be felt in Swedish church life during the past few years. In many ways, we have begun to experience a renewed openness to the Gospel. People dare to speak in a new way about personal matters and important questions of faith. The public dialogue on ethical and religious questions is more open than it has been in the past, indicating a new sense of the relevance of the religious community's contribution to social issues.

The international team saw signs of the future church in "new and vital forms of worship." There is a revival of worship in most Swedish denominations, partly in ecumenical cooperation. The most hopeful sign is that all denominations in Sweden, with the exception of the Orthodox Churches, have published a new hymnbook, partly or wholly in common. That means that the Church of Sweden, the Free Churches, the Pentecostal Movement, and the Roman Catholic Church now have hymnbooks in which the first 325 hymns are the same! Such a hopeful ecumenical sign cannot be seen in any other country, as far as I know. The road to full visible unity in Swedish churches is still a long one, but even here, ongoing dialogues have opened new doors for the future: dialogues between the Church of Sweden and the Mission Covenant Church; between the Methodist Church and the Roman Catholic Church in Sweden; and among the Mission Covenant Church, the Baptist Union, and the Methodist Church.

Through influences from the wider *oikoumene*, the Swedish churches are becoming more and more involved in questions of international economic and political justice. For years they have given moral and economic support to the African National Congress and other organizations working for democracy and against apartheid in South Africa. Today they are criticizing Swedish governments of different political persuasions for decreasing solidarity with the South. This is an important part of their Christian witness. Evangelism is a question of credibility.

Let me repeat that: Evangelism is a question of credibility. The Christian message is always related to the messenger, and the credibility of the message is always related in some manner to the credibility of the messenger. The life of the Church and the Christians who inhabit it is of great importance for people's understanding and believing in the Gospel. For years there has been a credibility gap between acts and words in the life of the Swedish churches. There are signs that this credibility gap is diminishing a bit, but the mission and evangelism of the Swedish churches is still not very successful, insofar as they can be measured. What then can the churches in Sweden learn from Kosuke Koyama, the missiologist? In short, it is this: Perhaps mission and evangelism are not a question of success at all, but of being true followers of Jesus, the crucified Lord.

THEOLOGY OF THE CROSS

Kosuke Koyama is an important renewer of Christian language and symbolism in our time. His theology is expressed through a rich variety of images and metaphors. Symbols and metaphors give genuine expression to the theology of the cross for Koyama. The cross is "a passionate event of God in search of humanity," "God's foolishness," and "the agitated mind of God." Jesus Christ is "the person of renewing self-denial," who is "affirming his centrality by giving it up." Jesus is "the centre becoming periphery," which means he is broken, not imperial. A characteristic feature of the theology of Kosuke Koyama is that the cross of the Lord's suffering servant is in the center. If we wish to understand his biblical thinking and learn from him, this will necessarily be a starting point.

The phrase *theology of the cross* (*theologia crucis*) was first used by Martin Luther to express the message of the Reformation in its early period. Of course it has its background in biblical teaching, for example, in the first letter from the apostle Paul to the Corinthians, where Paul writes:

> This doctrine of the cross is sheer folly to those who are on their way to ruin, but to us who are on the way to salvation it is the power of God. . . . Jews call for miracles, Greeks look for wisdom; but we proclaim Christ—yes, Christ nailed to the cross; and though this is a stumbling-block to Jews and folly to Greeks, yet to those who have heard his call, Jews and Greeks alike, he is the power of God and the wisdom of God (1:18-25, NEB).

Martin Luther used the expression *theologia crucis* not only in reference to the atonement, the central point of the Christian faith in salvation. He used it in order to interpret the whole Christian confession, the whole of theology. In his Heidelberg Disputation (1518), Luther drew a contrast between the theology of the cross and the theology of glory (*theologia gloriae*). With the latter term, the reformer was criticizing medieval scholastic and mystical theology. According to Luther, God is not known through God's glory, power, or creation, but through the cross of Christ, experienced through suffering. For Luther, the cross is thus the criterion of all things. "The cross alone is our theology," Luther would say. By such expressions, Luther was rejecting humanity's self-justification, whether accomplished by moral or intellectual deeds. Humankind is saved by faith alone, faith in the Crucified.

The whole biblical message has its center in the theology of the cross, according to Luther. Thereby he understood himself to be following not only the teaching of the apostle Paul but also of the entire Old Testament and of Jesus himself. What looks small is great in the eyes of God; what looks weak is strong. So the Lord says to Israel:

> It was not because you were more numerous than any other nation that the LORD cared for you and chose you, for you were the smallest of all nations; it was because the LORD loved you and stood by his oath to your forefathers, that he brought you out with his strong hand and redeemed you from the land of slavery, from the power of Pharaoh king of Egypt (Dt 7:7, NEB).

The prophecy of the suffering servant of God, which for the Christian Church is among the most important texts of the Old Testament, provides a description not of glory, but of the cross: "he had no beauty, no majesty to draw our eyes, no grace to make us delight in him" (Is 53:2b).

The teaching of Jesus is full of examples of what could be called theology of the cross. Jesus pays honor to those who are weak and poor, to the blind and lame, to children and women, to publicans and sinners. He offers a new style of living to his disciples: "Among you, whoever wants to be great must be your servant, and whoever wants to be first must be the willing slave of all—like the Son of Man; he did not come to be served, but to serve, and to give up his life as a ransom for many" (Mt 20:26-28). Jesus understands his ministry in the light of the suffering servant, and he compares the Kingdom of Heaven with a mustard seed, "smaller than any other" (Mt 13:31-32).

The theology of the cross was not always central in the teaching of the churches of the Reformation after the sixteenth century. In the twentieth century, however, it has returned in different church traditions. It can be seen in the Roman Catholic Church in the theology of Karl Rahner and Hans Urs von Balthasar, for instance, and in the writings of Nicholas Berdyaev and others within the Orthodox tradition. The Protestant theologian Karl Barth had a deep understanding of Luther's message of the cross. Barth insisted that the divinity of Jesus Christ is most clearly revealed in the humiliation of the cross, whereas his humanness is made known in his exaltation. The *theologia crucis* in this century has also been developed by other theologians from the churches of the Reformation, such as Dietrich Bonhoeffer, Kazo Kitamori, Jürgen Moltmann, and Eberhard Jüngel.

Along these lines special attention is due to Jürgen Moltmann. His book *Theology of Hope* is one of the most important theological works of the postwar period, influencing the churches in the West as well as in the Third World. Its eschatological and christological perspective gives hope for the future of humankind and the whole creation. Moltmann's "theology of hope" could also be called a "theology of resurrection," as he understands the resurrection of Christ as the first eschatological event, bringing hope to humankind. But Moltmann was criticized by some for being too optimistic and stressing the resurrection of Jesus at the expense of his death on the cross, thereby giving support to the mood of political optimism in the 1960s. Moltmann's second major work, *The Crucified God*, can be understood as an answer to that criticism.

The subtitle of *The Crucified God* is *The Cross of Christ as the Foundation and Criticism of Christian Theology*. In *Theology of Hope*, Moltmann states that eschatology is not only one of the theological issues but an essential dimension of Christian theology as a whole. In *The Crucified God*, he joins this eschatological perspective with the theology of the cross. Thus he writes, "*Theologia crucis* is not a single chapter in theology, but the key signature for all Christian theology," a statement which could also have been said by Martin Luther and Kosuke Koyama.[3] Reflecting the influence of Luther and Barth, Moltmann understands God to be revealed in the cross. He presses the meaning of this statement further, however, to understand the suffering and death of Jesus not in terms of theism and monotheism, but in a trinitarian context. The death of Jesus means that he is abandoned by the Father, while the Holy Spirit, in a powerful movement of love, brings salvation from the trinitarian God to all humanity. Moltmann's trinitarian understanding of the cross that is found in *The Crucified God* is developed more fully in *The Trinity and the Kingdom of God*, a trinitarian perspective that is much weaker in the theology of Koyama.

Both Jürgen Moltmann and Kosuke Koyama stand in the Reformed theological tradition. Both are deeply influenced by Martin Luther, especially his *theologia crucis*. Koyama wrote his dissertation on Luther's commentaries of the Psalms, and the German reformer continues to mean much for his talk about "the crucified mind of God." Koyama links up with both Martin Luther and the apostle Paul when he writes, "God's foolishness is wiser than men! These are the key words of the theology of the cross. . . . God's foolishness is the moment of judgment upon all theologies."[4]

One of the central biblical texts for Koyama is the words of the loving God, talking through the prophet Hosea: "My mind is turning over in me. My emotions are agitated all together" (11:8). Commenting on this passage, Koyama writes:

> I have no precise theological formulations by which I would connect the words of Hosea, about God and "the word of the cross" (1 Cor 1.18). But I find that the image of the agitated mind of God, given by Hosea, illuminates the "word of the cross" for me "from inside God," if we are allowed to say such a thing in all our theology. The word of the cross points to God's agitated emotions because of God's love towards us. The word of the cross heals our history by giving it hope and life.[5]

Certainly Christians have preached the crucified Jesus Christ, Koyama says. But in practice Christianity has presented him as a crucifying one, "the most serious missiological problem today in Asia."[6] The important question is whether we understand Jesus as the crucified or as the crucifier, as the Savior or as the representative of Western power and violence. For Koyama, the crucified Christ calls Christianity to repent of its crucifying tendencies, thereby becoming "deeply historical." The missiological response of repentance is movement into history, which brings with it the promise of a future. "The content of repentance is 'Go therefore . . . .' "

Go where? For Koyama the answer is clear:

> So Jesus Christ demonstrates his centrality by going to the periphery. Where is the periphery? The periphery is the place without honour, prestige and power. . . . This

understanding of periphery is important. The theology of the cross is fundamentally
different from a theology of honour, prestige and power.... The periphery is the place
of discipleship. If we follow Jesus we will come to the periphery with him.

The periphery is the place of the cross.... Jesus Christ is the center, therefore,
wherever he is becomes the center. If he goes to the periphery, the periphery, because
of his presence, becomes the center.[7]

Not only is the theology of the cross a critique of the crucifying tendencies of
Western power and a call to repentance of Christianity, but it is a call to go to the
periphery of human historical experience in order to experience the presence of the
crucified One. Koyama's theology of the cross introduces into the very heart of missiology a critique of human power and the historical distortions of Christianity. As
he made clear in his address at the 1980 World Conference on Mission and Evangelism in Melbourne, Australia, the themes of suffering and injustice that are on the
periphery of history must be at the very center of a missiology carried out in Christ's
way. This is why one reads in the "Message to the Churches" from the conference:

Jesus Christ affirms his lordship by giving it up. He was crucified "outside the gate"
(Heb 13.13).... People who suffer injustice are on the periphery of national and community life. Multitudes are economically and politically oppressed. Often these are the
people who have not heard of the Gospel of Jesus Christ. But Jesus comes to them.
He exercises his healing authority on the periphery.[8]

The image of the crucified Christ going to the periphery of history is a compelling missiological theme. Yet we must acknowledge that it has not been universally heeded or even accepted among Christians and theologians of the
contemporary world. If it is true that the theology of the cross has returned during
the twentieth century, it is also true that the theology of glory is increasing in our
time.

Theologia gloriae has had different shapes in church history. During the period
of the Reformation, Martin Luther used the phrase as a polemical term to criticize
scholastic theology. By it he meant that traditional theology in his time understood
salvation to be a work of human reason and speculation rather than a free gift from
God, a gift received by humanity in faith. The theology of glory postulated humanity's ability to achieve its own salvation. Luther argued, however, that salvation is
not achieved through any act of cooperation between God and humanity (syner-
gism), but is given *sola gratia* and accepted *sola fide*.

Today we find *theologia gloriae* in a variety of forms. The so-called church
growth movement, for instance has offered a form of theology of glory. It is often
said in this movement that the main goal of evangelism is church growth, which
means growth in numbers and membership. For church growth advocates, church
history must be a history of success. But this is not in the main the biblical perspective. In an article entitled "God's Arithmetic," the well-known Bible study
leader from the World Council of Churches, Hans Ruedi-Weber, declares, "The
early history of the Church is no success story." By that he means that the church

growth movement is using "man's and not God's arithmetic as the measure of growth." "God's purpose is the salvation of *all*, of the total *cosmos*, yet in order to achieve this, God elects, calls and converts a few." This is the biblical paradox for Weber: "In order to save the *cosmos* God sends the One, his own Son. Christ calls a few, the representative twelve, and he sends them into the whole inhabited world to be witnesses of his cosmic redemption." He continues, "Mission is not connected with statistics, but with sacrifice." The key question, according to Weber, "is not how churches can grow numerically, but how they can grow in grace."[9]

Weber's perspective on the mission of the churches is in accordance with Koyama's understanding of the theology of the cross. Over against the tendency to look for statistical success he poses a missiology of *theologia crucis* which sees in the weakness of the church God's strength at work. For its part, the church growth movement is not always dominated by "success theology," and when it is not, it presents to a high degree a healthy challenge to the churches and their mission. My own conclusion is that we have to learn solidarity with the oppressed from the missiology of *theologia crucis* and learn a concrete practice of disciplining and nurturing in mission from the church growth movement. These two dimensions don't necessarily exclude one another, and we can learn from both. But this requires that we do not follow the pathway of success given in the theology of glory.

There is a strong tendency to accept another form of the theology of glory, especially in Western church life and teaching, a tendency that must be firmly rejected. The individualistic life-style that is so prominent in the West today is also in the churches. Salvation very often means private happiness, and nothing more. Since the time of Enlightenment, the word *happiness* (French "*bonheur*") has figured prominently in European life and thinking. In the churches, we have developed an individualistic theology of happiness as well, what Koyama calls "protection-from-danger-religion" and "happy-ending-religion."[10] This type of theology exists in most churches and denominations in some form or another. "Become a Christian and you will get positive and happy!" it often proclaims. As an example, for a number of years we have had in Sweden a religious movement derived from the United States, from a teacher from Tulsa, Oklahoma, named Kenneth Hagin. According to its "theology of success" teaching, which must be looked upon as heretical, a Christian can demand of God to be happy, healthy, and rich—even beautiful!

This triumphalistic theology, with its anthropology of happiness and success, is not biblical. The Bible does indeed talk about being blessed, which means being a participant in the Kingdom of Heaven. It also includes suffering, however, as Jesus said in the Sermon on the Mount: "How blest are those who have suffered persecution for the cause of right; the kingdom of Heaven is theirs" (Mt 5:10, NEB). The theology of happiness and the theology of success are modern forms of *theologia gloriae*. They stand in real contrast to *theologia crucis*, to the life and teaching of Jesus. To be a Christian is not to be happy. It is to be baptized into the death and resurrection of Jesus Christ and follow him in joy and affliction. The life-style of baptism is a real alternative to the false theology of success, to happy-ending religion.

KOYAMA AND SWEDEN IN DIALOGUE

When reading Koyama or listening to him speak, one is struck by the fact that he is always eager to convince his fellow women and men that God's agitated mind, God's love toward us, is expressed in the incarnated Christ, dead and risen for our sake. Koyama is advancing the Reformation message of justification by grace and faith. God is a holy God. That truth, Koyama says, is Israel's unique contribution to humankind. Yet this holy God is often seen as stationary, keeping a distance from humanity. "A holy God cannot run," it might seem, according to Koyama. Yet the biblical God is not an Unmoved Mover but a God who runs toward the Prodigal Son. The holy God ran and embraced him and declared, "I will restore you and you shall stand before me" (Lk 15). The holy God is a loving and impassioned God; that is the gospel according to Koyama. "The cross is not a tranquil situation. It is a passionate event of God in search of humanity. Christians are committed to this impassioned event of God."[11] This is the basis for Koyama's missionary theology and for a theology of evangelism in secularized Sweden.

It is a basis that is drawn from the pages of Scripture. Koyama uses the Bible more than many other systematic and missionary theologians. With knowledge and imagination, he guides us into the biblical world in order to deal with today's issues. He certainly makes more use of the Old Testament than most Swedish theologians would do. In his study of the idolatries of Japanese and Christian spirituality, *Mount Fuji and Mount Sinai*, he locates his subject with the help of four questions taken from the Old Testament. In his lectures at the Stockholm School of Theology in 1994, he told the audience that during his basic studies in New Jersey he read Augustine and Aquinas, Luther and Calvin, Barth and Brunner. "So I had no time left to read the Bible!" His comment was met by a laughter of recognition from the Swedish students—a warning to theological faculties and seminaries in Sweden and elsewhere! A biblical foundation is, of course, as needed for the work of theology as it is for the work of evangelism. Here Koyama can teach us how to use the Bible not only in a traditional way, but in a more contextual way as well.

Like many other theologians from Asia and Africa, Koyama has strong criticism for the individualism of the Western churches. The Swedish churches ought to listen to him here, living as they do in a culture where the Christian faith has been confined in such a high degree to the private sphere. Christian faith is not a private affair according to the Bible and to the Christian tradition. It is practiced within the fellowship of the Church. In the ecumenical Faith and Order movement today, more is being said about the *koinonia* (*communio*, fellowship) of the Church than of the unity of the Church. With the word *unity*, one can get the impression that a mode of conformity of the Church is intended. With the term *fellowship*, one remembers that the faith is something we have in common and that there are varieties of gifts of the Spirit (1 Cor 12).

Koyama talks about fellowship in the worship of the Church, clearly expressed in the Holy Supper, where the broken Christ/bread is healing the broken community. "Christian theology then is fundamentally sacramental theology since Jesus

Christ is the central sacrament of our faith," he writes.[12] We are all invited to the Holy Eucharist, which represents a universality rooted in the self-denial of Christ, according to Koyama, leading to a missiology of eucharistic justice.

Fellowship has to be practiced more by the churches in Sweden, where so much of Christian faith is anonymous and loneliness is one of the main social problems. Fellowship does not exclude a commitment to, and a following of, Jesus. When one listens to Koyama, one hears a man talking about *his personal faith in Christ* in a sometimes old-fashioned, nearly pietistic way. But one sees that Christian faith is personal, not private.

Kosuke Koyama is consciously Asian in his theology, with deep roots in Japanese culture. But his concern for the indigenization of Christianity does not exclude international involvement. The particular God is the universal God. Koyama is not afraid of entering into dialogue with people of other faiths and ideologies. He thanks God for his dialogue partners, drawing upon Buddhist motives in his own thinking and learning from the indigenous traditions of a number of lands. Koyama argues that syncretism poses as great a danger in the Western capitalist culture as it does in Asia.

He is quite creative in using new metaphors fetched from the surrounding culture. He even makes drawings to illustrate his dogmatic books! Koyama can talk about the *Three Mile an Hour God* or tell us that there is *No Handle on the Cross* (both metaphors are titles of books). Sweden needs, as do many other Western countries, a contextual theology with new metaphors. Along these lines I have made a modest effort myself in a dogmatics in outline in Swedish, *Ny skapelse* (English: *New Creation*) where one chapter deals with "Liberation Theology in Swedish." But much more work is still needed to interpret the Gospel to the Swedish people today.[13]

Koyama is best known for the title of his first book, which he wrote as a missionary in Thailand. Soon after arriving there in 1960, he recognized that the theological systems of Aquinas and Barth were not understandable or applicable among the farmers in the rice fields. Thus he wrote *Waterbuffalo Theology*. Someone proposed half-jokingly that we should have an "Elk Theology" or a "Moose Theology" for Sweden. But we need a theology today for the affluent Western society. Why should we not be developing a "Volvo Theology"?

Sweden is said to be a secularized country. But the international ecumenical group mentioned above asked an important question: Maybe Sweden is not secularized, but nonevangelized? By that they meant that most Swedes have never really heard friends giving witness to the Gospel, nor taken part in a living, local church with worship, witness, and service. Perhaps that is what Koyama means. He is not talking about church growth, which to him is too technical a word. He is talking more about our task to witness about Christ and proclaim the Gospel. The proclamation should take place not in a crusading mind but in a crucified mind. What does that mean in a Swedish context? It is our task to give an answer.

Maybe it is not too dangerous if a country is involved in a process of secularization. The consequence could be that the Church is losing power, and that is often a healthy thing. Koyama tells us that Christ is gaining power by giving it up. The powerless Church is called to follow the powerless in God's mission.

The main contribution of Koyama to the Swedish churches is possibly his criticism of the efficiency and the high speed of Western society and Western churches.
God needs a long time to teach God's people a lesson. God decided to use forty
years in the wilderness for the chosen people, Koyama says. We need a less nervous
religious life. "In the wilderness our speed is slowed down until gradually we come
to the speed on which we walk—three miles an hour." "We believe in
efficiency. . . . I find that God goes slowly in his educational process of man."[14]

Is that the way of evangelism in Western countries, to get to know the wise God,
as Asians understand "the three mile an hour God"? To be silent and calm? To listen to God's Word in meditation? At least it is one important way in Sweden, where
rationalism and efficiency are understood as the highest values in society and where
a growing number of people are seeking Holiness and Wisdom. Is the "three mile
an hour God" the answer to the secularized but nevertheless religious people in
Sweden and other Western countries?

This does not mean that the cross is a silent and tranquil situation, Koyama says.
From the cross one hears the prophetic voice talking to all humankind.

> [T]he theology of the cross makes us aware of the presence of many gods. Some
> gods—gods of colour of skin, intellectual capacity, good income, guns and missiles—
> are very fascinating to us. . . . The theology of the cross gives us a criterion by which
> we can make a distinction between the true God and the false gods, and true prophets
> and false prophets.[15]

The cross is not a tranquil situation. The passionate event of God, according to
Koyama, means a challenge to all Christians to witness among our fellow humanity. The cross is a calling to discipleship to be practiced at the periphery. Evangelism is a question of credibility: the credibility of a church that claims to follow
Christ, and thus the way of the cross, to the periphery of history.[16]

The cross has ethical implications, both on a personal level and on the level of
social issues. There was no cheap grace for Bonhoeffer, nor is there for Koyama.
There is a cost of discipleship! Koyama reminds us of the sacramental and ethical
significance of the Holy Communion by quoting Jesus in his Sermon on the Mount:
"If you are offering your gift at the altar and there remember that your brother has
something against you, leave your gift there before the altar and go; first be reconciled to your brother, and then come and offer your gift" (Mt 5:23-24).

Those words, Koyama says, give us "the sacramental meaning of the altar." He
continues: "In the most holy moment at the altar we are to remember our broken
relationship with our neighbors. At the altar you will remember that your brothers
and sisters, hungry, poverty stricken, 'widows, orphans, aliens' and marginalized,
have something against you."[17] Koyama reminds us that the cross has moral importance in our lives: Come to the altar twice! Take a side trip to your brothers and sisters and be reconciled with them!

The cross has social and political implications. "For the salvation of humanity
we must say that we stand for creation and not for destruction. . . . Justice is not just

a sociological but a christological concept. . . . Christian ethics must be studied in the perspective of theology of the cross."[18] Mission is a critique of idols, Koyama tells us, and he doesn't hesitate to call into question the political and economic powers in his own Japan. The churches are often in a credibility gap in the West because they do not always call into question the political and economic powers of their own lands. (In this sense it is a missionary calling to criticize the churches that do not criticize the political and economic powers.) Mission needs prophetic voices and moral courage, especially in the West.

Secularized Sweden is in dialogue with Kosuke Koyama. He invites us to leave the God of happiness and power behind us and listen to the living God, the biblical God. In the modern context we are often tempted to talk about "an unbroken Christ, a powerful, conquering Christ."[19] But the hope for the world is the Crucified and Risen One. He is also the only hope for the Western secularized world.

NOTES

1. Shusaku Endo, *A Life of Jesus* (Tokyo: Charles E. Tuttle Company, 1985), p. 1. In this book he provides us with a picture of a tender and weak Jesus, appealing to contemporary Japanese. Endo writes: "The religious mentality of the Japanese is—just as it was at the time when the people accepted Buddhism—responsive to one who 'suffers with us' and who 'allows for our weakness,' but their mentality has little tolerance for any kind of transcendent being who judges humans harshly, then punishes them. In brief, the Japanese tend to seek in their gods and buddhas a warm-hearted mother rather than a stern father."

2. We should note here, however, that as Roman Catholics begin to play a more significant role in the ecumenical fellowship, they are able to make an interesting and important contribution to the discussion of evangelism.

3. Jürgen Moltmann, *The Crucified God: The Cross of Christ as the Foundation and Criticism of Christian Theology* (New York: Harper and Row, 1973), p. 72.

4. Kosuke Koyama, *Mount Fuji and Mount Sinai: A Critique of Idols* (Maryknoll, NY: Orbis Books, 1984), p. 252.

5. Ibid., p. 241.

6. Kosuke Koyama, *No Handle on the Cross* (Maryknoll, NY: Orbis Books, 1977), p. 109.

7. Koyama, *Mount Fuji and Mount Sinai*, pp. 251-52.

8. *Your Kingdom Come: Mission Perspectives. Report on the World Conference on Mission and Evangelism, Melbourne, Australia 1980* (Geneva: World Council of Churches, 1980), pp. 235-36.

9. Hans Ruedi-Weber, "God's Arithmetic," *Mission Trends No.2: Evangelization*, Gerald H. Anderson and Thomas F. Stransky, eds. (New York: Paulist Press, 1978), pp. 64f.

10. Kosuke Koyama, *Three Mile an Hour God* (Maryknoll, NY: Orbis Books, 1980), p. 4.

11. Koyama, *Mount Fuji and Mount Sinai*, p. 256.

12. Ibid., p. 243.

13. Lars Lindberg, *Ny skapelse* (Stockholm: Verbum, 1986).

14. Koyama, *Three Mile an Hour God*, pp. 5-6.

15. Koyama, *Mount Fuji and Mount Sinai*, pp. 259-60.

16. *See* Lars Lindberg, *En fråga om trovärdighet—evangelisation i vår tid (A question of credibility—evangelism in our time)* (Stockholm: 1976).

17. Koyama, *Mount Fuji and Mount Sinai*, p. 244.
18. *Your Kingdom Come,* p. 169.
19. Koyama, *Mount Fuji and Mount Sinai*, p. 242.

7

Faith and Justice

The Spirituality of the Hebrew Scriptures

HUMBERTO ALFARO

The spiritual experience narrated in the Hebrew scriptures is both theological and anthropological. On the one hand, this spirituality is theological since it is centered on the relationship between the human person and God. On the other hand, it is anthropological since it also seeks to understand and even to orient human interrelationships. In order to analyze such a complex idea of spirituality, even if just in sketch form, it is necessary to take into account the factors that have originated, motivated, and been stressed in the spiritual experiences of the Hebrew scripture's characters.[1] I suggest that a failure to account for these factors can lead to a debilitating alienation of the text's narrated spiritual experience and its historical embodiment.

In every stage of the biblical narration of Israel's history, certain fundamental questions arise which call into account the dynamic relationship between creator and a people. Some of these questions are: How and where can God be encountered? How can God's will be discerned or understood? What is the meaning of human life? These fundamental questions cannot be ignored, since they provide a framework of reference for understanding the type of spiritual experience propounded in the Hebrew scriptures. In the attempt to respond to these questions, it is important to keep in mind that Hebrew thought gives priority to those historical events that are understood as demonstrative of God's activity in human history. This historical understanding of God's activity is not a static idea but, rather, a dynamic dialogue. That is to say, it is understood as an interaction between the creator and creature, God and humanity. Using these introductory and orienting remarks as a starting point, I wish to examine the factors that form the spiritual experience of the Israelite people as narrated in the Hebrew scriptures.

A SPIRITUALITY ROOTED IN HUMAN HISTORY

A careful examination of the spirituality of the Israelite people, as it is presented by the writers and redactors of the Hebrew scriptures, will lead to the realization that this form of spirituality is not the product of abstract conceptualism. On the contrary, this spirituality is founded on the purposive activity of God in history. For this reason, large segments of the Hebrew scriptures' narrative represent a theological recounting of a kind of divine meddling in human history. An example of this idea can be found in the expression "thus says the Lord . . . " (Ez 7:2-4; 25:3-5; 37:1, for instance), which is usually utilized after the biblical writers have interpreted an historical event as a clear example of God's activity in the course of human history. What is interesting in this theological formula is that it assumes that the portentous acts of God are modes of revelation. That is to say, it assumes that any speech about God can only be derived from and traced through what we as humans take to be God's activity in history.

Thus, according to the theological thought of the Hebrew scriptures, God's activity in human and natural history provides a mode of revelation of God's self, and also provides a referential framework for an understanding of spiritual experience. This understanding provides the forum for the belief that, in every historical event in which God has intervened, Israel can discover a hermeneutical paradigm by which to understand its past, present, and future. This timely hermeneutical paradigm is not merely an intellectual exercise but a pragmatic tool that enables the Hebrew people to be agents of change in the course of history. The Hebrew deity found in the Hebrew scriptural narrative reveals the divine self as the God of history. God's actions are therefore to be understood as interpretative keys of the past and also as promises and models for further futuristic divine irruptions in history through the relational activity of God and God's creation.[2] In short, the relevance of history is foundational in the spiritual experience of Israel, and this understanding confronts us with the responsibility to discern God's activity and will in our historical context.

Yet the task of speculating or discerning divine will for the purposes of orienting human activity is never an easy one. One of the reasons contributing to the difficulty of such a task is the anthropological reality of evil.[3] In other words, because of their capacity for voluntary action (free will), humans are not puppets controlled by the strings of determinism. On the contrary, humans are fully responsible for the course of human historicity. The intention of the creator should never be conceived as the mutilation of human free will but, rather, as the energy that allows for and calls for the production of creative and progressive changes in history. In this sense, faith is inextricably and symbiotically related with justice.

After affirming the concrete activity of God in history and the free will of humans, we must conclude that the general spiritual experience of Israel does not eliminate the emotive reality of the particular actors in that history. Stated otherwise, the spirituality found in the Hebrew scriptural narrative is not a form of escape from the lived reality. According to the theology of the Hebrew Bible, a spirituality that merely offers an escape from lived reality equates to a kind of pseudospirituality that undercuts human dignity. Genuine spirituality does not suffer from a paralysis that impedes intervening activity in political conflicts, nor does it suffer from indifference in face of human pain and anguish. Rather, being rooted in history, genuine spirituality always seeks integral liberation. The spirituality that the Hebrew scriptures propound challenges us to become involved in the struggle to change the systemic structures that serve to oppress. To put it boldly, the spirituality of the Hebrew scriptures integrates faith with a mercy that fights for justice.

Genuine spirituality, according to the Hebrew Bible, is the stubborn event of a God that never tires from the incessant task of human integral emancipation. This idea serves as a hope that the God of history never abandons us in our earthly journey. This hope is not a product of a sudden emotional impulse or a product of isolated intellectual reflection; rather, it is a product of an existential risk of faith that leads to a belief in the concrete activity of God in history.

At the center of the Israelite faith exists a salvific history. This salvific history holds that God is actively shaping human history while at the same time participating in the relativity of all existence. History is the locale where humans encounter God and God's plan of salvation. History is the place where God's revelation is found; however, history is also the place where humans honor God. I suggest that the religious thought of the Israelite people moves from singular and concrete to the general and abstract. That is to say, it first verifies the originality of particular acts and then moves to consider their implications. It moves from the particular to the general, even when such a conceptual move serves to question and challenge faith.

Very often these particular events are minimized by theologians, religious scholars, and biblical interpreters. Yet such a depreciation equates to a catastrophic error that truncates the unfolding of biblical spirituality, since every event, no matter how insignificant it may appear, carries with it wide-ranging implications. The reason for this, as per Hebrew religious thought, is that when God reveals Godself in a particular moment of history, God is also revealing Godself as the God of all history. Yet this type of universality does not give way to mere abstractions and empty generalities. The particularity implied remains unrenounceable, since s/he who experiences the historical moment of God's revelation is not called to be a mere philosopher but, rather, a witnessing agent who participates in the course of human history.

This idea of spiritual experience embeds the Israelite people in concrete history, even when the events they experienced challenged the religious conception that Israel had of history.[4] Yet these challenges actually serve to disallow the concept of spiritual experience in the Hebrew scriptures from falling prey to a meaningless anachronism. On the contrary, these conceptually challenging events demand that Israelite religiosity uphold a kind of spirituality that is open to the provocative nature of such historical events. Genuine spirituality always remains in touch with concrete history so that it can fulfill the role of an agent of change that integrates faith with justice. Although the way of genuine spirituality is filled with risks and hardship, I maintain that it is nevertheless preferable to take on this challenge than to succumb to the false refuge that a pseudospirituality offers by divorcing faith from the task of doing justice.

A SPIRITUALITY ENCLAVED IN WORDS AND SIGNS

We have attempted to demonstrate the relevance of history in the spiritual experience of Israel. At this point, it is necessary to acknowledge that in the Hebrew scriptures salvific history appears in a fragmentary manner. Therefore, it is necessary to develop a kind of remembrance, a theological reconstruction of Israelite history. Among the noteworthy events in this theological reconstruction of Israelite history we can include the journey of the Patriarchs and the exodus of the Hebrew people from Egypt. This remembrance is embodied in words and signs. Yet this remembrance is not a fossilized memory, rather, it energetically merges the past with the present. It is the kind of historical retelling that merges the past, in which God is taken to have demonstrated redemptive power, with the present, wherein redemptive power is taken to continue. This memory, however, presupposes the creative participation of human beings. Brazilian theologian Rubem Alves rightly criticizes classical Protestantism for its tendency to eliminate the opportunity in history for human creativity.[5] This energetic merging between divine activity and human creativity, between past and present, generates a hope for the future through an orienting spirituality.

This remembrance, which is enclaved in words and signs, celebrates the feats of the Hebrew God. It retells these feats with the hopes that it will energize the faith of its listeners. It is here that we perceive the necessity of proclamation, and it is here that we realize that proclamation is impossible without a remembrance, without a memory of the past. It is for this reason that the Hebrew scriptures place great emphasis on names, symbolic markers, and the celebration of liturgical acts.

Liturgical celebrations bring to memory the activity of God in the past and serve to energize the faith of the believing community. The Israelite liturgy does not seek to entertain or divert the participants; instead, it seeks to remind them of God's activity in the past. In doing so the Israelite liturgy merges the past with the present without forgetting about the future.

In light of what I have said, it is necessary to ask a key question: Are we, in our liturgical celebrations, remembering God's activity in past history, or are we merely exalting humanly constructed institutions? Is our liturgical celebration a remembrance of God's love for all humanity, or is it a remembrance that promotes oppression and subjugation? Does our liturgical activity serve to remember those signs of the past that communicate integral liberation, or does it promote signs that transmit racism, sexism, and discrimination? The remembrance of God's redemptive activity in history within the religious thought of the Hebrew scriptures is a promise of liberation for all humanity, not merely for a particular group or elite. In the same way, our liturgy should declare equality, plurality, and a memory of integral liberation. It is certainly irritating when the present Church ignores the fact that a liturgy that does not liberate equates to a form of blasphemy.

A MESSIANIC SPIRITUALITY

While the Hebrew community is persuaded by the remembrance expressed in liturgical celebration that affirms God's activity in history, this divine activity in history is not circumscribed to the past or the present. Rather, divine activity extends itself to the future by way of its fondness to a messianic future. This messianic component is the third factor in our interpretation of spirituality in light of the religious thought of the Hebrew scriptures. It would be a great error to attempt to understand the spiritual experience of Israel without recognizing the relevance of the idea of a messianic future. The depressive reality of history experienced by the Israelite community led them to the development of a strong messianic eschatology. Besides relying on an active deity, the spirituality of the Hebrew scriptures insists that because God is faithful, human history cannot end in chaos. Even when history has not yet revealed a clear trajectory of liberation, Hebrew religious faith still affirms God's active generosity.

It is necessary to note that the messianic hope of Israel is not founded in a naive optimism that ignores the difficulties of history; rather, it is founded in an exclusive faith that believes in God's fidelity. As Leonardo Boff rightly notes, messianic hope should manifest itself through a complete openness to God and others.[6] It is an indiscriminate love without limits. It gives primacy to persons over things.

In the unavoidable confrontation between divine fidelity and history, the spirituality of the Hebrew scriptures does not seek paths of escape that deny the lived reality. This spirituality accepts this confrontation, but it also vehemently holds that God's final redemptive response has been reserved for the future. As a consequence, this form of spirituality extracts from the future the missing significance in the present moment. This propensity for a messianic future is a product of faith, but it also serves to nourish faith. It helps Israel confront the present with the hope that the future is not uncertain. In this manner, Israel constructs a religious paleography of history without distancing itself from concrete history.

A SPIRITUALITY BETWEEN
REMEMBRANCE AND NOVELTY

The factors of spiritual experience that we have been discussing are the relevance of history, the importance of remembrance, and the Hebraic fondness towards a messianic future. Each of these factors provides solidity to the biblical idea of spirituality. But in order to maintain an equilibrium in our interpretation of spirituality in light of the Hebrew scriptural narrative, a fourth element is needed: the equanimity between remembrance and novelty. God's activity in the present is a novelty of faith. This novelty is characterized by the constant newness or freshness of God's activity in history. Thus it is important to keep a balance between God's past and divine novelty. This balance is not merely an option but the imperative that we find in the whole trajectory of the biblical narrative.

Equilibrium is an indispensable requirement in Christian spirituality. The peculiarity of biblical spirituality exists in its need to balance the memory of God's past activity in history and God's present activity. Every time the Israelite community of faith accommodated itself to bygone modes of life, God is presented by the Hebrew scriptures as a God who perturbs the people with the presentation of new events, new interventions, and new forms of crisis.

This divine pedagogy impedes the ashes of conformity from putting out the efficacy of faith. It should be noted, however, that even the past activity of God can be alienating. This element of the spiritual experience separates, in a very tangible manner, Hebrew thought from Greek thought. The Greek mythology conceived of the world as a coherent and harmonious system regulated by immutable rules. Greek thought in the pre-Christian and early Christian era was interested in discovering the laws of the cosmos and accommodating itself to such laws. Its primordial intention was the discernment and respect of the natural order.

The Hebrews, on the contrary, were interested in searching for the independent free will of God. Their concern was therefore that of participating as agents for change in human history. The divine plan was believed to be in progress, and it required faithfulness to history and at the same time a novelty that prevails over simple nostalgia. In this sense, events from the past are taken to be revelatory reference, yet the unbalanced appeal to this past was also taken to be potentially debilitating. On this matter the prophet Isaiah tells the people, "Do not remember the former things, or consider the things of old" (43:16-21). The imperative here is to move forward, to advance toward the final goal where God's redemptive plan is to be consummated. Yet in this progress, we cannot forget our historical responsibility as moral agents.

The intention of this spiritual construction in the Hebrew scriptures is to maintain a difficult but necessary balance between the liberating events of God in history and an openness in faith to that which is new. That is to say, this spirituality is a challenge to live in an equilibrium between the past and what is to come, between history and an eschatological expectation. The danger here is that a distorted dependency on the past can curtail an active faith. Therefore, the relevance of this structure exists in its ability to liberate the people not from history but from an existentially meaningless nostalgia. It should be noted that this equilibrium is possible for those who hold to a linear conception of history that foresees a progression toward an ultimate goal of liberation.

The Hebrew scriptures do not pretend to conceal the ample cultural sharing that Israel experiences with adjacent cultures. This interaction with problems, concepts, and customs of neighboring civilizations engenders cultural forms of assimilation that reveal themselves in all the dimensions of Israelite spirituality. Yet, in this incontrovertible assimilation of other civilizations, there is one theological inheritance that Israel maintains.

This particular element of Israelite spirituality, just as our previously mentioned elements, arises from the premise that God is active in human history. This form of spirituality holds that God directs and operates in history and is also worthy of human trust and faithfulness. This sort of faith can be confused with a determinism that undercuts the voluntary capacity of human beings. But a careful analysis of the biblical narrative indicates that this is not the idea of faith proposed by Israelite spirituality. Rather, Israelite spirituality binds together the belief in God's purposive activity in history and human responsibility. The achievement of this sort of integration, which holds together a belief in divine action and human moral responsibility, makes the Hebrew scriptures' type of spirituality especially appealing and useful.

SPIRITUALITY AND THE PRESENCE AND ABSENCE OF GOD

The Israelite community of faith believed it experienced the active presence of Yahweh with such a fervor that declarations such as "God liberated us from Egypt" appear continuously in many segments of the Hebrew Bible. Even so, the Israelite people also experienced moments where God's presence seemed to be absent. This religious assumption that God was absent in certain pockets of history is articulated frequently by the biblical writers through a question: Where is God? God's activity in this sense is very disconcerting: First God liberates the Hebrew community, then it appears that God abandons it (*see* Ex 14:11; 16:3; 17:3; and Nm 11:4-6; 11:31-34).

In this journey, highlighted by divine activity and absence, we find another element of Israelite spirituality: God's abandonment. The objective of this element is not to do away with divine mystery, since this would be a fruitless attempt. Rather, in the Hebrew scriptures, God's absence and silence is interpreted as an actual part of God's pedagogy. That is to say, these chaotic moments in history where God appears to be absent and silent are taken to be pathways to greater human maturity. Yet even in light of these kind of assertions, in moments of existential and sociocultural chaos, the Israelites often felt compelled to search for other gods. Essentially, they wanted a deity that would be less disturbing than Yahweh. Yet time and time again, the Hebrew people were compelled back into the belief and worship of Yahweh because of the attractiveness of a concept of God that upheld divine activity and human responsibility in the course of history.

Under the framework of Israelite spirituality, those chaotic moments where God seems to be absent from history are interpreted as moments in which God's salvific activity remains undetectable by human intellect. In other words, God's activity is assumed as being present, even when it is not discernible or understood. We should note that certain tensions arise from this element of Israelite spirituality. God is transcendent, but God is also taken to be immanent in history. God is the protagonist of history, but history is also shaped by human autonomy. God is Lord of history, but yet evil exists in history. God acts in favor of humans, but God is not swayed by human action. Interestingly, the biblical narrative accepts, declares, and even supports these antinomies, but it does not resolve them. The narrative's framework, however, does suggest three things. First, the God of history always allows for human freedom of choice and thus allows a space for evil. Second, although God allows space for human freedom and evil, God remains the protagonist and Lord of history. Third, God's absence and silence are not simply pedagogical, but are a necessary space that force us to take responsibility.

SPIRITUALITY AND THE TEMPTATION OF IDOLATRY

Each one of the elements mentioned in the above paragraphs plays a crucial role within the spirituality propounded by the Hebrew scriptures. It is necessary to note, however, that these reflections would remain incomplete if we were to ignore the fact that every authentic spirituality must be tested by the experience of temptation. The particular type of temptation that Israel repeatedly encountered was that of idolatry.[7]

A large part of the biblical narrative deals with the Israelites' spiritual combat with the seduction of idolatry. Evidence of this combat is reflected in the prophetic tradition of the Hebrew scriptures. These prophets of God greatly stressed the importance of monotheism and ridiculed idolatrous worship. An exemplary biblical passage that demonstrates this point is Isaiah 44, where the folly of idolatry is exposed. According to this passage, as well as others, the mistake of idolatry exists in its confused identification of creature with creator. That is to say, idolatry confuses creation with creator: Idolatry makes that which is created or humanly constructed a God. Idolatry, in Israelite spirituality, is the placement of trust in another God than Yahweh. It is also the restriction of God's mastery through the imposition of selfish human desire and activity. In this sense, it is important to note that idolatry transcends the actual tangible idol or object that is worshiped. Idolatry, in a more concrete and meaningful manner, equates to the prostitution of human values that leads to or allows for the oppression of other persons, groups, and even the natural world.

In the biblical prophetic tradition, many human sins are discussed and eschewed. However, the prophetic framework holds that at the core of all sin is idolatry. As I see it, there are three elements in idolatrous acts: distrust in God, a search for false securities, and a corrosive desire for independence. In this sense, idolatry is not merely the rejection of God. Once God is rejected, God is substituted by something or someone that is held in higher esteem, something or someone that is believed to be more immovable than God. That is to say, idolatry strips God from the ultimacy that only God deserves. Theologian Gordon Kaufman, following Paul Tillich's earlier insights, rightly notes that:

> By "God," then, we mean the ultimate point of reference for all understanding of anything; by "God" we mean the ultimate object of devotion for human life. . . . It is precisely this ultimacy, however, interpreted mythically or metaphysically, that distinguishes God from all idols, and it is only because of this ultimacy that God can be considered an appropriate object of worship, a reality to which self and community may properly give themselves in unlimited devotion. To give oneself in worship and devotion to anything less than "the ultimate point of reference"—anything less than God—would be to fall into bondage to some finite reality, eventually destroying the self and making true human fulfillment (that is, salvation), impossible.[8]

Similarly, speaking about the subject of God and idolatry, the prophet Jeremiah offers the following words from God: "for my people have committed two evils:

they have forsaken me, the fountain of living water, and dug out cisterns for themselves, cracked cisterns that can hold no water" (Jer 2:13).

There are two basic types of idolatry. The first type can be called an open idolatry. This type of idolatry renounces a monotheistic faith in order to search for other gods, to which one's worship and devotion are given. The second type of idolatry equates to a legalistic religiosity. I suggest that this second type of idolatry is even worse than the first because it is hypocritical. This type of idolatry is very dangerous, for it enlists appeals of divine approval for particular actions that can at times be corrosive and irresponsible. This kind of religious legalism usually insists on the observation of strict rules of conduct that benefit the purposes of its practitioners. It should be noted that this kind of idolatry does not renounce allegiance to God and, in the case of Israelite religion, it does not renounce allegiance to Yahweh. Rather, this type of idolatry makes God part of a plurality of gods. In this manner it can superficially continue giving the appearance that the practitioners of this legalistic form of idolatry remain people of God.

The narrative presented in Exodus clarifies this point. This biblical passage narrates that the Hebrew people constructed a golden calf in the desert that came to symbolize the power of God. In this case, allegiance to Yahweh was not completely renounced; rather, allegiance to Yahweh was shared with another god. I suggest that both types of idolatry lead to the same conclusion. Whether through total renouncement or through a partial renouncement, both forms of idolatry lead to despair. Giving ultimacy to any sort of idol leads the idolatrous person to a destructive self sacrifice and also to the trampling of other peoples' dignity. In short, idolatry is a lessening of God's supremacy, and it always leads to human destruction.

I believe it is necessary to examine how this idea of idolatry finds significance within various kinds of temptations that contemporary Christianity faces. A religious temptation that still continues today is that of legitimating an oppressive status quo. Another religious temptation is that of reading the biblical narratives in a closed minded manner that only seeks to restore or maintain past ecclesiological models. I believe that the task of any religious or theological construction is not to return to old models but to evaluate those models continuously for the purposes of constructing new meaningful models of religious/theological orientation. I believe feminist theologian Sallie McFague eloquently makes this idea clear when she states:

> No longer is it possible to insist without question on the "fixed canonic and binding" character of metaphors and the concepts built upon them that have come to us "after long usage." The constructive character of theology must be acknowledged, and this becomes of critical importance when the world we live in is profoundly different from the world in which many of the traditional metaphors and concepts gained currency. Theologians must think experimentally, must risk novel constructions in order to be theologians for our time.[9]

On this note, I believe that culture provides a necessary source for the birth of a meaningful evangelical proclamation. It is in the realm of lived history where we can affirm that our religious commitment is to the transformation of humans. This I believe to be the core message of the biblical narratives: the transformation of human relationships. This message, in Leonardo Boff's words, requires a "total/integral liberation" of human beings.[10]

In the theological perception of the Hebrew scriptures, true blessing comes from and after liberational activity in favor of the people. As a result of this assumption, Israelite spirituality holds that those who say they love God must demonstrate that love through acts of benevolence, mercy, and justice (for example, *see* Hos 6:6; 10:12; 12:7). The ethical demand of this sort of spirituality calls for the transformation of the social structures that serve to oppress society's losers. In sum, in the Hebrew scriptures, the proper relationship of the Israelite community with its God is determined by a faith that is committed to salvific action in favor of the oppressed in history. In the framework of this spirituality, God is a benevolent actor who works in history, leading those who allow themselves to be led by God's Spirit toward greater love, mercy, compassion, and justice.

SPIRITUALITY AND THE HISPANIC
CONDITION IN THE UNITED STATES

The kind of spirituality that I have traced in the Hebrew scriptures most basically equates to a manner of living in or living out life. To put it in Justo Gonzalez' words, "spirituality is first of all living in the gospel—making faith the foundation for life. And it is also living out the gospel—making faith the foundation of action and structure."[11] In this sense, the spirituality we have traced can be used as a model for other communities of faith. Being a Hispanic/Latino, I have in mind the Hispanic/Latino[12] community in the United States. I am careful not to suggest that a particular kind of spirituality can be forced upon a people without being mindful of the uniqueness of a people's culture. However, I will suggest that some general insights could be carried over from the Israelite model of spirituality into other sociocultural contexts without falling prey to a naive kind of universality. I submit that United States Hispanics can make use of some general insights that the Israelite spirituality of the Hebrew scriptures present. Most notably, I believe that the idea of idolatry found in the Hebrew scriptures can be a useful one for United States Hispanics who wish to make sense of the evils in American culture and wish to be critical of these evils with the hope of transforming the structures that oppress segments of the American population.

The Hispanic community is a rapidly growing community in the United States. By many accounts, it may become the largest so-called minority group in the United States by the year 2000. Nevertheless, the Hispanic population within the United States sociocultural scene suffers greatly from disproportionate poverty, unemployment, harmful racial stereotypes that promote racial discrimination, deteriorating housing conditions in city slums, and a multitude of other oppressive situations. The dismal lived reality of most Hispanics is not a result of internal choice but results from external pressures that serve to oppress this segment of the American population. Hispanics must struggle against certain discriminatory perceptions that serve to stymie the upward social mobility of this social group (Hispanics are wrongly perceived as lazy, unproductive, undisciplined, unskilled, unintelligent, inferior welfare recipients who are simply a drain on the American economy). In light of these sociocultural pressures, Hispanics must come up with a spirituality that could help them combat and survive these oppressive forces. As I see it, this spirituality, among other things, will need to engage in a struggle against those social conditions that serve to oppress, seek conscientization (the development of a critical consciousness among the Hispanic masses), and affirm the practical worthiness of community/solidarity. Toward this goal, I believe that the idea of idolatry found in the Israelite spirituality can be useful as an orientative model for United States Hispanics.

As we have seen, idolatry in the Hebrew scriptures is most properly understood as the bestowal of ultimate value on any human construction. Idolatry equates to confusing God (or that which is worthy of human admiration and worship) with other gods (those things which are not worthy of human admiration and worship). It is important that Hispanics in America not bestow any ultimate value on those sociocultural, sociopolitical, and socioeconomic structures that serve to oppress them. Hispanics need to develop a critical consciousness that fights against feelings of conformity with the status quo. As Eldin Villafane rightly notes, "all social structures and institutions have moral values embedded in them. They can be good or evil. To speak of sinful structures and institutions is to speak of structures and institutions that have become distorted, misguided, destructive or oppressive."[13]

These sinful structures and institutions that have served to promote injustice against Hispanics must be unmasked. They must not be treated as a god that deserves our unquestioned allegiance. This sort of unquestioned allegiance would equate to idolatry and a corrosive form of spirituality. A genuine spirituality serves to promote freedom, equality, and justice. To achieve this goal, a social spirituality that serves to promote Hispanic liberation must keep in mind, and in the people's mind, that social structures are not a god and any social structure or institution that serves to promote injustice must be spoken against and not conformed to as if it held some kind of ultimate value. Our active struggle against oppressive social conditions, our process of conscientization, our affirmation of community and liberation require that we expose reigning oppressive social conditions and their consequences without fear and for what they really are—social idols that are not worthy of our admiration or worship. This orientative insight can be gained by looking back into the integration of faith and justice that occurs in the Hebrew scriptures' form of spirituality. The practical spirituality that ensued from the integration of faith and justice in the Hebrew scriptures continues to be a useful model for those groups of people who still fight for their freedom, equality, and liberation.

NOTES

1. I should note that in this essay I am speaking from the perspective of a religious-theological practitioner/minister, rather than from the perspective of a Hebrew Bible scholar. Nevertheless, as a religious-theological practitioner who is called upon to apply the biblical

message in real lived experiences, I am willing and also able to join in the dialogue of interpreting the biblical message in light of our contemporary context. I have been encouraged in this endeavor by Kosuke Koyama, who has likewise sought to interpret the Bible in light of his context. In doing so, Koyama has challenged the notion that biblical interpretation belongs exclusively to the academically trained elite.

2. I should note that I particularly have in mind human activity. Although I would include the serendipitous activity of the greater natural context in this phrase, I particularly focus here on the human capacity for moral reflection and action.

3. Specifically, I have in mind moral evil. I refer here to the actions of human agents that carry the intent of harm (inclusive of the greater natural world as well as humans). For a clear, concise, and helpful explanation of moral evil, *see* Patricia L. Wismer, *A New Handbook of Christian Theology*, ed. Donald W. Musser and Joseph L. Price (Nashville: Abingdon Press, 1992), pp. 173-75.

4. For a further explanation of this idea, *see* R. De Vaux, "The Presence and Absence of God in History According to the Old Testament," *Concilium* 50 (1969): 494.

5. Rubem Alves, *A Theology of Human Hope* (Washington, DC: Corpus Books, 1969), p. 142.

6. Leonardo Boff, *Jesus Christ Liberator: A Critical Christology for Our Times* (Maryknoll, NY: Orbis Books, 1978), p. 110.

7. Here I find my dialogue with Kosuke Koyama's *Mount Fuji and Mount Sinai: A Critique of Idols* (Maryknoll, NY: Orbis Books, 1985) to be especially helpful.

8. Gordon Kaufman, *Theology for a Nuclear Age* (Philadelphia: Westminster Press, 1985), p. 25.

9. Sallie McFague, *Models of God: Theology for an Ecological, Nuclear Age* (Philadelphia: Fortress Press, 1987), p. 6.

10. Boff, *Jesus Christ Liberator*, pp. 290-91.

11. Justo L. Gonzalez, *Mañana: Christian Theology from a Hispanic Perspective* (Nashville: Abingdon Press, 1990), p. 157.

12. The term *Hispanic* accounts for five historical and geographical divisions: those whose origins are found in Middle America/Mexico, Central Americans; Caribbean peoples (Cubans, Puerto Ricans, and Dominicans), The Andean peoples, and the borderlands peoples of the American Southwest and California. It attempts to account for a large number of ethnic communities that now live on a permanent basis in the United States. For a helpful analysis of who the Hispanics are, *see* Allan Figueroa Deck, "The Spirituality of United States Hispanics: An Introductory Essay," in Arturo J. Bañuelas, ed., *Mestizo Christianity: Theology from the Latino Perspective* (Maryknoll, NY: Orbis Books, 1985), pp. 226-35.

13. Eldin Villafane, "An Evangelical Call to a Social Spirituality," in Arturo J. Bañuelas, ed., *Mestizo Christianity: Theology from the Latino Perspective* (Maryknoll, NY: Orbis Books, 1985), p. 214.

8

Mount Fuji, Mount Baekdu, and Mount Sinai

The Echoes of the Mountains

DAVID KWANG-SUN SUH

HAN OF AUGUST MOON

Choosuk is the ancient thanksgiving day for Koreans. This is the day for all Koreans to offer the year's harvest to heaven and pay their respects to their ancestors' spirits at the family graves. Family members scattered around the world come back to the family grave sites on the hills of their hometowns to celebrate Choosuk. This is also an annual family reunion day; family members living in this world gather together in the presence of the spirits of family members in the other world. This is the time of reconciliation—some arguments, some crying and weeping over a little rice wine—in memory of the deceased or some family feud, but departing with a feeling of consolation and reconciliation in the names of the ancestors' spirits.

During the three-day Choosuk holiday, Seoul was almost empty, while all the highways were jammed with cars carrying people to the countryside. I drove up to my parents-in-law's graveyard with my family. When our son was a teenage boy, he used to ask me about my father's graveyard, but he stopped asking me about that because now he knows why we don't go there and because he often saw me getting upset and even angry. Even this year I knew he wanted to ask me this deadly question: "Do you still think that you can go to the North and find your father's grave in your lifetime?" But he would not, because I wouldn't know the answer. Instead of an answer, I might have given him a deep sigh with tears in my eyes. For Koreans, not visiting one's ancestors' graveyard at least once a year during the Choosuk holidays is a sin violating filial piety. This is what Confucianism taught us from time immemorial.

Millions of North Koreans left home during the Korean War, promising they would come back home to celebrate the next Choosuk at their family grave sites. I left my father's grave on the southern hillside of Pyungyang, the capital city of North Korea, looking over the evergreen Daedong River, and for over four decades, I have never been able to take care of my father's lonely grave.

POLITICAL THEOLOGY OF MOUNT FUJI[1]
AND MOUNT BAEKDU[2]

My father was a freedom preacher. When he was young, he refused to worship at the Japanese Shinto shrine. Most of the Korean preachers under the Japanese colonial rule preached on Moses' Exodus as if the liberation stories of the Hebrews were the stories of the enslaved Koreans under Japanese colonialism. My father was no exception. When I was old enough to understand the language of the Bible, I understood why the stories of Exodus, Daniel, and Esther were so important to the Koreans. The language of the Bible is the language of liberation, the stories of the Bible are stories of the salvation of oppressed people, and the image of God in the Bible is the God of justice. For Korean preachers, God was the one who would correct the wrong history of Japanese colonialism and bring forth justice, freedom, and independence. In their faith they were firm about God's political action in the world of human history.

My preacher father could not stand the fact that I was forced to pay respect to the Shinto shrine. As a third-grader, I had no way of refusing the forced group activity on the mountain behind the primary school, where the shrine was located. He even visited my school's Japanese principal and requested permission for me to stay away from the Shinto worship. My father thought that every Christian had the right to stay away from such idol worship. My father truly believed that Shinto worship or the thought that the Japanese emperor was divine was wrong because it was idol worship. He himself refused to attend Shinto shrine worship with other preachers in town. He was taken in by the Japanese police and beaten up. I remember my father saying that the Japanese police asked him, Who is higher, the Christian God or the Japanese emperor? His answer was clear and stubborn: Of course the Christian God is much higher than any human being, and the Japanese emperor is just a human being. My father had to stay in bed for a week after the beating and decided to quit the ministry and go into a grocery business in another town.

The small village church preacher of Korea seemed to have understood intuitively the political meaning of the first two commandments of iconoclasm: "You shall not make for yourself an idol," and "you shall not bow down to them or worship them" (Ex 20:4a,5a). These commandments encouraged the American missionaries to demand the first Christian converts destroy literally all the Shaman rituals and artifacts, Confucian ancestor worship, and home sanctuaries. Those things that were Korean and not "Christian" were considered idols by the missionaries, and they were to be destroyed as one became a Christian. The Korean con-verts followed the missionary teaching. It was therefore quite natural for them to refuse the Japanese order to pay religious respect to the emperor and to the Japan-ese Shinto shrines. They were neither Christian nor Korean. It was not only a reli-gious idol, but also a political idol. The Korean village preachers intuited that worship of the emperor and Shinto Shrine was not only religiously forbidden, but also politically so. To bow down to the Shinto shrine was not only a religious act of idol worship, like worshiping woods, stones, or graven images, it was also a politi-cal act of idol worship—like heiling Hitler. Refusal of the Shinto shrine was a mat-ter of *status confessionis* for Korean Christians under Japanese occupation.

Kosuke Koyama is one of the few Japanese Christian theologians openly critical about the "divine emperor." He does not think the Japanese divine emperor is "through God." He says, " 'Through God' is the principle of the critique of idols. The holy God refuses to tolerate the divine emperor for the sake of his holiness. This is the way God experiences history." But Koyama thinks that "This line of thought . . . is quite foreign to Japanese cultural heritage," and that "Japan made the divine emperor quite openly without 'guilt feeling'. "[3] If he said this sort of thing in the 1940s in Japan or Korea, he would have been thrown into prison with other Korean preachers, many of whom died in prison cells. However, in 1938, the Gen-eral Assembly of the Korean Presbyterian Churches adopted a forced resolution that "there is no contradiction between the Christian faith and Shinto shrine worship."[4] Korean Christian delegates to the assembly perhaps unwillfully accepted the divine emperor publicly, with guilt feelings. Korean Christian leaders could not resist the orders of the Japanese colonial authorities to make the divine emperor and Shinto shrine holy, neither religiously nor politically, realizing fully they are both religious and political idols.[5]

IDEOLOGY, WAR, AND MARTYRDOM

In defiance of the Korean church leaders' decision on the Shinto shrine issue, my father stubbornly refused to join other preachers and pay respect to the local shrine. Finally he left the church and opened a grocery store in a northern border town on the southern bank of the Yalu River,[6] facing a Chinese village that can be reached by crossing a railroad bridge. I was happy because the whole family had enough to eat. My father was a better businessperson than a preacher, I thought. The business was flourishing, and our economic situation was better off. But one severe winter morning, he announced to the family that he would leave for Manchuria.[7] He had been appointed by an American missionary-teacher-mentor to a Korean church in Manchuria. In that severe cold winter of 1941, when the Japanese emperor declared war against the United States, our family crossed the Yalu River by train over the iron bridge.

I remember the heavy snow and cold wind of the deserted flatland of Manchuria, a small village school, and a run-down church where my father ministered as an itinerant preacher. The church was rapidly growing, and my father had to move to another place because the local police noticed his nationalistic preachings on Exodus and Daniel. He was, through and through, an anti-Japanese preacher, denouncing the divine emperor and Shintoism as idol worship. His theology was an intuitive, gut-level, political theology. He was a nationalist Christian, as most conscientious preachers of the time were. One of his favorite passages in Paul's letters was Romans 9:1-3: "I am speaking the truth in Christ—I am not lying; my conscience confirms it by the Holy Spirit—I have great sorrow and unceasing anguish in my heart. For I could wish that I myself were accursed and cut off from Christ for the sake of my own people, my kindred according to the flesh" (NRSV).

An anti-Japanese nationalist like my father could use this passage as a proof text to prove his or her position. Many Christians have used this passage in their resistance against oppressive colonial power and to fight revolutionary wars in national independence movements. But this passage cannot only be used by oppressed or colonized people. It can be used by oppressors and colonizers as well. In the name of nationalism, Christians in powerful oppressor nations could be on the side of the oppressors and justify their actions.

Paul was not arguing for the nationalist or racist point of view. He was a nationalist and a Jew among the Jews, arguing against racism and insisting upon the opening of the Christian mission among the Gentiles. His nationalism is under the judgment of God. He quotes Hosea:

> "Those who were not my people I will call 'my people,'
>   and her who was not beloved I will call 'beloved.'
> "And in the very place where it was said to them, 'You are not my people,'
>   there they shall be called children of the living God."
>
> (Rom 9:25-26, NRSV)

Koyama and my father would argue on the same point that their respective nationalism is under the judgment of God, who is the source of any political power. A country preacher like my father understood it intuitively in his faith, while theologian Koyama presented his argument more powerfully. For Koyama, the Japanese nationalism that is the backbone of the divine emperor is an idol. Like Paul, in spite of Koyama's love for his country and Mount Fuji—the symbolic mountain for all Japanese—and because of his patriotism and nationalism, he has stood up to say in his book that the divine emperor is "not through God" and therefore is an idol for Christians. He presents and comments on the passage from Hosea:

> They made kings, but not through me. They set up princes, but without my knowledge (Hos 8:4).

> They [kings and princes] must not have the ultimate authority. They are subjected to the Higher Authority. In the very process of making kings and setting up princes the whole community must know that politics independent of God will lead eventually to the destructive influence of idolatry. . . . "Through God" is the principle of the critique of idols. The holy God refuses to tolerate the divine emperor for the sake of his holiness.[8]

Professor Koyama and my father both insist that the divine emperor is an idol, and both of them are ardent nationalists. The only difference between the two was that Koyama was a citizen of the oppressor nation of Japan and my father was one of the oppressed people in the colonized country, where Christians were victimized as enemies of the state. They were both nationalists and Christians, but for my father, obedience to the commandments and the name of God reinforced his nationalism, while Koyama, on account of his faith in God, had to denounce his nationalism.

LIBERATION AND DIVISION

When I heard the radio announcement of the divine emperor on the end of the Second World War, I was in a ditch that my Japanese classmates of the ninth grade in a Manchurian middle school were digging. We were digging antitank ditches on the hillside of a Manchurian mine town[9] to defend the town from the invading Soviet army, which declared war against Japan on August 8, 1945. We were immediately sent home. When I went home, my parents were already in the process of packing to leave for Korea. "Korea is liberated." This is the only thing my father repeated as he told my mother what to pack and what to leave. The next thing I remember, we were on the last train to leave for Korea.

My father decided to take his family to his hometown near the Yalu River, some 150 miles northeast of Pyungyang, the North Korean capital. He did not know at the time that the Korean peninsula would be divided for good. Actually, no Korean knew about the division. The only ones who knew were a few generals in the Pentagon who had deliberated on the advance of the United States forces on the island of Japan and procedures for disarming the Japanese soldiers and establishing the military occupation of Japan. A line was drawn on the 38th parallel, and it was agreed that north of the line would be occupied and ruled by the Soviets and that south of the line would be at the hands of the United States armed forces. We thought that all the soldiers, Soviets and Americans, would leave soon after the Japanese soldiers went home.

There were a number of attempts to leave Korean affairs to the Koreans, but all failed, and the foreign soldiers stayed on until in 1948 a pro-American government was established in the south and a pro-Soviet government in the north. The Soviet soldiers left Korea immediately after the establishment of the two separate governments, but the American soldiers stayed on. Korea was divided not only for military reasons but for political and ideological reasons as well.

After he came back to our North Korean hometown and settled in a new parish church, my father became an anti-Communist preacher. He decided that the Communist state in the north was a state of anti-Christ and the Christians in the north were in a "Babylonian captivity." Once again he preached on the Exodus and liberation. As a student activist against the oppressive school curriculum and organization of the Communist Youth League at school, I had frequent dialogues with my father. I challenged him as to why he was an anti-Communist, when he came from a poor farming family, had been ministering to a poor congregation for so long, and preached about equality and justice in society. As a conservative preacher, he opposed Communism as atheism, a godless ideology, and he despised Communist police brutality against those who had land and money. My father lost many church leaders who were brutally tortured and chased out of their households and land because they were bourgeois landowners who "sucked the blood of the working class." He once again denounced self-made political idols, this time of the Communist Party and their politics. He did not think, according to Hosea, that the North Korean Communist regime was "through God."

On the eve of the Korean War, which started on June 25, 1950, he was taken into custody by the North Korean police. A bloody three-month battle ensued that almost unified the country by force. The North Korean People's army retreated when the United States army, led by General MacArthur, launched a surprise attack. MacArthur's army occupied most of the North Korean territories and was prepared to go home by Christmas of the same year. But then the Chinese People's army marched into the north to fight against the United Nations forces, and the totally unprepared United States army had to retreat south of the 38th parallel. While the United States troops were in the city of Pyungyang as the occupational force and Pyungyang was celebrating its liberation from the oppressive Communist regime, my family and parish members and I searched for my father. After a week-long search, I finally found his bullet-ridden body on the Daedong riverbank on an evening of freezing October wind. After a church funeral for my father, we had to leave home for the south, along with the columns of retreating South Korean and United States soldiers.

POLITICAL ECONOMY OF THE HAN OF DIVISION

When the August moon is full and bright, millions of us separated in the north and south swallow tears that well out of our broken hearts of deepest han—longing for the family members left behind, with shame and guilt for our "escape" from danger to safety and comfort. Millions of Koreans on both sides lost family members in combat and bombings. Thousands of men who left their wives in their North Korean homes and remarried in South Korea are still weeping silently, thinking about the whereabouts of their family members in the north. Hundreds and thousands of South Korean families cannot openly visit their family graveyards because their sons, brothers, sisters, husbands, and fathers were tortured and killed, standing on firing lines in dark nights of horror in South Korean army massacres of innocent villagers. They were framed as pro-Communists who were helping North Korean spies and guerrillas hiding in the villages. There are people who have no graveyards to visit, neither in the south nor in the north, because their fathers and sons were missing in combat or in kidnapping. Because of the division, people were killed for being pro-Communist as well as for being anti-Communist: they killed anti-Communists in North Korea and pro-Communists in South Korea. Not only were they killed because of their ideological convictions, but many were killed just because they happened to live in this divided and wartorn country.

Even as we heard the sound of the Berlin wall breaking down on television, the 200-mile-long Demilitarized Zone barbed-wire fence was becoming higher and tighter. Since 1972 (some twenty years after the armistice agreement was signed by North Koreans, Chinese, and the United States), when government leaders from the north and south announced the so-called July Fourth agreement on the reunification of Korea, there has been a considerable amount of governmental and nongovernmental exchanges in Korea and abroad, and there have been significant changes in inter-Korean dialogues for the establishment of peace on the peninsula. Twice a limited number of North Korean civilians were able to visit their missing family members in South Korea, and a limited and select number of South Korean civilians visited their missing family members in the north with a large entourage of reporters and entertainers. Although North Korean sports teams refused to come to Seoul to participate in the 1988 Olympics, sports teams from the north and south meet quite often in the international sports arena, and sometimes they organize joint teams to compete against other nationals. South Korean musicians were invited to the north and North Koreans to the south. In 1993, South Korean women leaders went north and visited Kim Il Sung, the North Korean President for nearly a half-century, and a return delegation of North Korean women visited Seoul. Since 1986, some South Korean Christian leaders have been able to meet North Korean counterparts in Switzerland, Japan, the United States, and Canada to talk about reconciliation, peace, and the reunification of Korea.

In spite of the glittering record of these inter-Korean exchanges, the accumulated han of the divided people of Korea has not been released. There is no crossing the DMZ to visit families and family graveyards on the other side, even just for one day. There is no postal service across the border. South Koreans cannot subscribe to North Korean newspapers, nor can North Koreans turn on some of the decadent South Korean show programs. In the early summer of 1994, former president Jimmy Carter visited North Korean President Kim Il Sung, and we heard the surprising news that North Korean President Kim would meet and talk with South Korean President Kim. In the middle of preparations for this inter-Korean summit in the late summer of that year, North Korean Kim died of old age.

Han is primarily a psychological feeling experienced when a person's desire is not satisfied. One might have the unsatisfied han of wanting to fill his or her stomach, or the never-fulfilled desire for education, political power, or wealth. But when one's desire is not satisfied because of unfair reasons one cannot control, the feeling of han mounts up. And when a person is unjustly and even inhumanely treated and is not allowed to speak up or protest against the unjust treatment, the feeling of han accumulates. And when that feeling has to be repressed for survival, the whole existence of that person becomes nothing but a han.

The han of division is not only a personal han, but also a structural one. The han of the division of the Korean people is not limited to a feeling of sorrow and a sense of shame and guilt for not being able to visit graveyards of war victims or not being able to have a family reunion across the DMZ barbed wire. In itself, of course, the han of the division is heartbreaking for those of us who have no hometown to return to. But more than that, the han of the division of Korea has been accumulated because of its history and structure. The han of division has been imposed upon the Korean people by the superpowers since 1945. This is the han that has been accumulated since the end of the Second World War, the liberation, division, and the Korean War. For Koreans, the Second World War will not be over until the state of division is over, and the Cold War will not be not over until the north-south confrontation and conflict are over.

Since 1953, when the Korean War was officially over, the political economy of Korea has been built on the basis of national division, military confrontation, economic competition, and ideological degradation. North and South Korea define each other as mortal enemies, and both sides have armed their 2 million soldiers to the teeth with the most sophisticated modern firearms, at the expense of nearly 6 percent of the South Korean GNP and 20 percent of the North Korean GNP. In the so-called peacetime military camps, combat-free army generals became ambitious. They grabbed political power with the justification that the fate of the nation was in danger from a North Korean Communist invasion. The division of the nation was a convenient excuse for the army generals to come into the political arena, where they suppressed the parliamentary process, rigged the national elections, reneged on their public promises to go democratic, and forced the people to accept their lifelong tenure in power. In maintenance of the politics of division, the basic rights of the press, assembly, and free expression of political opinion were all suppressed. The country's prisons filled with protesting students, intellectuals, opposition party leaders, and conscientious religious leaders.

The leading ideologies of the last three decades have been national security and anti-Communism. Around these "national" ideologies, the military culture has set the life-style of the people. A culture of hate, suspicion, vengeance, and violence against the Communist north has become our mind-set. From primary school curriculum to college required courses on "national ethics," the North Koreans are regarded as less than animals and Communism is depicted as the archenemy of humankind. Hatred of Communism led the government to say that all criticism against the military government on any issue was collaboration with the enemy and therefore pro-Communist, and should be eliminated by law—the national security law. Furthermore, any knowledge about the north was forbidden, and any discussion of the reunification of Korea, or any way of making connection with people in or from North Korea, would be punished severely by law. Most fundamentally, the Korean people were alienated from the process of government, from basic human rights, and from participation in the decision-making process that determined their own destiny. Because of the division, we had to give up democracy and our God-given human rights. This is the most fundamental political han of the people of the divided Korea.

A THEOLOGY OF HAN: MINJUNG THEOLOGY

Korean minjung theology is an articulation of the han of the Korean people. It has grown out of the political context of 1970s and is primarily a political theology.

The political theology of minjung has been developed out of reflection on the praxis of resistance against the military dictatorship. It is the Christian mission to stand with God against oppressive political powers. The minjung theologians called the military dictatorship an idol, for it absolutized its power and stood against human rights.[10] Any power that stands above a human person stands against God. No power should stand above a human person, for power comes from the people and is to serve the people. Minjung theologians believe that their God stands against absolutizing political powers, stands in judgment of them, and relativizes them.

The political theology of the minjung theologians is a reclaiming of the minjung critique of idols against the Japanese divine emperor and the Shinto shrine, and against the oppressive Communist regime in North Korea. It is also an ecumenical discovery of the political theologies in the contemporary West. Most minjung theologians were deeply influenced by political theologians such as Karl Barth and Dietrich Bonhoeffer in the German Confessing Church, as well as Jürgen Moltmann. The American Civil Rights movement and the Latin American Liberation movement have also been avidly discussed in theological schools and among the student Christian movements in Korea.

If the theological concerns of minjung theology in the 1970s were struggle against the antidemocratic military dictatorship and the critique of political idol making and worshiping, its main concern in the 1980s was the han of the division, the root cause of militarism in the post-Cold War era. People came to realize that the division of the country is the real root cause of many other political problems. Continuous military dictatorship appears inevitable, once one accepts the ever-present threat of war. The presence of United States forces likewise seems inevitable in order for South Korea to defend itself against a possible North Korean invasion. Freedom of speech and other human-rights issues have been curtailed, seemingly in order to fight the Communist north. The national security ideology divides the country and keeps pushing it further apart. The Korean minjung continued to suffer under the perpetual division of the country, because they were mobilized for military service, while the labor movement was also weakened, and most human rights could not be advocated under the national security ideology.

THE INTERNATIONAL STRUCTURE OF DIVISION

National division is a collective han of the Korean people. As I mentioned above, right after the liberation of 1945, the 38th parallel line was drawn across the peninsula by the Soviet and United States governments without a single consultation with the Korean people. The Korean people are a han-ridden people with a long history of colonialism, foreign invasion, and subjugation. A small country surrounded by such great powers as China, Japan, and Russia, Korea has been a prey of imperial advances. The Korean people have accumulated in their collective consciousness a han of people who have been oppressed and exploited by foreign powers. The division of Korea is another heavy addition to the already accumulated national han of the Korean people.

With the liberation of 1945, the occupying Japanese armed forces were disarmed and left Korea for good. But the victorious liberation armies of the United States and the Soviet Union, who came to Korea to disarm the retreating Japanese soldiers, stayed to solidify not only geographical but ideological division. During the Korean War, some fifteen national armies landed on Korean soil and sacrificed their lives under the United Nations flag, and millions of Chinese soldiers pushed into the north to fight beside the North Korean army. Japanese soldiers stayed in Korea for about thirty-six years (1910-1945); United States troops have been stationed in the south for fifty years (1945-1995). About 43,000 United States soldiers are in Korea. Their supreme commanding general is in control of the United Nation's command and the United States army, and exercises operational command of the Republic of Korea (ROK) army. United States soldiers are placed at the front line of defense against the north, and their police guard the Panmunjum Joint Security Area. Millions of dollars are paid to the United States government to make the soldiers stay as long as the land is divided and as long as there is a threat of a North Korean invasion.

Until three years ago, every springtime the whole Korean land—the mountains, rivers, woods, and rice paddies—were alarmed by soldiers conducting massive Korea-United States joint military exercises. During these exercises, some 200,000 United States troops participated in land, air, and water exercises. Rivers were polluted, wooded mountains devastated, farmland destroyed, and women of the villages harassed and raped. In a recent visit, President Clinton announced again that the United States troops will be in Korea as long as the Korean people want, but it is the han of the divided people of Korea to endure the presence of alien troops in their backyard.

The women of divided Korea carry most of the collective han of the Korean people. The wounds and scars of Korean women under Japanese colonialism were deep and painful. During the Japanese Pacific War of the 1930s and 1940s, an unknown number—probably 100,000 to 200,000—young women were kidnapped and arrested by the Japanese authorities. They were taken everywhere, from the coal mines of Japan to the jungles of Indonesia and Cambodia, as "comfort women" to be raped by the soldiers. Even before the wounds and scars of Korean women during the Pacific War were healed, military prostitution was begun on and around United States military camps. Some women married the soldiers and were taken to a strange land, carrying their deep han of division and separation as they struggled to adjust to a new language and new way of life.[11]

Since the implosion of the Soviet Union, the reunification of the two Germanies, and the resolution of the Cold War, significant progress has been made in the areas of north-south talks on reconciliation and peace on the Korean peninsula. However, no one is certain about the international arrangements on the issue of future progress toward the reunification of Korea. The United Nations has invited the two Koreas to sit in on their meetings, and flags of the north and the south fly side by side at the United Nations in New York City. But some believe that this has to be a temporary thing until one unified Korean flag will be hoisted, and some would insist that two flags would have to stay for some time to maintain peace on and around the Korean peninsula. Since 1993, North Korea's nuclear capability has been one of the hottest issues in the international community. The North Korean government refused to allow inspection by the International Atomic Energy Agency and has withdrawn from the Nuclear Proliferation Treaty, actions that are regarded as the gravest current threat to the maintenance of peace in northeast Asia. As long as we are threatened by the potential of nuclear war, our hope of reunification is gone. Even more gravely, our survival itself is in danger. Fortunately, United States and North Korean negotiations on the issue have resolved these threats for the time being. In October 1994, an agreement was reached: As North Korea terminates its nuclear activities, South Korea will help build nuclear power plants in the north, and diplomatic relations between the two countries will be established in a year's time. The agreement offers hope for a peaceful resolution to the Korean nuclear issue.

HEALING THE WOUNDS OF DIVISION

In 1988, the General Assembly of the Korean National Council of Churches adopted a policy statement, "Declaration of the Churches of Korea on National Reunification and Peace." This document was produced by a group of Christian activist theologians as a result of several large-scale consultations with ecumenical church leaders. It is a theological document calling for the work of healing and reconciliation. It is a political document challenging both governments to come to terms with the national division, with the suffering of the people, and with the vision and hope of peace and reunification. It is an ecumenical Christian document announcing the Jubilee, the second liberation of the Korean people, looking toward the year 1995, the fiftieth anniversary of the division.

The first part of the declaration calls for the repentance of all Christians. The declaration stated:

> As we Christians of Korea proclaim this declaration for peace and reunification, we confess before God and our people that we have sinned: we have long harbored a deep hatred and hostility toward the other side within the structure of division.
>
> 1. The division of the Korean people is the result of the structural evil reflected in the world's superpowers in their east-west Cold War system, and this reality has also been the root cause of the structural evil present within the societies of both north and south Korea. Due to the division we have been guilty of the sin of violating God's commandment, "You shall love your neighbor as yourself (Matthew 22:37-40)."
>
> 2. We confess that the Christians of the south especially have sinned by turning the anti-communist ideology into a virtual religious idol, and have thus not been content to treat just the communist regime in the north as the enemy, but have further damned our northern compatriots and others whose ideologies differ from our own....

This was the most difficult part for the South Korean Christians to swallow. Repentance in abstract terms may perhaps be easy to make, but in concrete terms such as this, it is dangerous, especially in a country whose national ideology is anti-Communism. For people like myself, whose relatives and friends were killed by the

Communist North Korean secret police in torture chambers or in combat, "love your enemy" is the most difficult command to follow. But we have come to realize that this is a necessary condition we must come to terms with, in order to heal the deep wounds of the division. For this is a transcendental judgment upon the structural division, to be able to see the reality of the division and open up the hidden wounds of the hearts of the people suffering the han of the division. Once we repent of our sins of hatred, we can open our eyes and see the real structure of our sins, our han-ridden history, and our oppressive politics and economy.

The second part of the document moved forward with concrete policy recommendations to both governments. The Korean National Council of Churches document has adopted the three basic principles articulated in the first North-South Joint Communique of July 4, 1972: independence, peace, and national unity transcending the differences in ideas, ideologies, and systems; and it has added two more, namely humanitarian principle and people's participation in the process of reunification. The most sensitive recommendations had to do with the establishment of peace on the peninsula. The KNCC suggested the reduction of arms on both sides, a nuclear-free Korea, and withdrawal of all foreign troops, including the United States military forces. Political repentance of hatred can only be shown through peace talks and peace negotiations, with trust that there is no preparation for aggression. The wounds of war can only be healed with a clear vision that there will be no war, no killing, and no bloodshed. Christians working for peace and building up genuine trust between former enemies are healing the wounds of the han of division.

The third part of the KNCC document pronounced the 1995 Jubilee Year for Koreans and called the Korean churches to celebrate and take the responsibility of the mission of God to heal the wounds of the Korean people suffering under the structure of national division. The establishment of peace and peaceful reunification of Korea is the mission of God on this earth and in this country of divided Korea. We are called to the mission of healing the wounds of the people in the divided Korea and to the mission of reconciliation.

THE KOREAN JUBILEE

It did not take too much historical or theological imagination to understand the proclamation of the Korean Jubilee. The year 1995 is the fiftieth anniversary of the liberation of the Korean people from Japanese colonial rule. But the year 1995 also marks the fiftieth year of the division of the Korean people and their land. Therefore, the proclamation is a desperate expression of the hope and aspiration of the Korean people to be liberated once again by overcoming the division and achieving peace on the peninsula. And the theological motive for proclaiming 1995 as the Jubilee Year for peace and reunification of Korea is in the spirit of the Jubilee proclaimed by Jesus (Lk 4:16-19), and in the Old Testament (Lev 25:8-12; Is 61:1-4). The proclamation of the Jubilee Year for peace and reunification is our commitment to strive for true liberation, shalom, and the favorable year of the Lord in our concrete historical situation.

In Korea, we have this unresolved feeling that World War II will not really be over until the Korean peninsula is reunited in peace and harmony. The reunification of Korea is unfinished business of the Second World War, for the division of Korea is the result of World War II, and the Korean War was a consequence of the Second World War and the result of the Cold War. The Korean people are still suffering from World War II and still struggling to be free of the Cold War. It is our understanding that the basic reason for the division of Korea was that Korea was under the yoke of Japanese imperialism. Japan is at least in part responsible for the division of Korea. At the defeat of the Japanese army in World War II, Japan was not divided, but Korea, which was in no way responsible for the war, was.

We also feel that the war is not over because the Japanese imperial mentality is not over. For too long the Japanese government ignored the historical fact that Japan invaded Korea against the will of the Korean people and colonized the land and ruled with brutality for nearly forty years (1905-1945). Recently Japan officially acknowledged their aggression against Korea and offered an apology. But for too many years we have also heard from the Japanese press that some responsible government ministry-level people have argued in public that the Japanese occupation of Korea was for the benefit of the development of Korea. The Japanese feminist scholar Yuko Suzuki, talking about Japanese ignorance concerning the war crimes of the Japanese Imperial army, writes:

> The reasons for this [ignorance] are rooted in the following:
>   1. The Japanese people lack any understanding of war responsibility.
>   2. The Japanese people have never truly evaluated the colonization of other coun tries.
>   3. The Japanese people have not recognized the Emperor's war responsibility and have exempted him from war crimes. . . . [12]

This is an appalling analysis. I take it to mean that the divine emperor cannot take responsibility for the war, and therefore he is not responsible for war crimes and the crimes of violence against the colonized people of Korea. Kosuke Koyama reveals the Japanese consciousness of their defeat in the war in his most candid reports of the end of the war on August 15, 1945. "Exactly at noon" Koyama heard the "Diamond Voice of the emperor" in Tokyo, the devastated capital of Japan.[13] I heard the same voice on a radio in the hills of Manchuria, at exactly noon of the same day. For him perhaps it was a defeat, but for me it was a victory and liberation. But "the Diamond Voice" of the emperor only said that "We have ordered our Government to communicate to the Governments of the United States, Great Britain, China and the Soviet Union that our Empire accepts the provisions of their joint declaration."[14] Koyama recalls that "On the same day that General MacArthur, the conqueror of Japan, arrived in Tokyo, 30 August 1945, the Prime Minister, Prince Higashikuni, gave his first press conference after the war. 'All one hundred million Japanese must repent' . . . in order to start a new national life."[15] Koyama was surprised to hear the argument that "the Japanese people were victims, not perpetrators, of the crimes committed by their military and fascist rulers. Our leaders must repent, but we are innocent."[16]

Koyama says boldly in his book that "we should repent before the defenceless peoples upon whom we had inflicted injury: the Chinese, Filipinos, Koreans, Malaysians, Burmese, Indonesians and others."[17] But he criticizes his own people:

> Japan had perpetrated a great injury outside herself. Yet when the moment of repentance came she retreated into her own parochial mythology, to "the hallowed spirits of the imperial ancestors." . . . It is perhaps the lack of a sense of responsibility for historical events that made even personal repentance difficult for the Japanese people.[18]

As of the Fiftieth Anniversary day of August 15, 1995, no official apology came from the divine emperor of Japan. As long as the Japanese people cannot come forward to the people of Korea and Asia and publicly say, "We have sinned against heaven and before you" (Lk 15:18), and continue to stay within their "parochial mythology," we still need another day of liberation, and struggle for it. For Koreans, with "the Diamond Voice" of the Japanese emperor, the land and the people were divided into two.

The proclamation of the year of Jubilee in 1995 is a declaration of our commitment to strive for the second liberation and independence from Japan and for the restoration of human rights and property. It declares the true end of the Cold War, the end of the confrontation and conflict between East and West, between hostile ideologies. It proclaims the end of the age of idols—religious, political, ideological, and economical—"anything that is in heaven above, or that is on the earth beneath, or that is on the water under the earth" (Ex 20: 4b).

As Mount Fuji is the holy mountain of Japan, Koreans regard Mount Baekdu as sacred. The voice of God on Mount Sinai is echoing on the hills of these mountains, and Christians around the world must hear the resounding echoes of the two mountains.

NOTES

1. Professor Kosuke Koyama's book is entitled *Mount Fuji and Mount Sinai: A Critique of Idols* (Maryknoll, NY: Orbis Books, 1985). He writes in that volume about Mount Fuji, the tallest mountain in the Island of Japan:

> Mount Fuji is a beautiful symmetrical mountain, the subject of many poems throughout the centuries.
>
>> When going forth I look far from the Shore of Tago
>> How white and glittering is
>> The lofty Peak of Fuji
>> Crowned with snows!
>
> Mount Fuji can be a dangerous mountain if we try to climb up to the top in the bad weather. Otherwise, it is basically a safe mountain (9).

2. Mount Baekdu (White Head) is the tallest mountain in Korea, located at the border of northern China and North Korea where the Yalu River originates to the west and the Duman River to the east. Koreans regard this mountain a sacred mountain, a symbol of the Korean people. Mount Baekdu carries its name, "white headed mountain" due to its perpet-

ual snow at the top. The mountain is famous for the bottomless lake at the top.

3. Koyama, *Mount Fuji and Mount Sinai*, p. 49.

4. One of the most authoritative studies of the issue of Shinto shrine worship and Christian responses to it in the war years is in Korean: Kim Seung Tae, ed., *Hankuk Kidokkyo Wa Sinsachambae Munjea* (*Korean Christianity and the Problem of the Shinto Shrine Worship*) (Seoul: Research Institute of Korean Christian History, 1991). In this volume, Lee Jin Ku's article, "The Korean Christian Responses to the Issue of Shinto Shrine Worship," p. 311, is a thorough study on the issue. *Also see* my book, *The Korean Minjung in Christ* (Hong Kong: Commission on Theological Concerns, The Christian Conference of Asia, 1991), pp. 54-55, and endnotes.

5. In the five years of the Pacific War, more than 200 churches were closed down because of the refusal. More than 2,000 Christians were imprisoned and some 50 church workers died in prison. *See* Suh, *The Korean Minjung in Christ*, p. 55.

6. The Yalu River is the longest river bordering China and North Korea. It flows from Mount Baekdu westward to the Yellow Sea.

7. Manchuria is the northeast portion of China, with Siberia to the north and northeast and North Korea to the south. It was penetrated and developed by Russia with the building of the railroad from the Russian border down to the Yalu River that borders North Korea. The Japanese interest in Manchuria clashed with the Russian advance, which caused the Russo-Japanese War (1904-1905). After that, Manchuria was under the strong influence of Japan, and in 1931 the Japanese crowned a puppet king of Manchukuo and controlled the whole area. It is now completely a part of China.

8. Koyama, *Mount Fuji and Mount Sinai*, p. 49.

9. Benshifu is where the Japanese steel industry was built. Around the steel factory the Japanese population had grown to create a town called "Miyahara" where I was admitted to a Japanese middle school.

10. This was clearly and powerfully expressed in the Theological Declaration of 1974 which I signed with sixty-four other leading Korean theologians, most whom became "minjung theologians." *See* Suh, *The Minjung in Christ*, p. 82.

11. See Marion Kennedy Kim, *Once I Had a Dream: Stories Told by Korean Women Minjung* (Hong Kong: Documentation for Action Groups in Asia, 1992).

12. Center for Christian Responses to Asian Issues, *Asia Tsushin: Eyes on Asia* (Japan: NCC, August 1995), p. 15.

13. Koyama, *Mount Fuji and Mount Sinai*, p. 25.

14. Ibid.

15. Ibid., pp. 26-27.

16. Ibid., p. 27.

17. Ibid., p. 30.

18. Ibid.

9

Craven Images

The Eiconics of Race in the Crisis of American Church Historiography

JAMES MELVIN WASHINGTON

"Our buried past is mighty; the ghosts of our fathers and of the selves that we have been haunt our days and nights though we refuse to acknowledge their presence." [1]
—H. Richard Niebuhr

"John Bunyan introduced me to the image of history as linear progression." [2]
—Kosuke Koyama

Kosuke Koyama's fertile assumption[3] that theological intellection is deeply influenced by our conceptions and uses of *symbolic space* is a signal contribution to theological and ecumenical studies. Granted, the notion of *space* is my interpolation rather than Koyama's focus, since he is more concerned with using its symbolic implications for theological concerns. His use of space qua images inspires me, however, to think about the images of spatiality privileged by American church historians. Indeed, his style of thinking provides a segue to the main topic of this essay. Koyama's notion of "the image of history," and his belief that idolatry is "a misuse of centre symbolism"[4] provide intellectual capital, if not leverage for discerning how race often unconsciously has been the *axis mundi* of most American religious historiography. In order to explore this generalization, I will need to ask certain questions. What is meant by the ideology of race or white supremacy as the "symbol of the center" of American religious historiography? Why and how did race capture the center of the axiological space of the psyche of American religious historians? But before I pursue these questions, I need to highlight some of the problems with re-envisioning the historiographical process.

I proceed with some trepidation because anyone who ventures to challenge the regnant ideology[5] of an academic discipline might seem to be asking for trouble. On the contrary, I am not asking for trouble. I am troubled. I am disturbed about the slow response of the guild of religious historians to the intellectual and moral implications of not having far more religious historians who are deeply conscious and knowledgeable about the history of pseudospeciation. I am not interested in becoming a gadfly, however. Stinging colleagues is too often counterproductive; they focus more on the sting than on their own offense. Emotional jabs do not encourage empathy. They legitimize self-pity. Challenges to the "sly civility" of the recipients of the gadfly's sting mask their own unconscious agency in perpetuating the suppression of disfranchised worldviews.

But revisionists are also historical beings who are subject to all the vicissitudes of agency and contingency. Beyond the temptation to be a gadfly, perhaps the most troublesome burden of servants of the revisionist[6] impulse is how much they too can also be affected by various events in the complex theaters of unconsciousness. Revisionists and consensus historians are occupants of time and space. Scientists and philosophers of cognition have taught us that these mental events engender ego-centric frames[7] which operate like *psychic prisms*. Of course a prism can be defined as "a medium that misrepresents whatever is seen through it."[8] By *psychic prism* I am referring to that axiological space within which writers of history perceive other persons and peoples who have not shared their cultural experience. This cognitive *terra firma* usually feels threatened by the *terra incognita* of the unknown. Not surprisingly, one of the definitions of terra incognita is "a new or unexplored field of knowledge."[9]

The theories and myths of objectivity help ease the anxiety spawned when the vast regions of the known and the unknown confront each other. Indeed, the myth of objectivity has too often dominated the cognitive history of unwitting historians who convince themselves that fidelity to "scientific" principles and research would protect them from charges of bias. But devotion to psychological determinism is not a prerequisite for subscribing to the wise uncertainty implicit in William James's questioning observation:

> Sleeping, fainting, coma, epilepsy, and other "unconscious" conditions are apt to break in upon and occupy large durations of what we nevertheless consider the mental history of a single man. And, the fact of interruption being admitted, is it possible that it may exist where we do not suspect it, and even perhaps in an incessant and fine-grained form?[10]

Yes. Despite enormous scrupulosity, it can creep into the mental space of both well-meaning critics and defenders of historical revisionism as well. The horns of this historiographical dilemma are graphically evident in a recent gratuitous recognition of this problem on the part of two esteemed church historians:

> It has taken the work of women historians and African American theologians to convince us that a person's socio-political setting and personal history profoundly shape

both the content and the methods of his or her scholarship. The rapid maturing of the new fields of women's history and the history of ethnic and religious minorities has raised in an acute form the question of whether it is possible for historians to attain any reasonable degree of detachment and objectivity in reconstructing the past.[11]

The authors then proceed to defend the myth of objectivity by confessing the need for historians to be continuously aware of its limitations. An awareness of the gravity of the problem seems to elude them. How do we explain the seemingly invincible ignorance and even indifference to the historical knowledge and implications of the new fields of vision they mention?

First of all, the limitations of our own experience oftentimes discourage us from intuiting, seeing, and accessing alternative worldviews. We know that they exist, but their existence is relegated to the periphery of reconstructions of the past. Symbols are ensembles of signs that signify how to gain access to the experience of the other, but if we fear those symbols and images, we avoid them. The praxis of objectivity becomes a tool for protecting the profession from hoaxes, false consciousness, ideology, and idolatry. Historians may try to avoid these pitfalls by invoking the sanitizing, if not sanctifying, authority of verification. Of course this aspect of the praxis of objectivity is located in the historian's notes. But what if the notes themselves become an end rather than the means to achieve the purposes of objectivity? The notes themselves become a fetish.[12]

Verifying the verification consumes gargantuan amounts of the historian's time and energy. More than the charge of pedantry is involved here. The problem is much deeper. The crucial dialectic between "distanciation and appropriation" is disabled. Distrust ensues, indeed predicates objectivity itself. Objectivity surely can be seen as the agent of alienation, because it is the linchpin of an intellectual technology that conquers and manages ignorance and falsity. In this verbal virtual-reality scenario, ignorance and falsity are the mortal enemies of objectivity. The praxis of objectivity purports to establish a hegemony over these aliens attacking the citadels of cognition and consciousness. But what is often forgotten is that the conqueror fears the power of the vanquished. It is not always clear how much knowledge and how much verification is required to keep the conqueror from becoming the vanquished. Intellectual certainty is both foolish and forbidden in the political economy of the praxis of objectivity. Not just a hermeneutics of suspicion, but an axiology of distrust and disciplined skepticism must prevail in order to calm and manage this fear, with all its attendant craven images. The promise of the distrust of pathos is that it will enhance cognition. What is at stake is the meaning of a text. Paul Ricoeur states this point quite succinctly: "In other words, what has to be appropriated is nothing other than the power of disclosing a world that constitutes the reference of the text."[13]

If "a symbol somehow *connects*"[14] two or more ideas or objects that ordinarily seem to have no relationship, symbols reflect and disclose what they have in common. Kenneth Boulding coined the word *eiconics* to describe the "science," the cartography, of making connections between various symbolic communications[15] that disclose the tain in the mirror of cognition. Images, as primal agents of cognition, are mirrors, not pictures,[16] that reflect other reflections. Discovering the qualities of the mirror is the specialty of the eiconicist. Koyama is a theological eiconicist. He is also a cartographer of the soul. If this sounds familiar, it is because this is an ancient, indeed Platonic paradigm for discerning the difference between appearance and reality.

Yet how do we understand those belletrists and scholars in particular who insist that appearance is comparable to reality? I have often found this to be the case in the way too many intellectuals understand the worship experience of African American people.

Macabre and often voyeuristic descriptions of African Americans at worship seem to dominate the vast and rich landscape of American literature and history more than the powerful and inspiring experiences that I have had. One in particular fascinates me. It appears in Herman Melville's *Moby Dick*. Ishmael, the protagonist of this quintessential American novel, arrives in New Bedford, Massachusetts, late on a Saturday night, wanders into a strange neighborhood, and immediately begins looking for a place to lodge. He describes how he mistook a black church for an inn:

> Such dreary streets! blocks of blackness, not houses, on either hand, and here and there a candle, like a candle moving about in a tomb. At this hour of the night, of the last day of the week, that quarter of the town proved all but deserted. But presently I came to a smoky light proceeding from a low, wide building, the door of which stood invitingly open. It had a careless look, as if it were meant for the uses of the public; so, entering, the first thing I did was to stumble over an ash-box in the porch. Ha! thought I, ha, as the flying particles almost choked me, are these ashes from that destroyed city, Gomorrah? But "the Cross Harpoons," and "The Sword-fish?"—this, then, must needs be a sign of "The Trap." However, I picked myself up and hearing a loud voice within, pushed on and opened a second, interior door.
>
>   It seemed the great Black Parliament sitting in Tophet.[17] A hundred black faces turned round in their rows to peer; and beyond, a black Angel of Doom was beating a book in a pulpit. It was a [N]egro church; and the preacher's text was about the blackness of darkness, and the weeping and wailing, and teeth-gnashing[18] there. "Ha, Ishmael,["] muttered I, backing out, ["]Wretched entertainment at the sign of 'The Trap!' " [19]

Many white belletrists concluded that religion fomented passivity and ignorance among African American denizens. More specifically, they concluded that the tocsin of predestination ominously was sounding the pending demise of those Black Parliaments (congregations) of Doom that meet at their symbolic Tophet to commit infanticide against the youthful modern spirit of openness and freedom. It is not immediately evident why Melville inserts this peculiar scene. Perhaps it demonstrates the reach of the expansive power of Calvinistic determinism.[20] This is not an unwarranted surmise. The evolving ideology of white supremacy supported the interests of slavery and so possessed the nation that civil war seemed to be a certainty by the 1850s. "The Black Image in the White Mind"[21] threatened the individual and collective self-identity of white America. Indeed, an entire chapter of

Moby Dick is devoted to the meaning of whiteness. Meville places these arresting questions in the mouth of Ishmael:

> Is it that by its [whiteness] indefiniteness it shadows forth the heartless voids and immensities of the universe, and thus stabs us from behind with the thought of annihilation, when beholding the white depths of the milky way? Or is it, that as in essence whiteness is not so much a color as a visible absence of color, and at the same time the concrete of all colors; is it for these reasons that there is such a dumb blankness, full of meaning, in a wide landscape of snows—a colorless, all-color of atheism from which we shrink?[22]

Like other belletrists[23] of the "American Renaissance" of the 1850s,[24] Melville sought to unmask and disclose evils engendered by such professed goodness. Exposing the stark nakedness of humanity is the chief duty of modernists. Captain Ahab, the infamous antagonist of *Moby Dick*, expresses the depth of this process in response to Starbuck, the advocate of conscience:

> All visible objects, man, are but as pasteboard masks. But in each event—in the living act, the undoubted deed—there, some unknown but still reasoning thing puts forth the mouldings of its features from behind the unreasoning mask. If man will strike, strike through the mask! How can the prisoner reach outside except by thrusting through the wall? To me, the white whale is that wall, shoved near me.[25]

Those of an existentialist bent, like myself, would call this wall the absurd.

Indeed, Melville's fictive odyssey reflects and foreshadows modern struggles with the absurd. He seems to parody the western habit of making whiteness a fetish as well as a synonym for visibility and consciousness. But Melville also suggests that whiteness, as the great sign of positivity, is simultaneously a crucifix. It mirrors both power and terror. His narrator states it is the vast oceans of what we call "unconsciousness" in our post-Freudian worlds that we find most terrifying and inexplicable. What we assume and think we know is often nuanced and even subverted by our unwitting fidelity to habits of the mind and heart[26] that belie our certainty, not only what we do not know. It is what we think we understand that we keep discovering has a mercurial quality. But the guild of American church historians has come a long way from the days when the great Philip Schaff could believe, as a child of Romanticism,

> All nations however are not historical, any more than all individuals; but only such as have made themselves felt in a living way upon the actual development, inward and outward, of the world's life as a whole. The Hottentots, Caffrarians, Negroes and New Zealanders, for instance, have thus far played no part whatever in the grand drama of history. Paganism in general, since the introduction of Christianity, is to be regarded as material merely, which must be Christianized in the first place, before it can fall into the stream of historical development; like the child, which has yet come to years of responsibility, and can take no position of its own accordingly in human society.[27]

I believe the notion of field of vision is a double-edged sword for proponents of historical revisionism, but I do not see how we have an option. We must continue to contribute to the perpetual reconstruction of the narrative lines and analytical foci of American religious history. But more theoretical work is necessary in these times of expanding horizons. At the same time, we need to be cautious about claiming too much or too little, because we are always subject to the temptation of "idols of the mind," spirit, and culture.

In other words, historians employ distinct fields of vision or paradigms to offer imaginative reconstructions of the past with the raw data provided by the testimonies of artifacts, documents, and even living witnesses. In fact, no self-respecting historian who has studied the vast history of modern Christianity can escape the responsibility of bringing it into some kind of focus. As William H. McNeill argues in his delightful treatise on *The Shape of European History*,

> It is a matter of some importance to link teaching and research, even very detailed research, to an acceptable architectonic vision of the whole. Without such connections, detail becomes mere antiquarianism. Yet while history without detail is inconceivable, without an organizing vision it quickly becomes incomprehensible.[28]

This insight certainly holds true for modern and American church history. One must have an interpretive framework before delving into this gargantuan field.

What Handy has rightly said about American Christianity should be applied as well to modern Christianity in general: "American Christianity is so diversified and confusing and its material of such a vast extent that the scholars who have worked at the broader aspects of its history have had to bring to their study certain interpretive theses in order to find their way through the material at all."[29] His own well-known paradigm has been the idea of "A Christian America" which he sketched in a monograph with that title and embodied in his magnum opus, *A History of the Churches in the United States and Canada*. Unlike many other scholars, Handy rejects the idea that the reality and ideal of Christendom died with the Middle Ages. To the contrary, he shows how the wedding between Christ and culture in its Protestant guise helped foster American and Canadian nationalism and in turn depleted the spiritual integrity of the churches. In other words, he gives us what I would characterize as a detailed portrayal of the weal and woe of Teutonic and Anglo-Saxon Protestantism as it shaped modern American culture with intermittent success.

This outlook is what Handy calls an interpretive thesis. In post-Foucaultian historiography, Handy's notion of interpretive thesis is comparable to what is called paradigm or field theory. This statement could be construed as a crass reliance upon historical determinism to explain historical events. But before we dismiss this concept too readily, perhaps we should recall that the New Testament era itself, with our shifting and differing interpretations of it, functions for many in the Christian church as the normative, regulative, and constitutive ideal of the essence of the Faith. The vision of God in New Testament canon[30] and its understanding of human nature have often functioned as the paradigm for *regula fidei* as well as correct behavior. Other paradigms have also shaped the course of Christian history, such as the ideas of wilderness and paradise.[31] I believe one can use the models provided by church historians like Handy and Williams to deepen our understanding of how race, class, and sexism have influenced Christian history, just as the older generation of American church historians has examined the tendrils of nationalism and intellectual modernism within the Christian story.

I am acutely aware, however, that communities of discourse find it difficult— Kuhn would say highly improbable—to expand or alter their views of reality. This is not less true of religious liberals than racist bigots and black nationalists. But what strikes me as most significant in this observation is the powerful role minority consciousness plays in human history and historiography itself. Such consensual groups predicate a reality out of several possible worldviews and project it upon the stage of time and space. Thus when we speak of paradigms we touch the very nerve center of the corporate and individual consent that sustains community. But the perennial problem is not how to create human solidarity, given the complex nature of communities and the conflicts between human communities. One sees this problem all too clearly in the complex streams and tributaries of the Christian movement. It is a movement that intentionally searches for community as its means for survival, but most importantly as its very goal.

Therefore, the intellectual challenge posed by the problem of expanding the historian's field of vision is more than a methodological difficulty for church historians. It is an epistemological and cosmological problem as well. New approaches to the difficult processes of discovering and presenting historical knowledge are always useful. But if the data to be organized and disseminated has no organizing principle beyond mere celebrationist or chronological ones, then its value is highly suspect. Without blueprints outlining the vision of the architect, no builder can begin construction. Simple-minded, naive, or pious narratives will not do either. They insult our intelligence as well as the beautiful complexity of the Creator's universe. If we are to deal with the tough intellectual challenges posed by modernity's assaults upon the old theories of knowing and seeing truth advanced by Christian intellectuals, the church's historians need to develop a new aesthetic that would allow them to value and see more of the grand panorama they are so privileged to survey.

This is one reason why I believe the history of the victims of Christian history, as well as the history of downtrodden Christians, is so vital. We need their views not simply to critique our own elitist views but because we need to discover when, where, and how we failed to love them as the Lord commanded us to do. Church history at its best must become concerned and interested in the oppressed. Otherwise it runs the risk of betraying the Gospel's allegiance to the downtrodden. It would remain, as it often is, the history of pious elites written by sometimes pious, sometimes irreverent elites.

There are some like Karl Popper who argue that the history of the oppressed cannot be written. He rightly understands that the viewpoint of the oppressed seldom gets into print:

The life of the forgotten, of the unknown individual man; his sorrows and his joys, his suffering and death, this is the real content of human experience down the ages. If that could be told by history, then I should certainly not say that it is blasphemy to see the finger of God in it. But such a history does not and cannot exist; and all history which exists, our history of the Great and the Powerful, is at best a shallow comedy; it is the opera buffa played by the powers behind reality (comparable to Homer's opera buffa of the Olympian powers behind the scene of human struggles). It is what one of the worst instincts, the idolatrous worship of power, of success, has led us to believe to be real. And in this not even man-made, but man-faked "history," some Christians dare to see the hand of God![32]

These eloquent convictions are enshrouded in the Barthian conviction that revelation of God should not be identified with history. But both Popper and Barth are wrongheaded on this point. The kerygma itself testifies that "God with us" is the *modus operandi* of the Holy Spirit. As poor folk have repeatedly said, "God moves in mysterious ways." History is one of those ways. It is true that God's will is not revealed in historiography (both religious and secular). But God's will is revealed in human history. Where else can it appear? The historical enterprise is, after all, an industry, a cultural artifact, the highest form of ideology (which is the penultimate vindication of particular human self-interests). But human history is different from the historical enterprise. Human history is the story of the entire human race. Historians can never tell all that story. We tell only part of it, and the part we tell reflects our basic interests. I do not believe there is such a thing as innocent curiosity, however.

W. D. Gallie argues with great force that historians "show an almost pathological disinclination to commit themselves to any general statements about their work, its aims, subject-matter and methods; but on the whole, both by occasional precept and general practice, they give the impression of wanting—perhaps not unreasonably—to have things both ways."[33]

He correctly sees that historians demand the professional privilege of freely choosing their topics "with whatever predominant interest seems good" to them. But at the same time they insist on the need for a belief and search for the "interconnectedness of events." The problem with this classic formulation of historical liberalism is that it rests upon what Hans-Georg Gadamer calls the Enlightenment's prejudice against prejudice.[34] We need to recognize and confess that the hypocrisy of classical liberalism in all its various forms rests on the unfortunate presupposition that white western culture is the prism through which the nature and destiny of humanity should be seen. Robert Solomon rightly locates this myth in the rise of bourgeois ideology. Ideology is the key concept here, because it highlights the need for discerning the contours of the idolatrous cultural and political vindication of a tribal worldview. There is, of course, nothing inherently wrong with seeing western culture as a set of diverse tribal worldviews. But when this outlook masquerades as universal history or as the chief bearer of the revelations granted the universal church, the burdens that idolatry and unregenerative ideology place upon us have frightening consequences.[35] Two consequences deserve mention here. One relates to the rather fallacious assumption on the part of classical historical liberalism that history is a value-free praxis. The other is the assumption that people and topics that have previously been neglected were neglected because there was insufficient data to reconstruct their story.

In the first instance, we need to remind ourselves that all authors have a point of view,[36] and that every worldview (*Weltanschauung*) has political consequences, if not political motives. Although he overstates it, Frederic Jameson correctly spurns all pretensions to innocence and objectivity when he opines that "there is nothing that is not social and historical—indeed, that everything is 'in the last analysis' political."[37] Certainly Christians, and some other religious persons, would want to leave room for the possibility of altruistic motives on the part of religious scholars, but there is a thin line between the love of learning and learning as a narcissistic commitment. As Howard Thurman, a noted African mystic, has said, "It is possible for a man to make an idol of commitment."[38] I do not see why scholarly bigotry should be exempted from this charge.

Oscar Handlin is a classic example of this syndrome. He offers an exquisite jeremiad against those in the history profession who have been responsive to the social and cultural revolutions of the 1960s and 1970s:

> The crisis in history is the result not of the death of the past but its misappropriation. Its negligent guardians have lost command. Confused by gadgets, internally divided and distracted by the racket outside, they have allowed their subject to slip into the hands of propagandists, politicians, dramatists, novelists, journalists, and social engineers.
>
> Mostly I draw comfort from the reflection that, whatever may happen to the community of investigators, the historian, when all else is stripped away, remains a creative individual.[39]

He is convinced that what Charles S. Peirce called the community of investigators is both necessary to the historical enterprise and superfluous to it. He cannot have it both ways. Actually, as far as investigation is concerned, no historian can function well without that community of investigators. But when it comes to the actual job of drafting a manuscript, the historian becomes an author with a definite point of view. It is at this point that the very purpose of research is realized. Peirce himself advanced a similar point when he argued that "opinion which would finally result from investigation does not depend on how anybody may actually think. But the reality of that which is real does depend on the real fact that investigation is destined to lead, at last, if continued long enough, to a belief in it."[40]

The problem with this formulation, which Handlin accepts without comment, is that it is a pragmatist's argument for an idealist's position. Peirce argues that truth and reality are more than community decisions. They are, for him, constituents of the real, which is an objective fact obtained through "scientific" investigation. Historical research is a far more complicated endeavor. But my central point here is that when the historian moves from the archives to the task of writing, we are talking about two different phases in one politically and socially significant act. To think otherwise is to disregard the necessity to uncover why historians neglected minority religious history in the first place. We may never fully understand how what Hume called spontaneous discrimination[41] operates.

Nonetheless, as a black Christian permitted to rise out of the depths of Afro-America's working class, and now as a scholar, teacher, and preacher, I believe I see a glimmer of intellectual and spiritual hope. That hope emanates from a strange and faint light. It resides in what may seem like a cynical, obvious, and even groundless rumor: Afro-Americans are a homeless people. James Baldwin, in his unflagging inimical way, crafts this point with agonizing eloquence: "Behind them was the darkness, nothing but the darkness, and all around them destruction, and before them nothing but the fire—a bastard people, far from God, singing and crying in the wilderness."[42] Despite the fact that this observation is born of despair, I still believe there is hope. Black homelessness has taught us something about how to cope with modernity that may be useful to Christians and pagans alike.

As children of the infamous Atlantic Slave Trade, we were the first modern people to encounter what the existentialists call absurdity. It came upon us on a massive, continuous scale. Sartre defines the absurd in *Being and Nothingness* as having an existence whose "contingency finds no external justification."[43] Of course he believed human existence itself is absurd. Yet even the absurd is experienced in specific contexts and situations. Too often the bourgeois propensity to spawn sameness and universality erroneously homogenizes human experience. Diversity is located in the nuances of human experience.

But I believe one has to make a distinction between the makers of history and the victims of history. Mircea Eliade offers a rather handy definition of the victims of history in his *Cosmos and History* as those who know the terror of history firsthand. He says, "We are concerned with the problem of history as history, of the 'evil' that is bound up not with man's condition but with his behavior toward others." This particular evil is experienced by those who happen to be in "the pathway of history."[44] What other people of God in the history of modern Christendom have carried the opprobrium of victimization more consistently and courageously than people of African descent in the western hemisphere? Rabbi Arnold Jacob Wolf wrote, in the midst of the Black Revolt of the 1960s, that "what one sees in the Negro revolution is men not trying to get what they want . . . but seeking what they have been made to know is wanted on high. The revolt of the under-privileged against us who are over-privileged is not simply a war for redress; it is also incipient revelation."[45] If we have in the black story a new revelation of the Lord's purpose for our lives in these latter days, then the black story is not merely interesting. It is vital. Now, thanks to industrialization, technology, the reality of a probable nuclear holocaust, and Nietzschean "transvaluation of values," all of us live oblivious to the absurdities of our era at our own peril.

We need what Ernest Becker calls an anthropodicy to deal with what we have done. But history as theodicy should be understood not in the way Hegel understood it, not as a justification of the ways of God before the judgment bar of reason,[46] but as a faithful narrative that brings its own judgment and clarity to our tormented age. More, not less historical knowledge is the antidote to the problems of historical knowledge. History in this sense becomes a moral mirror that discloses our misdeeds, misconceptions, and misjudgments. As Walter Rauschenbusch, a church historian known more for writing theology than history, reminded us, "The future of Christian theology lies in the comprehension of Christian history. The future of Christianity itself lies in getting the spirit of Jesus Christ in history."[47] As long as we remember our sins, learn from them, and allow them to judge us, the possibility exists that the future holds liberation for both victimizers and the victimized. But this faint possibility of earthly redemption escapes the realm of the possible if the stories of historical victimization remain in the past's unexplored caverns. This is the central reason why I believe the story of Afro-American Christianity is so vital.

Peter Berger would probably satisfy my *raison d'etre* for Afro-American Christian history as the use of the inductive approach to provide another "possible model for thinking about religion."[48] I would not demure too loudly from this hypothetical classification. But I would conjecture that Berger has not come to terms with the central problem of modern consciousness, the problem of historical consciousness from the standpoints of the victimizers and their victims. The history of each is vital to understanding each other. Hegel made this painful reality quite explicit in his famous analysis of the master and slave relationship: The negative self-image of the slave is rooted in a perverse symbiotic relation with the master and vice versa, because each self-definition is shaped by the prevailing perversity of the reality of what Orlando Patterson calls social death.[49] The human struggle for ego satisfaction, for recognition, is at the heart of this struggle.

Certainly, I agree with Berger that historical method "brings forth and dissolves one structure of consciousness after another."[50] But what about the problems posed by the consciousness of the historian? As Franklin H. Littell said recently, "Presuppositionless history does not exist. The facts do not speak for themselves. Every translation, however careful, is an interpretation."[51] Berger's blanket endorsement of Leopold von Ranke's rather naive view that history can let us know "how it really was" (*wie es wirklich gewesen ist*) ignores what Nietzsche called "The Advantage and Disadvantage of History for Life" (*Vom Nutzen und Nachteil der Historie für das Leben*). Moreover, questions of the psychological, cultural, and moral limitations of historians also come into play in very subtle and often insidious ways.[52]

This attitude has often misled such major church historians as Cyril Richardson to argue that church history is not "the meticulous study of any institutions which happen to call themselves churches."[53] There may indeed be some justification for ignoring self-proclaimed churches as churches in the New Testament, medieval, or Reformed views of what constitutes a church.[54] But let us define what we mean. Unfortunately what has too often been meant by ignoring some churches has not been only a presupposed but unshared notion of orthodoxy on the part of the church historian but also commitments to cultural values which simply leave the historian powerless to know how to include religious "weirdos." The discovery of such cultural myopia as this has led Sydney Ahlstrom to predict that the basic paradigm for a renovation of American church history is the black religious experience, which has been virtually closed out despite the obvious fact that any history of America that ignores the full consequences of slaves and non-emancipation is a fairy tale, and that the black churches have been the chief bearers of the Afro-American heritage from the early nineteenth-century revivals to the present day.[55]

Ahlstrom's proposal was part of what Handy characterizes as the scholarly side of the civil rights movement.[56] We must certainly give the liberal tradition of American church historiography—of which professors Williams, Handy, and Ahlstrom are prominent voices—credit for advancing this scholarly civil rights movement. But as with most compromises, this fails to satisfy all, so it should not be surprising that I'm dissatisfied with Handy's suggestion that the black religious experience should be seen as an important addendum to a basically honest story. If one translates the issue of the place of black church history in the history of modern Christianity into the intellectual challenges presented by the issue of the church's role in the human rights struggles of the modern era, fresh paradigms and methodologies are allowed to surface.

For example, instead of stressing the history-of-ideas approach to church history, one begins to see that social ethics, politics, popular hymns, religious novels, architecture, art, and social history become as important. We need to teach our students to see the relation of the churches to other ideational systems. Modernity disqualifies all apologetic attempts to view Christian history as a closed system. Post-Christendom religious history is forced to view Christian history as a competing, evolving complex of values, beliefs, and behavior. In a recent book review, John Lankford put the same point in these words: "What is called for is a much more complex model of the interplay among symbols, rhetoric and other aspects of human experience (most evidently the political and economic spheres) conceived of as an interconnected system. Then we will be able to see the relative importance of each component, both in terms of change and in relation to the whole system."[57]

Besides these, as well as other methodological issues and alternatives, philosophical problems arise out of these concerns. For instance, after a helpful analysis of the treatment of race in the histories of American religion by Handy, Marty, and Ahlstrom, Roger D. Hatch concludes that "the most important step in adequately integrating the issue of race into the story of Christianity in America comes at the very beginning, it comes in defining the subject matter."[58] Although Hatch's use of the term "subject matter" is ambiguous, the point is well taken. I would talk about the axiological blinders that affect the historian's vision. A historian must have some perception of the past before reconstructing it in written form. As R. W. Southern said in his Rede Lecture, "nothing in the past is usable until it has been the subject of a vivid perception, and it is important to know what it is we are expecting to perceive."[59]

Certainly the most obvious reason is that the legacies of slavery and racism still stalk the hall of academia in the form of institutional racism. This assertion, however, besides being palpably very self-serving, obscures the intellectual dimensions of the problem presented by minority, what I prefer to call alternative views of Christian history. Perhaps if we examine this problem briefly, not as a problem of inclusiveness, as it is often mistakenly viewed, but as the problem of the impact of cultural and psychosocial diversity upon the traditionally closed guild of American church historians, we might come to a better understanding of at least one intellectual manifestation of institutional racism.

Determining the value of my own area of specialization in the context of modern and American church history is another matter. This is needed largely because little is known about the history of people of African descent in the western hemisphere. But such a discussion is also needed because racism has left an indelible imprimatur on the western psyche. This stamp has been so impressive that one in my position dares not assume one's colleagues agree that the study of Christian people of African descent is a crucial pursuit. This is especially true in the light of comments coming from such prominent historians of Christianity as William A. Clebsch who believe "Negro religion in America imitated white religion."[60] Obviously unaware of the racial implications of this earlier remark, he recently wrote something that is equally disturbing to one with my social background and intellectual interest. He says, "The Christian religion has been primarily, although by no means exclusively, a European religion, and the principal religion of European civilization has been Christianity. It is generally agreed that to study the history of Europe involves studying the history of Christianity and vice versa." Then he contradicts himself by adding, "Consensus rapidly fades when one asks how the two stories are related."[61] Clebsch believes this methodological problem raises anew the problem of the relation between religion and culture.

I agree with Sir Richard Southern that historians too often "write of the church as if it could be separated from secular history," and that to do so is to repeat "the mistake made by medieval ecclesiastical reformers, who were never more clearly the captives of their environment than when they spoke of their freedom from it."[62] But I must add that this should not be a license for cheap shots or slipshod research and writing.

The struggle to achieve a balance between in-depth research and judicious reporting is indeed difficult. But the problem is often ignored or delicately clothed in the name of artistic consistency or as a result of a kind of explicit or latent tribal consciousness. One way to account for this prevalent agenda within church historical circles is by recalling Franklin H. Littell's excellent observation that church members in the United States are first- or second-generation Christians. He argues that their problems are not different from "those which are found in all periods and places in church history where large masses of new converts affiliate with a religion whose implications they but vaguely grasp." One of the central problems which obtain as a result of this situation is the dominance of "racialism (the practice of religion as a tribal cult)."[63]

I believe this situation is reflected in the scholarly praxis of American church historians—no matter how liberal they happen to be in their social and political ideologies. The way they practice history reveals a racial provincialism that feeds on a very steady but fattening diet of "historical objectivity" which intends to produce a lean and broad historiography but actually produces one that suffers from scholarly obesity. Minority people are simply viewed as not being important figures in the history of the Christian church. With this kind of racialist ambience, it is not difficult to see why most white scholars find it difficult to understand why anyone other than themselves would be seriously interested in church history, which of course is primarily the history of white people.

No professor of church history in this venerable tradition has been more energetic and emphatic about preserving this view than Philip Schaff, the founder and first president of the American Society of Church History. He declared, in his inaugural address of October 25, 1844, as Professor of Church History and Biblical Literature in the Theological Seminary of the German Reformed Church (Reading, Pennsylvania), that "Protestantism springs, as all know, from the *German* life, which may be considered constitutionally its proper womb and cradle."[64] It is one thing to assert quite correctly that the Reformation received its major impetus in the German states; it is quite another thing to suggest, as Schaff does, that the Reformation received its major initiation in Germany because of some *Geist* in German culture. Heinrich Heine was certainly more emphatic about this than Schaff. He simply declared that "we Germans are the strongest and most ingenious of nations."[65] H. Richard Niebuhr calls such cultural nationalism "henotheism," which is a "social faith which makes a finite society, whether cultural or religious, the object of trust as well as of loyalty." He believed that this ideology "tends to subvert even officially monotheistic institutions, such as the churches."[66]

The history of a distinct and variable African American Folk theological tradition can be recovered. More work certainly needs to be done. But we need to know that since the late eighteenth century, oppressed people began to find ways of developing and communicating their own point of view. They left significant tracings of their experience. A revolution along these lines took place in the nineteenth century with the publication of slave narratives, black sermons, denominational minutes of minority religious communities, as well as their newspapers, etc. Church historians of this period can no longer overlook these resources when they write the history of modern Christianity.

Regardless of the sparsity of resources in some periods, I'm convinced that church historians must identify those Christian communities that have lived and believed in redemptive suffering. I have been deeply encouraged along these lines by statements made by two of my mentors at Harvard and Yale. After giving a masterful review of the state of the church historical discipline of 1950, Professor George H. Williams concludes that the history of American Christianity presents the greatest challenge to the quest to develop adequate interpretive schema to reflect the widest range of data. He then ends his essay with this amazing and stimulating prophecy:

And finally, if we follow James Hastings Nichols' suggestion as to the relationship of crisis, catastrophe, and momentous decision to the writing of autobiography and history, perhaps we may expect some comprehensive (I should like to say momentous) historical interpretation of the nature and destiny of American Christianity. It is quite possible that it will be written by an American Negro historian of the Church, reaching back for basic categories of interpretation to the Judaeo-Christian experience of redemptive suffering and to the concept of God's Covenant with His ongoing Israel of history.[67]

It would certainly be grossly arrogant of me to suggest or even to declare that I am that historian. On the other hand, I would be dishonest not to confess that I would like to be. Without large and great goals, who can endeavor to strive toward excellence?

From a more sober standpoint, church historians must not only come to grips with the exclusion of minority people from their histories of the church, but they must also try to determine why they overlooked them in the first place. This is a large task. But it is a task that may indeed lead to a much-needed renovation of the discipline as it tries to regain its composure once it realizes that it is in the grips of an enormous epistemological and cosmological crisis. Again, Sydney E. Ahlstrom believes that that renovation will be ushered in by black religious history.

What would be the impact upon the discipline of Church history if we entertained Karl Rahner's idea of anonymous Christianity?[68] Recovering the history of Invisible Christianity and its legatees might indeed become as engaging and challenging as the practices and beliefs of Roman Christians in the catacombs.

NOTES

1. H. Richard Niebuhr, *The Meaning of Revelation* (New York: Macmillan Company, 1941), p. 83.

2. Kosuke Koyama, *Mount Fuji and Mount Sinai: A Critique of Idols* (Maryknoll, NY: Orbis Books, 1985), p. 6.

3. I characterize Koyama's use of space as an "assumption" rather than an "insight," because he does not offer a clear-cut and sustained treatment of the use of space as a critical dimension of intellection. For an engaging philosophical analysis of spatiality in cognition, *see* John Campbell, *Past, Space, and Self* (Cambridge, MA, and London: MIT Press, 1995).

4. Koyama, *Mount Fuji*, pp. 83-102.

5. I am using "ideology in the descriptive sense" defined by Raymond Geuss, *The Idea of a Critical Theory: Habermas and the Frankfurt School* (Cambridge, England, and New York: Cambridge University Press, 1981), pp. 4-12. I agree with Geuss that the indicative use of the word *ideology,* is an attempt to describe a set of beliefs, attitudes, and habits that nurture and serve individual or social interests. Although those interests are often material ones, they could just as well constitute a praxis that is comfortable to continue, or bring discomfort if discontinued. Religious ideology often falls into this latter category. I do have some sympathy, however, for deterministic materialists who argue that all, or nearly everything, either directly or indirectly reflects material concerns and interests—even one's belief or disbelief in God. This is partly what Clifford Geertz means when he asserts that the problem of evil inevitably leads to the problem of suffering. *See* Geertz, *The Interpretation of Cultures* (New York: Basic Books, 1973), pp. 105-6. A very helpful examination of this problem can be found in Kenneth Thompson, *Beliefs and Ideology* (London and New York: Tavistock Publications, 1986). A fine etymology of "ideology" is in Raymond Williams, *Keywords: A*

Vocabulary of Culture and Society (New York: Oxford University Press, 1976), pp. 126-30.

6. For weal or woe, *revisionism* itself has become a cross-disciplinary enterprise. One of the numerous examples of this largely postmodern phenomenon can be found in Harold Bloom, *Agon: Toward a Critical Theory of Revisionism* (Oxford and New York: Oxford University Press, 1982), esp. chapt. 1, "Agon: Revisionism and Critical Personality," pp. 16-51.

7. Campbell, *Past, Space, and Self*, pp. 8-19.

8. This definition of prism can be found in *The American Heritage College Dictionary*, 3d ed. (Boston and New York: Houghton Mifflin Company, 1993), s.v.

9. Ibid., s.v.

10. William James, *The Principles of Psychology* (1890; rpt. Cambridge, MA, and London: Harvard University Press, 1983), pp. 197-98.

11. James E. Bradley and Richard A. Muller, *Church History: An Introduction to Research, Reference Works, and Methods* (Grand Rapids, MI: William B. Eerdmans Publishing Company, 1995), pp. 47-8.

12. Somewhere in his insightful writings, Bruce Lincoln once characterized the footnotes as a form of ancestor worship.

13. Paul Ricoeur, *Interpretation Theory: Discourse and the Surplus of Meaning* (Fort Worth, TX: Texas Christian University Press, 1976), p. 92.

14. F. W. Dillistone, *The Power of Symbols in Religion and Culture* (New York: Crossroad, 1986), p. 14.

15. Kenneth E. Boulding, *The Image: Knowledge in Life and Society* (Ann Arbor, MI: University of Michigan Press, 1956), p. 148.

16. *See* Nelson Goodman, "Pictures in the Mind?" in *Images and Understanding: Thoughts about Images, Ideas about Understanding*, ed. Horace Barlow, Colin Blakmore, and Miranda Weston-Smith (Cambridge, England, and New York: Cambridge University Press, 1990), pp. 358-64.

17. Topheth was "an illicit open-air sanctuary or High Place in the Valley of Hinnom" mentioned in Jeremiah 7:31 where "children were sacrificed as burnt offerings in honor of Baal, who is mentioned in parallelism with Molech" (Jer 32:35). *See* G. A. Barrois, "Topheth," in George Arthur Buttrick, et al., eds., *The Interpreter's Dictionary of the Bible: An Illustrated Encyclopedia* (Nashville: Abingdon, 1962), p. 673.

18. *See* the King James Version translation of Matthew 8:12; 13:42; 13:50; 22:13; 24:51; 25:30; and Luke 13:28.

19. Herman Melville, *Moby Dick or The White Whale*, vol. 40: Everyman's Library (1851; rpt. New York: Alfred A. Knopf, 1991), pp. 9-10.

20. *See* R. W. B. Lewis, *The American Adam: Innocence, Tragedy, and Tradition in the Nineteenth Century* (1955; rpt. Chicago: University of Chicago Press, 1980).

21. *See* George M. Frederickson, *The Black Image in the White Mind: The Debate on Afro-American Character and Destiny, 1817-1914* (New York and London: Harper & Row, Publishers, 1971).

22. Melville, *Moby Dick*, p. 195.

23. Given the extensive prejudice in the academy against religious intellectuals, I want to underscore that I include them when I use this term. *See* H. Shelton Smith, *In His Image, But . . . : Racism in Southern Religion, 1780-1910* (Durham, NC: Duke University Press, 1972); and H. Brook Holifield, *Gentlemen Theologians: American Theology in Southern Culture, 1795-1860* (Durham, NC: Duke University Press, 1978).

24. *See* F. O. Matthiessen, *The American Renaissance* (Oxford, England: Oxford University Press, 1941).

25. Melville, *Moby Dick*, p. 164.

26. *See* Robert Bellah, *Habits of the Heart: Individualism and Commitment in American Life* (Berkeley: University of California Press, 1985).

27. Schaff, *What Is Church History? A Vindication of the Idea of Development* (Philadelphia: J.B. Lippincott and Co., 1846) p. 39. A facsimile of this classic statement can be found in Charles Yrigoyen, Jr., and George M. Bricker, eds., *Reformed and Catholic: Selected Historical and Theological Writings of Philip Schaff* (Pittsburgh, PA: Pickwick Press, 1979), pp. 17-144. This quotation can be found on page 55 in *Reformed and Catholic.*

28. William H. McNeill, *The Shape of European History* (New York: Oxford University Press, 1974), p. 4.

29. Robert T. Handy, "The Protestant Quest for a Christian America," *Church History* 22 (1953).

30. The long process of the canonization of the New Testament was of course partly an accommodation to *Pax Romana. See* Harry Y. Gamble, *The New Testament Canon: Its Making and Meaning* (Minneapolis: Fortress Press, 1985); and Peter Brown, *Authority and the Sacred: Aspects of the Christianisation of the Roman World* (Cambridge, England, and New York: Cambridge University Press, 1995).

31. George H. Williams, *Wilderness and Paradise in Christian Thought: The Biblical Experience of the Desert in the History of Christianity and the Paradise Theme in the Theological Idea of the University* (New York: Harper, 1962).

32. Karl R. Popper, *The Open Society and Its Enemies*, vol 2, *The High Tide of Prophecy: Hegel, Marx, and the Aftermath* (Princeton, NJ: Princeton University Press, 1966), p. 272.

33. W. B. Gallie, *Philosophy and Historical Understanding*, 2d ed. (New York: Schocken Books, 1968), p. 53.

34. Hans-Georg Gadamer, *Truth and Method* (New York: Crossroad, 1982), p. 242.

35. *See* a fuller discussion of these matters in Robert C. Solomon, *History and Human Nature: A Philosophical Review of European Philosophy and Culture, 1750-1850* (New York and London: Harcourt Brace Jovanovich, 1979).

36. *See* Søren Kierkegaard, *Point of View for My Work as an Author* (New York: Harper, 1962).

37. Frederic Jameson, *The Political Unconscious: Narrative as a Socially Symbolic Act* (Ithaca, NY: Cornell University Press, 1981), p. 20.

38. Howard Thurman, *Disciplines of the Spirit* (1963; rpt. Richmond, IN: Friends United Press, 1977), p. 35.

39. Oscar Handlin, *Truth in History* (Cambridge, MA, and London: Harvard University Press, 1981), pp. 20, 21.

40. Philip P. Wiener, ed., *Charles S. Peirce: Selected Writings (Values in a Universe of Change)* (New York: Dover Publications), p. 134.

41. Mary Warnock, *Imagination* (Berkeley and Los Angeles: University of California Press, 1976), pp. 131-95.

42. James Baldwin, *Go Tell It on the Mountain* (New York: Dell Publishing Co., Inc., 1953), p. 137.

43. Jean-Paul Sartre, *Being and Nothingness: An Essay on Phenomenological Ontology*, trans. Hazel E. Barnes (New York: Philosophical Library, 1956).

44. Mircea Eliade, *Cosmos and History: The Myth of the Eternal Return*, trans. Williard R. Trask (New York: Harper & Row, 1959), pp. 150-51.

45. Arnold Jacob Wolf, "The Negro Revolution and Jewish Theology," *Judaism* 13 (Fall 1964): 480-81.

46. Georg Wilhelm Friedrich Hegel, *The Philosophy of History*, trans. J. Sibree (New York: Dover Publications, 1956), p. 15.

47. Walter Rauschenbusch, "The Influence of Historical Studies on Theology," *American Journal of Theology* 11 (1907): 111.

48. Peter Berger, *The Heretical Imperative: Contemporary Possibilities of Religious Affirmation* (Garden City, NY: Anchor Press/ Doubleday, 1979), p. 127.

49. Orlando Patterson, *Slavery and Social Death: A Comparative Study* (Cambridge, MA: Harvard University Press, 1982).

50. Berger, *The Heretical Imperative*, p. 120.

51. Franklin H. Littell, "The Periodization of History," in F. Forrester Church and Timothy George, eds., *Continuity and Discontinuity in Church History: Essays Presented to George Huntston Williams on the Occasion of His 65th Birthday* (Leiden: E.J. Drill, 1979), p. 18.

52. *See* John C. Biddle, "Historical Study and Theological Education," *Reflection* 76 (April 1979): 9-11.

53. Cyril Richardson, "Church History Past and Present," *Union Seminary Quarterly Review* 5:1 (November 1949): 13.

54. Eric G. Jay, *The Church: Its Changing Image Through Twenty Centuries* (1978), as well as Martin E. Marty, *A Short History of Christianity* (2d ed., revised and expanded, 1987) offer helpful profiles of the churches' self-understanding throughout their history.

55. Sydney E. Ahlstrom, *A Religious History of the American People* (New Haven, CT, and London: Yale University Press, 1972), pp. 12-13.

56. Robert T. Handy, "Negro Christianity and American Church Historiography," in Gerald C. Braver, ed., *Reinterpretation in American Church History* (Chicago and London: University of Chicago Press, 1968), p. 102.

57. John Lankford, review of *American Apocalypse: Yankee Protestants and the Civil War, 1860-1869* (1978) by James H. Moorhead, in *Church History* 48 (March 1979): 119.

58. Roger D. Hatch, "Integrating the Issue of Race into the History of Christianity: An Essay Review of Sydney E. Ahlstrom, *A Religious History of the American People*; Martin E. Marty, *Righteous Empire: The Protestant Experience in America*; and Robert T. Handy, "A Christian America: Protestant Hopes and Historical Realities," *Journal of the American Academy of Religion* 46 (December 1978): 567.

59. R. W. Southern, "The Historical Experience," *Times Literary Supplement* (London) 24 (June 1977): 771.

60. William B. Clebsch, *From Sacred to Profane in America: The Role of Religion in American History* (New York: Harper & Row, 1968), p. 97.

61. William B. Clebsch, *Christianity in European History* (New York: Oxford University Press, 1979), p. 3.

62. R. W. Southern, *Western Society and the Church in the Middle Ages* (Baltimore: Penguin Books, 1970), pp. 15-16.

63. Franklin Hamlin Littell, *From State Church to Pluralism: A Protestant Interpretation of Religion in American History* (New York: Macmillan, 1971), p. xv.

64. Philip Schaff, *The Principle of Protestantism* (1845; rpt. Philadelphia, 1964), p. 61.

65. Heinrich Heine, *Religion and Philosophy in Germany: A Fragment*, trans. John Snodgrass (rpt. 1882 ed.; Boston: Beacon Press, 1959), p. 51.

66. H. Richard Niebuhr, *Radical Monotheism and Western Culture* (New York: Harper, 1960), p. 11.

67. George Huntston Williams, "Church History: From Historical Theology to the Theology of History," in Arnold S. Nash, ed., *Protestant Thought in the Twentieth Century: Whence & Whither?* (New York: Macmillan, 1951), pp. 177-78.

68. *See* the following three essays: Karl Rahner, "Anonymous Christians," in vol. 6, *Concerning Vatican Council II*, trans. Karl-H. and Boniface Kruger, *Theological Investigations*

(Baltimore: Helicon Press, 1969), pp. 390-98; Rahner, "Anonymous Christianity and the Missionary Task of the Church," in vol. 12, *Confrontation*, trans. David Bourke, *Theological Investigations* (New York: Seabury Press, 1974), pp. 161-78; and Rahner, "Observations on the Problem of the 'Anonymous Christian,' " in vol. 14, *Ecclesiology, Questions in the Church, the Church in the World*, trans. David Bourke, *Theological Investigations* (New York: Seabury Press, 1976), pp. 280-94.

PART THREE

NEIGHBOROLOGY

10

Neighborology

A Feminist Ethno-Missiological Celebration of Kosuke Koyama[1]

VICTORIA LEE ERICKSON

OIKOUMENE: THE NIPA HUT THAT IS NOT A SHIP

The way of *Being that is* Kosuke Koyama *is the nipa hut* that shelters my soul. When the rains come, the nipa hut can be turned upside down and used as a life preserving raft. After the rains are gone, sometimes the winds come and blow the nipa hut and soul around, separating fragile shelter from fragile life. It is a Koyama-way-of-being that recognizes that there are common and local materials within our reach to rebuild and reshelter the soul. The material and spiritual nipa hut is crafted from centuries of sheltering traditions that refuse to go away. In order for you to know what Kosuke Koyama's rediscovery, and hence remaking, of ancient sheltering means to me, I must tell you something about myself. This is not an egocentric act. It is in community that our bodies and souls are created as one body; each of us is a part of one another.

I am a missionary ordained in the United Church of Christ, USA. I am also a feminist well trained by Marxists at the Graduate Center, City University of New York. A Norwegian-American, I have grandparents who fiercely defended the future of cooperatives by procuring from them all their daily needs: dairy products, foodstuffs, seed, grain, electricity, farm machinery, clothing and, not least of all, knowledge about the way we should live. I grew up in farming communities and the small towns that served them; I educated myself in cities where I lived with my husband in cooperative housing. My children were raised in New York City while I served ecumenical ministries for the elderly, poor, and homeless. Until now, every community that shaped me was a community on the verge of collapse; their memberships held themselves together by sharing what they had and what they hoped for: strategies for survival and peace. The communities that produced me, and that I produced, all loved story telling. Somehow we all knew, growing up in rural and small-town Lutheran evangelical and mission-oriented churches, that it was in the stories of our lives that we found life itself: God with us. It could not be any other way. Stories did not make sense without God, without our ground of Being.

To surrender to the power of the story's embrace was to surrender to the well-being of our neighbor, whose story we listened to and told as well.

Telling the stories of the world's poor precipitated a variety of liberation theologies. For all the declarations of God being on the side of the poor, feminism, popular/populist movements, and most all liberation causes, I find myself halfway through life preparing dirges for communities of liberation that are about to become museum pieces. They do not know how to change, to rebuild, to become new. The Land O'Lakes butter cooperative seems to have survived with a viable future, but we know what happened to Marxism. The Protestant church is leaking like a sieve. Missions have shrunk to academic ecumenical and interfaith dialogues, with almost everyone afraid of announcing any contribution that Christians might make to the world. Feminism is in such trouble that we are now reduced to squabbles over who owns and who stole the heart of feminism. The church became the voluntary nerve center for the building of low-income housing and the attainment of affirmative action as a tool to achieving civil equity, but we do not seem to remember why we did these things. We live as if we have forgotten our stories.

In my pain and sadness for what was collapsing around me, Koyama's books reminded me that feminism, Marxism, and liberal Protestantism were not who I am. Who I am is deeper and richer than they ever were. I am of a people (*ethnos*) that answers to our very Being for the condition of community life. While I live in my town, I am responsible for the boredom of children who need opportunities to work at creating life for others. I am, then, standing in the middle of a deep sense of hope that has generated a vision of neighborliness that seeks and takes seriously the joy and goodness of daily life.

It is partly his way of retelling our daily story life that has endeared Koyama to us. From New York City to Stockholm to Manila, I have met people who not only know that Koyama loves to tell their stories but that he also loves people. Perhaps we will all, one day, love to tell our neighbor's story. Perhaps, one day, we will love our neighbors.

When it is not the wind and the rain, but the human heart that threatens the soul, Kosuke Koyama has learned how to protect fragile-soul-life by flattening the nipa hut to the ground, by surrounding the soul with his very being and the Being of God. This is what Kosuke Koyama is: a living nipa hut that knows how to rebuild itself over and over again, storm after storm, on the ground of Being. I would like feminism, liberation movements, the church, and communities of all kinds to learn how to do this. I would like to learn how to do this myself. In this essay we shall attempt a start. In great Koyama tradition, we will make it up as we go along. We shall not be afraid of those who threaten our lives, our tenure status, or our livelihood. Being on the bottom, close to the ground, surrounded by the love of Being, is the safest place to be.

NEIGHBOROLOGY

Kosuke Koyama accomplished his theology/ministry through a very special kind of listening. He listened to his neighbors. Because he listened well, he learned how neighbors become neighbors and then he learned how to become their neighbor himself. Koyama knew what a neighbor was, how to become one, and how to be a good one, long before he learned how others know these things. His theological education was not insignificant to this learning process, but it was not the site of his learning, either. He learned how to be a good neighbor (and as a result, how to build a good nipa hut—that is, he learned how to shelter the soul) by doing. In the mission fields of Southeast Asia, where understanding a new theological worldview is not, at first glance, worth much to local people—but good neighboring is—Koyama let go of theology and theory and became a local actor in a complicated system of accountabilities. When he did this, he discovered that the contents of everyday actions brought with them their own answerability. People's understanding of themselves and their actions, people's systems of accountability, stood in sharp contrast to the theory/theology he had brought back to Asia from Western academies.

In the process of releasing his grip on Western theology, Koyama did not let go of his identity as a Christian (shaped by crucified mind). In fact, his identity was strengthened. In conversation with Buddhism and the peoples of Southeast Asia, Koyama discovered that the dualist nature of the difference-similarity conversations dissolved. In its place grew an appreciation for the great variety of human experiences. This appreciation became an intentionally reflexive project that he has called "neighborology."[2] In the following pages we will explore the socio-theological product of Koyama's neighborology and compare it with nontheological, "secular," sociological understandings of "neighbor, neighboring and neighborhoods" produced in Western academies. I shall conclude by suggesting why it is that feminism, Marxism, and liberal Protestant churches are heading for a home in cardboard boxes on a cultural museum shelf.

COMMUNITY IS NEIGHBORS INTERACTING: KOYAMA'S ENCOUNTER WITH GOD

Life is liturgy for Koyama. In that culture is liturgy oriented, society organizes itself around moments of coming together, around a common understanding of what is right and good. Since culture is multilayered, with overlapping communities and their varied understandings of what is right and good, communication between memberships is critical for maintaining peaceable community. The missionary as peace educator attempts to learn all the languages people speak in order to maintain communicative networks of empowered members. "The power that enlivens communication is love.... God is love. God is communicating. Both of these go together even though it is 'hidden' from us. Hidden yet most communicating communication. An unusual manner of communication, indeed."[3]

Koyama understands God's communicating action in the way that people understand theirs. People's ritualized coming together hides, or keeps silent, the great communicative work of society. In ethnomethodological terms, common sense goes without saying, it builds itself around everything we take for granted.[4] The rules for everyday life are left unspoken. In Koyama's experience, we meet God in the communicative actions of our neighbors. Reading these actions is done through the Holy Spirit. And what a difference the Spirit makes! When Koyama encounters old Russian women, he is moved to write a poem about their wrinkled faces.[5] (Max Weber, on the other hand, does not find them beautiful and declared old women a detriment to the future of civilization.[6]) Koyama calls us away from theological and theoretical abstractions. He wants us to talk about "the people I know."[7] When we focus on theoretical and theological abstractions, we open ourselves to hatred and violence when the people we know do not march to the drums of our "isms." Our "isms," Koyama contends, often generate a tyranny of doctrine through a focus on the self, or, a tyrannical selfishness.[8] The task is to give up selfishness (not self-knowledge). "Personality is an event. It takes place when there is meeting between myself and others."[9]

If this is true—that we cannot know Buddhism, we can only know Buddhists—we can only speak practically of the local setting. When speaking of the local setting, we must be careful to not talk abstractly about religion. Koyama argues that on the local level the Christ and the Buddha have more important things to do than argue theology. They must think about human suffering. In this sense, local people are very much like the Buddha and the Christ and not very much like Buddhism or Christianity.

By listening to the stories of our neighbors and participating in the stories themselves, we achieve community. To have community we must have neighboring. Neither are achieved by efficient confrontation but by inefficient patience. Community is achieved by walking slowly with a neighborly three-mile-an-hour God.

Building community takes time. Taking our neighbor's questions into account is so time consuming that it is better to forget about time. It is better to learn how to be patient. We must learn to speak our neighbor's languages and understand our neighbor's memberships in overlapping communities. We must come to know what makes our neighbor laugh and cry. Once we come to love our neighbor, we realize that our love is rooted in the pain of God, the pain God feels when our neighbor is not loved.

SELF IN COMMUNITY: NEIGHBOR TO NEIGHBOR

Loving our neighbor often means that we must overcome our tendency to focus on our individual selves while strengthening our ability to grow in self-knowledge, that is, knowledge of who we are in relation to community Being. Self-denial reorients our focus to the present moment and the possibility of capturing the present as a meaning-filled moment. To live this one moment well is to understand that our lives are as fragile as a butterfly, and not as enduring as a temple bell.[10] In each moment the butterfly creates a foundation for life.

The self-identity that creates a foundation for life is, for Koyama, Abraham's dust and ashes identity.[11] A dust-and-ashes identity realizes one's limitations but does not give into self-rejection and despair. This fully awakened identity is also a buddha identity. A dust-and-ashes identity leaves no room for bribery. What can anyone threaten to take away from dust and ashes? Dust and ashes, a buddha-self, is free to possess a political power unknown to egocentric identities given to affinities with tyrannical orthodoxies.

A buddha mind is for Koyama a crucified mind. Self-denial without hesitation emancipates psychological, spiritual, and physical energies for encounters with the Other. When God introduces us one to another, each introduction is an event filled with interactions requiring massive amounts of energy to absorb all that the other person is. A good share of this energy is returned to the self by the other as it protects the self from crisis, as we create an understanding of who we are together in the context of historical, global, national, and communal life. The crisis created by the egocentric pull is that the self-centered person wants one history, and usually one's own particular "ism," to define all experiences. Rather, what we need is an ability to live in a varied universe of multiple meanings. We teach one another how to live together. The elimination of the egocentric "I" is the resurrection and restoration of a shared identity of peace.[12]

When we accomplish a shared identity, we are also free from time and space. Time cannot grip us, and we have no need to grasp after time.[13] Sexuality is decentralized, and we are profoundly liberated to encounter the journey of human beings whose suffering is the rightful center of our lives.[14] The sexualized egocentric self is no small player in the self-righteousness that always brings violence and death as it arbitrarily creates boundaries where no boundaries exist in shared communal identity.[15] The shared self-identity soon realizes that it is nurtured by grace. It is in those moments of wholeness and hospitality that philosophy's questions are answered by a community's practical/action theology. There is no great drama here. There are simply actions of hospitality. Theology is people doing.

The critical question is: People doing what? People doing egocentric action is destructive theology. People doing neighboring is peace-oriented theology as actors "accept the claim the neighbor makes on our lives."[16] The claim that the neighbor makes is that we experience the neighbor without a cushion.[17] When we allow ourselves to encounter others without the cushions of ideology, we hear and see our neighbors as they really are.

With all of this receiving of the neighbor, what is the role of the educator and the missionary? For the Buddha, ignorance only shields our unwillingness to change.[18] The educational goal of the Buddha is to learn why people let what is changable shackle their minds. People teach the Buddha their limitations, and the Buddha teaches people how to free themselves from these limitations. The problem, Koyama argues, is that Christians suffer from a teacher complex.[19] We are not interested in being taught by people. This is not a Christ problem but a Christianity problem. Christianity has found a powerful and wrongful method to control others. Jesus, Koyama reflects, asks the madman to "tell me your name."

Education is for personality formation. If our personalities are formed through events when we encounter others, education must help us encounter others in concrete material situations where we hear God asking: "Where is Abel your brother? How is he? Is your brother enjoying shalom in his community life?" But, writes Koyama with a note of sadness, we are too much like Cain. We respond, "Am I my brother's keeper?"[20]

And, finally, what of the missionary? For what reason does the missionary become a neighbor? To conquer the other? No. The missionary as neighbor pulls theology out of people's lives and helps them see how they really live. Mission as healing agent agitates culture and history so that people see their lives in new ways. The missionary as neighbor provides a gift, or is an act of grace, in that the other says "I am heard, I am known." The one who speaks my language and cocreates community with me is known by me and knows me. The one who knows me finds Being in me. When we find Being in each other, we are able to transform culture through respeaking, new acting, and doing. In response to Being, we intentionally shape those daily occurring events that create common-sense rules, define that which goes without saying, and determine our shared identity.

For Kosuke Koyama, being a neighbor/missionary means making an unconditional surrender to the embrace of God. This surrender leaves behind the glory of the empire for the privilege of inviting people, who may not invite you back, to share your table. When we surrender to God, we belong to the One who compassionately suffers for us—the One who is known in the suffering of others. The beginning of community is not confrontation but neighborly embrace. We start our life not with the hermeneutics of suspicion but with a hermeneutics of embrace. This embrace is elastic. Its large arms allow resistance to missionary/educator thinking. It invites surprise. It adjusts to the one "who cannot adjust to me." Continual adjusting to the other is a state of being in permanent transition. Koyama reminds us that only in a moment of transition, as he walked to the cross, did Jesus accept that he was God.

THE SOCIOLOGY OF NEIGHBORING

The neighbor has long been of interest to social scientists. The university settlement houses helped spur on this academic interest in the United States as they collected rich stores of data on neighborhood life. The founding purpose of the settlement house was to experiment in neighborliness or give hospitality. Through hospitality, it was hoped that the university could impact the needs of urbanites, mostly immigrants, through conversation, classes in sewing, economics, reading and writing, and lectures of many sorts. In the late 1880s, Northwestern University opened a settlement house in Chicago's 17th Ward, the smallest but most populated ward, teeming with Poles, Germans, Jews, and Scandinavians, all of whom had to learn how to get along and how to become American. Assigning itself the role of teaching culture, the settlement house monthly news journal promoted neighborliness as a moral good.[21] The settlement worker was seen to benefit equally from the engagement with the neighborhood. Such work invigorated moral health and facilitated self-improvement through self-abnegation.

> The joy of living in a certain community naturally is accompanied by a love for the persons composing it. That continual association with one's neighbors which a person has in a settlement draws him away from thoughts of self into a love for those around him, which perhaps extends to even himself, and which we choose to call self respect rather than love.[22]

By 1904, Harvard's Nathaniel Southgate Shaler was tracking down the "natural history of human contacts" because "individuals are in relations that determine their lot."[23] A strong country and city required strong neighborhoods. Strong neighborhoods were created by people who gave up self-centeredness and worked at loving the person one lived next to. Loving the person one lives next door to is not easy. In documenting how we learn to live next to each other, most sociological investigations into neighboring focus on how good neighbors are created, such as the study of saving face in Benin. Face-saving allows conflict between neighbors to be nonconfrontationally expressed. The Baatombu people of northern Benin devised a way to save face when criticizing a neighbor's behavior. They have cultivated names for their dogs that carry proverbial meanings. By calling the dog, the owner sends a message to the listening neighbor![24]

Face-saving might seem like a small task neighbors perform. But, in contexts where violence could easily be a result of humiliated, demeaned, angered, even annoyed neighbors, face-saving becomes a crucial element of the work neighbors do. Yet, from culture to culture, understanding why neighbors do not get along becomes cause for serious study and contemplation. It appears to be rather indicative of human community that we attempt to explain unneighborliness. When encounters escalate and complaints against neighbors arise,[25] all manner of resources are employed to explain why neighbors do not get along. The Coastal Miwok Indians argued that sorcery pitted neighbor against neighbor.[26] Sorcery makes bad neighbors in some contexts; in others, religion itself is seen as a source of good ones. Georgianna's survey of 715 persons in 12 neighborhoods finds no significant difference between religious and nonreligious participants' beliefs in the value of being neighborly. However, both groups do act differently in the neighborhood, and both value religious activities aimed at creating good neighbors.[27] Church attendance increases the likelihood that one will have faith in people.[28]

Across cultures, the neighborhood is a primary site for testing out values.[29] Deutsch's study of Arabs and Jews living together in apartment blocks in Israel showed that close neighborhood situations produced positive relationships. Yet, despite satisfaction, both groups wanted to maintain enough social distance to preserve their religious and cultural identities.[30] Preservation of identity is the major work of community members. Often it takes place in opposition to other social processes that seek to control it or dominate it in the interests of a few. Poyer's fascinating study of the people of the Sapwuahfit Atoll finds them, during a time of increasing inter-atoll hierarchy, promoting an intra-atoll egalitarian ethos through public events such as feasts. Through the act of feasting on shared food, a symbol of public caring for the public good, the public itself managed to challenge ideologies that threatened its communal identity.[31] The ideal of communal well-being became the practice of protecting communal well-being.

Maintaining an ideal neighborhood is a cross-cultural occupation, and not always an easy one, given the variables of class. Cukrowicz discovered that French and non-French origin families preferred to live next to French families with few children and high incomes.[32] Dyer's study of Texans indicates that higher income frequently means higher education, both of which bring increased acceptance of minority group contact.[33] It took some time for researchers to notice race and gender variables in neighboring.[34] Religion, however, has remained a consistent research focus in neighborhood studies. Researchers find that people know how to construct their lives and order daily events in order to accomplish social goals, and they have assigned to religion (in its humanist and holy forms) key tasks in the work of building community and creating neighbors.

SELF IN COMMUNITY: WE ARE
BREAD FOR ONE ANOTHER

As a final example of sociological neighbor studies and as a way into the practical role of religion in neighboring, let us look at Sandra Ott's exploration of the role of blessed bread in the French Basque Catholic commune of Sainte Engrâce.[35] Located between France and Spain on the southeastern edge of the Pyrénees-Atlantiques, the Basque community is about 1,400 years old. We know that it was an established Catholic community by the tenth century. Ott found that the Basque shepherding community organizes its life around notions of rotation and alternation. Evidence for this worldview is first found in the basic description of where the community lives. They claim not to live in a valley but "in a circle of mountains." The circular nature of their social world is maintained ritualistically. Ott's presentation of ethnographic data is particularly helpful, in that her descriptions are anchored in people's local/practical analysis of what the ritual is designed to accomplish.

The goal in the ritual exchange of blessed bread is the creation of "first neighbors." After the family household, "first neighbors" is the primary social institution of "permanently linked as interdependent and mutually supportive socio-economic units. . . . The people one knows best are not one's relatives but one's 'first neighbors.'"[36] "Closer than kin," first neighbors fill three categories: first-first (spatially to the right of one's own house), second-first, and third-first (spatially to the left of one's own house). No two households can have the same first neighbors. At a community-wide level, first neighbor relationships form an unbroken chain around the 500-member commune. "This is an empirical fact of which people were clearly aware."[37] First neighbors provide daily assistance and support in time of crisis. Quotes Ott: "If I do not get along well with my 'first neighbors,' who do I turn to if I lose sheep or a cow in the hills? Who will help me with my maize or fern? And worst of all, who would look after my soul and my *etxenkuak* [the members of my household] when I die?"[38]

The first neighbor relationships of looking after were especially critical during the Second World War, when occupying soldiers demanded each household to produce meat on a regular schedule. First neighbors would be called upon to provide the ration if the household lacked it and would ask for a return favor when it was their turn to produce meat.[39]

Blessed bread and mortuary services between first neighbors are the two most socially significant ritualized exchanges described by Ott. In a well-known Catholic community, it is interesting that very few people attended church. Everyone, though, respected the *indarra* or power of the priest. This power was from God. The same word, *indarra*, describes male semen, manna, and grace. Proclaiming and distributing blessed things were acts of grace. Ott records an offertory song where "God is invited to take our heart, our good bread, clean bread, our seed of *indarra*, our life. . . . "[40]

Although the priest was important ritualistically in the provision of blessings (hence one could refer to blessed bread, blessed water, blessed candles, etc.), the community owned responsibility for ritualistic maintenance of community-based liturgies/rituals. Every Sunday through a two-year rotation, the female first neighbors (*etchekandere*) sponsored a mass for the souls in Purgatory. They brought the priest two blessed candles to burn for them and baked leavened whole wheat bread to be blessed, and hence embodied, with special supernatural power from God. The first neighbor whose turn it was distributed this bread to the priest and worshiping community, to her family, and to her first neighbor. Interestingly, the unleavened Host (communion bread) was received on the tongue, but the blessed bread was served from a basket from which everyone helped themselves. After the service, the blessed bread was brought to the first neighbor. As the bread crossed the threshold, it was announced to be a gift of "our [women's] semen or seed."[41] Giving blessed bread was a woman's act of grace. This seed brought blessings for health and protection in the household. Ott finds that many "elderly women felt certain that the disciples were 'first neighbors' and that the custom of giving blessed bread to the first-first neighbor originated during the lifetime of Christ." One old woman said, "By giving our semen in the form of bread we women give life [*bizi*] to one another and to our respective households." [42]

Interestingly, Ott does not make much of the power of salvation the people find in blessed bread. It is taken after the eucharist and the consumption of the Host, the Catholic Church's great sacrament of salvation. Yet it was when consuming the blessed bread that the people said, "Blessed bread, engendered in the earth, blessed on the altar, if I should die this week, my soul will be saved."[43] For these women and men, salvation happened in community through the giving and receiving of leavened bread.

The second ritual exchange included mortuary services and happened between men and women in first-first neighbor relationships. The first-first neighbor family who received bread from the deceased became at death the primary special assistant to the first-first family and to the deceased. The first-first neighbor helped the bread giver's soul into heaven and the bread giver's family through mourning.

Through first neighbor ritual exchanges by men and women, Ott found that the Sainte-Engrâce commune preserved and perpetuated social relationships. These ritual exchanges were expectations—requirements—of daily living. It was unthinkable that one would not give or receive blessed bread or help one's first neighbor through death. Through ritual exchanges, the community created occasions for interaction that defined for the members who they were and what was expected of them.

THE MISSIONARY AND THE SOCIOLOGIST

Ott's ethnography provides insight into the ways a community constructed itself on the local, everyday level. But what of professional missionaries, theologians, and sociologists, with our theoretical constructions which are, by definition, abstracted from the everyday? Do we have something comparable to bread to share with each other and with a community beyond our intellectual disciplines? If we do, then there are good reasons for us to become first-first neighbors. Ultimately our work is not worth very much if we do not listen to people—and people themselves will decide how well we've listened and what value to place on our reflections. With this in mind, personal humility is the appropriate garb to wear as we trudge through data representing bits and snatches of people's lives.

Sociologists might call Koyama's social research methodology participant observation and his product "an ethnographic account of his experiences in Southeast Asia." Whereas Koyama the theologian defines good neighboring as how well one answers the questions, Where is your neighbor? How is your neighbor? Is your neighbor at peace in his/her community well-being? for all practical purposes sociologists are satisfied to document what neighbors do. The sociologists we have encountered above have used quantitative and qualitative methods to secure their data. Taken together, theologians and sociologists have produced remarkably similar observations: Without good neighbors, there is no good community. Without neighbors, there is no community at all. People need neighbors and devise all manner of processes through which good neighbors are produced. A primary location for the skills needed for creating worthy community members is religion's ritual/liturgical events. People encounter in their neighbors, whom they have constructed and who construct them, their most profound sense of self as shared identity. Racism, classism, sexism, and all the other "isms" impact the wholeness of neighborhood life and skew people's deepest aspirations. All neighbors are expected to act like neighbors and support the community through life-giving actions.

Koyama's listening-neighbor-heart and crucified/buddha-mind is an ancient way of being that is known to people who neighbor. The people I know who value being and creating good neighbors respond to Koyama as an expert witness to their lives. What Koyama discovered hidden in bombed-out Japanese cities, in Thai rice paddies, and on Mount Sinai is the key ingredient that produces meaning in our lives:

answerability. Social scientists have come close to Koyama's understanding of how we form identity. Most closely related to him are ethnomethodologists, whose work seeks to understand how in everyday practices people construct their moral world and create systems of accountability within it. Through ethnomethodology, sociology's gift to theology is an intentional method with which to document these accounting processes. Expanding our understanding of accounting practices to include answering practices is a gift theology gives to sociology. In that both focus on moral accountabilities and answers, ethnomethodology and theology are partners in the service of humankind.

ANSWERABILITY AND ETHNOMETHODOLOGICAL ACCOUNTING PRACTICES

I once bumped into a theologian whose arms were loaded with Max Weber's massive *Economy and Society* volumes. He announced cheerily that anything sociologists could do, theologians could do better. I prefer partnership, myself, although examples of it are difficult to find. The last great partnership in my estimation was between Max Weber and Ernst Troeltsch, but their relationship ended in disaster. Koyama's project could be seen as a merger of sociology and theology in what one might call ethnotheology. I would like to invite Koyama into a partnership.

Unbeknownst to Koyama, as he was graduating from Princeton Theological Seminary with his doctorate in theology, Harold Garfinkle was graduating from Harvard University with a doctorate in sociology and was about to forge the discipline of ethnomethodology. Both have had a history of being agitators of established academic discourses, and both have been willing to break the boundaries of their intellectual disciplines that would separate theoretical production from common sense.

What is ethnomethodology? Watts summarizes it quite simply:

> Ethnomethodology studies the procedures by which we go about constructing in our own minds and conversations a view of the social world around us. . . . We are interested in what everybody knows. What everybody knows is found in language. Language is both accomplished and transcendent. [44]

Ethnomethodologists look to the method to "analyze common everyday life in the formal properties that make up commonsense actions."[45] Maintaining the integrity of the action, ethnomethodologists find that there is no point in arguing with common-sense activity. They do not seek ways to "correct" it, they seek to understand it.

What ethnomethodologists have learned about everyday reality is used to form the small presuppositional base for ethnomethodology. Having said this, it is important to say immediately that ethnomethodologists are quite willing to give up this tiny base if it is shown that the membership under study does not use it. The following presuppositions are pulled out of everyday practices themselves and can be said to make up the formal properties of action. For ethnomethodologists, the inter-woven character of these properties insures that they will be found together, allow-ing actors to create and maintain meaning for the collectivity of actors.

Following are the formal properties of action identified by ethnomethodologists:

Practical Rationality

People produce rationality. They produce the settings they then take for granted. That is, people accomplish everyday life. Everyday life is socially constructed. Soci-ety is a purposeful construction of actors who work very hard every day to keep the meaning system in good repair.[46]

Reflexivity

Reflexivity means that life is contextual, self-descriptive, incarnate.[47] The social setting is maintained through a set of practices that constitute the social setting. The activities that produce and manage everyday life are the same as the procedures for producing accountability. Social life is contextual, so that one cannot understand actions without looking at the context in which action takes place. "Constituent fea-tures . . . are self-same with that which embodies them"; activity is "accountable in itself."[48]

Indexicality

Reflexivity establishes contextuality. Indexicality documents contextual mean-ing. Everyday life has meanings that one can count and index. Social life is an inter-pretive process involving documentary work, which is another way of saying that social life is made up of routine actions which can be observed and talked about (i.e., indexed) and which have observable meanings attached to them. Eth-nomethodological "analysis is concerned with the relation of action-to-action, rather than with the relation of sign-to-referent."[49] Activity is always "intelligible (accountable) to its participants"[50]; "ordinary users have no difficulty grasping it."[51] All action is meaningful in that meaning is embedded in the concrete situation.[52] Ethnomethodologists study the accounting practices found in society between its members.

Language

The notions of reflexivity and indexicality require an emphasis on language. Lan-guage is the mechanism by which the social world is created.[53] It is a rational process, as well. People, we have said, produce rationality; rationality allows peo-ple to plan and execute daily life.

In outlining rational behaviors, Garfinkle finds that rationality is the ability of a member of a community in conducting his or her everyday affairs: to calculate, to act deliberately, to project alternative plans of action, to select a fall of events, to pri-oritize selection of means, to predict surprise in small amounts, to prefer analysis to improvisation, to exercise choice, to insist on fine as opposed to gross situations, and to trust a vast array of features in the social order.[54] This concept of rationality, along with the notion that society is language in action, allows us to dispense with the notion of a free-standing agent. There is for the ethnomethodologist no such being as an individual, if we understand the individual to be an isolable entity that stands apart from culture or society. What exists are members of a course of activity. Members contribute to the shape of the culture or society they belong to, but they do not exist apart from a membership in some culture or some society. These members master a common (natural) language and participate in a text of speech acts, a system of practices.[55] This common (often experienced as "natural") language is highly pragmatic, highly contextual.

Language is created through interaction and is not therefore a "system of signs or symbols but a medium of practical activity."[56] Language, then, is not just a resource for studying social life; language is social life itself. It exists prior to and independent of the speaker, it constrains the speaker while simultaneously creating immediate and transcendental social reality. Language simultaneously accomplishes society and biography. These accomplishments are public, observable, controllable events. . . .[57] "*The* fundamental sociological activity [is] reflecting upon and repairing language."[58] This activity is a corporate activity that pushes sociological analysis beyond traditional liberalism's human action as center model, displacing human consciousness as the original source of theoretical and practical language.[59] Ethnomethodologists focus on the occasions where members gather. We do not focus on individual people as if they were independent of the context, as if they could be the center of it. Occasions have no centers; they are events of members interacting.[60] Gatherings bring together a multitude of members and often entertain new members. The pulling apart and regathering of community life requires continual renewal of language.

MEMBERSHIP IN COMMUNITY/COLLECTIVITY: MEMBERS INTERACTING

By our very membership in a common language/action system, we participate in constructing our identities and those around us. This claim does not diminish the uniqueness of each member and the contributions the member brings to shaping membership. By documenting ethnomethodologically how men and women produce everyday life through language and conversation analysis, we document indigenous moral structure. Contained in this structure is indigenous theory/rationality.

Everyday interaction depends upon an appeal to common-sense understandings so that a million tiny interpretations can be made. All rationalities have what ethnomethodologists have documented as results expected from behaviors. In the following, I will briefly use ethnomethodology's properties of rationality and show a connection between them and studies of neighboring.[61]

Categorizing and Comparing

Rationality depends upon the ability to compare two or more situations. People categorize and compare their experiences all day long. The people in Chicago's 17th

Ward know when the neighborhood is at peace and when it is not. Neighbors in France have figured out that life is better for them when their neighbors belong to the affluent cultural majority.

Tolerable Error

Actors pay close attention to what they observe and what they expect to find. The degree of fit marks one occasion more rationally constituted than another. People work to decrease the chances of making an error. The Sapwuahfit Atoll members observed the increasing power of hierarchical polities surrounding them and moved to protect their egalitarian values through publicly sponsored feasts.

Search for Means

People have rules for procedures that bring about the effects they desire. These rules are based on techniques that worked in other situations. The Basque commune maintained a highly structured system of first neighbor accountabilities that produced systematic caring for one another's daily and crisis needs. The rules and procedures were reenforced through the giving of blessed bread. This system worked so well that mortuary services were run in the same manner.

Analysis of Alternatives and Consequences

Rationality includes the anticipation of the reactions one's actions will produce. The consequences to one's actions are rehearsed in the imagination in advance. The old women knew that if they ceased to give blessed bread, the community well-being would suffer and relationships would dissolve. They explained their actions as rational ones: they followed Jesus' disciples, who created the custom.

Strategy

People plan ahead, they make strategies for action. When the ability to make a rational decision is considered low, people reach into a storehouse of what-to-do-in-case-of alternatives. The wider the gap between what people have experienced and the alternatives at their disposal, the more unpredictable the responses. The blessed bread community produced a male who would take the part of the female bread giver if a female head of house had died or was no longer there. This male would do all of the ritual practices assigned to the female bread giver. In contrast, an Alameda, California, study shows that when neighbors know that reporting domestic violence almost always results in a negative relationship with the reported neighbor, they are hesitant to report abuse.[62]

Concern for Timing

People tend to limit the activities they consider not very rational. People time events to produce desired results. The Basque community reminds people of their obligations to each other through ritual bread giving spaced every two years. It is the responsibility of first-first neighbors to watch the dying person and call the priest in time for last rites. At death, the first-first neighbor opens the window to let the soul fly home.

Predictability

People like to reduce surprise and increase predictability. Wanting surprise in small amounts is a typical way of measuring rationality. For Koyama, the liberated buddha-mind is free to accept our neighbor's anxieties as we invite our neighbor's surprise into our arms.

Rules for Procedure

There are many kinds of rules: tribal rules, western "economic man" rules, feminist rules, and the like. People evaluate right and wrong based on the rule set(s) they carry around with them. When immigrants arrive in a new country, they need to learn a new set of rules. Settlement houses provided a safe space for learning new rules.

Choice

People are aware of opportunities to choose, and they know when they make choices. Maximizing choice maximizes perceived rationality. Choices are made in the overall context of common-sense practices.

Grounds of Choice

There are grounds upon which people are aware of making choices. The ability to set their actions in context is called rationalization. The Atoll members were clearly aware of their decision to resist power hierarchies that destroyed egalitarian relationships.

Compatibility of Ends-Means Relationships and Logic

People often arrange an action and see it as a solution to problems. The ends-means relationship is evaluated in the context of logic. The physical construction of housing as a source for modeling successful multicultural living is a worldwide activity.

Semantic Clarity and Distinctiveness

People strive to come up with a definition of the situation that increases the rationality of the event. The Coastal Miwok Indians named sorcery as the reason for bad neighboring. No reasonable person would be a bad neighbor.

Clarity and Distinctiveness for Its Own Sake

How much clarity one needs and of what quality depends upon one's rule set and logic for rational accounting. The old Basque women were quite clear that the blessed bread tradition originated with the disciples during Christ's lifetime. This clear historical mandate explained why neighbors (as disciples) were closer than kin.

Simply put, ethnomethodologists find people to be rather brilliant. People are busy all day long, constructing and reconstructing their lives. Each member must give a communal account of, and answer for, her or his actions. In answering to the community, the member participates in the creation of moral life. In evaluating accounts, the membership establishes a way of being that transcends the content of previous actions. However, being is renegotiated in the next moment, when new actions are accounted for. The accounted-for actions that happened in the past no longer have a meaning that is available to us in their full truth-of-being-in-event. We may never know the meaning of past actions. In the absence of meaning, people transcend unavailability of meaning by creating meaning in the answer they give for their present actions. In this sense, being becomes an ongoing event that is both transcendent and immanent.

GOD AND THE ANSWER: BEING AS ON-GOING EVENT

There are two domains of theory of communication before us at this point: theory produced in the academy for its unitary being and theory produced in the everyday world for its unitary being. The Russian philosopher M. M. Bakhtin sought to bring these theoretical worlds together. Bakhtin's philosophy of the "act" and his understanding of everyday lived practice challenges academic work not to focus only on its own voice.[63] He saw the academic project for what it was: a departure from the reality of everyday life and therefore in danger of disregarding the truth-of-being-in-event that everyday life generates and then uses to maintain itself. What has not been fully appreciated in Bakhtin's work is that he was profoundly Christian. On the surface, Christianity and the church have little to do with his writing, but his power was and is the power generated by 5,000 years of answerable, moral community found in the dust-and-ashes identity of Abraham, Sarah, Mary, and Jesus.

What Bakhtin knew was what the developing tyrannical Russian leadership feared: The people knew the difference between the moral life they wanted and the ideological program they were offered. Kosuke Koyama learned the same thing about "isms" from Thai Buddhists. Bakhtin wrote for a very small dissenting voice of academicians who wanted the majority of academics not to miss their opportunity to make real contributions to everyday life—the kind of contributions Kosuke Koyama has made. Given the political geography of the time, Bakhtin's project was the more treacherous one. It is very hard to convince people that the everyday mundane world they left behind as profanely unenlightened is a better judge of what is real than their world of abstractions. Koyama chose what Bakhtin describes as the practical route of living sincerely, without an alibi, in worlds few academics are able, much less willing, to answer to. The dust-and-ashes-crucified-buddha-mind of Koyama and Bakhtin take on first-first neighbor obligations in order to insure that the entire community is cared for and survives, both in its material and soul life.

Bakhtin's project was to build a bridge between events and systems of registering events; the bridge determines the relations between now and after now.[64]

Now ——————— bridge ——————— After Now	
once-occurrent-event of Being	consequences of such events
experience	representations of experience
actual performance	theoretical world

Resisting Kant's transcendental conception of an a priori synthesis of sensibility and reason, Bakhtin argued that the unity of an event and meaning is always something that is to be achieved. The direction of his thinking was from actual events to the theoretical world. Bakhtin reflected: "All attempts to force one's way from inside the theoretical world and into actual Being-as-event are quite hopeless."[65] This is where ethnomethodology and Bakhtin agree: resistance to Kant's "as if" (the realm of possible experience or possible Being) requires what Bakhtin called a "no alibi" model of living as answerable deed.

Liapunov and Holquist point out that Bakhtin sought to replace Kant's a priori meaning system with the notion that meaning is achieved when people account for actions. Gone is Kant's universalized theorization that speaks for any/all people at any/all time. Instead, Bakhtin argues that we must account for each action. (This particular people oppress these particular people at this time by doing these acts.) Ethnomethodology's list of presuppositions is directly related to establishing a no-alibi accounting of events. What ethnomethodologists enjoy is what too many philosophers and scholars of objectivity have avoided: the messy, mundane, everyday world of awkward, inconsistent variety. What Bakhtin sought to defend, and what Koyama preached in Thailand, is that the everyday world is a moral world, and to act responsibly in it, one has to account for one's actions to the "neighbor I know." In this sense, there are no systems of power that pass on through time that are independent of the actors. Actors construct systems of power in daily accounting practices.

When I answer for what I did or thought to the neighbor I know, I unite the content of my experience with its accomplishment into a whole act Bakhtin calls *Being*. The act must answer for both its content and its being.[66] Since one act follows another, Bakhtin and ethnomethodologists speak of the ongoingness of Being. Bakhtin argues that science is wrong to separate the content from the moral answer given in the accounting process.[67] When science does not unite the two, the act it speaks about is a dead act, a meaningless act. The theory science produces then is not a true judgment on the act and cannot judge its moral value. The community of scientists that *ex cathedra* judge acts of the communities under observation has no power to insist that these observed communities let them in, let them speak, or let them work there.

> There is no aesthetic ought, scientific ought, and—beside them—an ethical ought; there is only that which is aesthetically, theoretically, socially valid, and these validities may be joined by the ought, for which all of them are instrumental. These positings gain their validity within an aesthetic, a scientific, or a sociological unity: the ought gains its validity within the unity of my once-occurrent answerable life.[68]

> Any kind of *practical* orientation of my life within the theoretical world is impossible: it is impossible to live in it, impossible to perform answerable deeds. In that world I am unnecessary. . . . for it is not the being in which I live, and, if it were the only Being, I would not exist.[69]

Self-renunciation is an important concept for Koyama, Jesus, Buddha, and Bakhtin. My place in Being looks very different from the theoretical world of sci-

ence. By separating content from answerability, theorists lose the self in self-renunciation. However, when I answer to my community/my membership/my neighbors,
self-renunciation means that I accomplish full Being. Self-renunciation is the claiming of a communal neighbor-self. Full Being-in-event requires a surrender of
self/act to the moral system that judges the value of my act. This surrender can only
happen in the world where I live.

WHERE WE LIVE

The giving of blessed bread only has meaning—is only real—in communities
that demand answerability for the act. If I give blessed bread and then do not assist
my neighbor in hauling manure, scrounging up meat for the enemy soldiers, or
attending to my neighbor at death, my act is valueless and has no meaning.

What happens when the community and I disagree about how one should act?
One cannot appeal to ethical norms constructed outside of my community of being;
one must appeal to what is practically valid from within. The time necessary to construct a possibility into an answerable deed must be taken. This construction
process can only happen in occasions where being-in-event is answerable to both
content and account. It must be performed in the community where I live. In the
Basque Sainte-Engrâce commune, care for the whole community's well-being
determined a valid rendering of accounts. Situated knowledge is not situated for/in
the individual but for/in the community. As such, there is no ought with determined
content before the act.[70] Bakhtin believed that individual answerable acts oriented
themselves to participation in Being. For Koyama, God is found when we answer
for our neighbor's well-being. Theologically, ultimate answerability *is* God.

The answer is performed in context, in front of a community that remembers the
stories of faith and whose narrative structure circles communal practice and law.
The stories of Judaism and Christianity revolve around a moral axis of grace. Goodness can only exist with an act of grace. Jews and Christians define and identify
themselves as people whose origins are held in a performed (done and spoken) act
of grace: In the beginning was the Word/in the beginning God said. In the beginning we are taught to love our neighbors and to seek the *shalom* of their community well-being. Buddhists would agree that the ultimate answerability is
compassion free from the attachments of greed, compassion that brings about
peace. In the beginning, or at the center of our lives, is peace.

If theology answers the questions that philosophy asks, it does so as well for the
questions of sociology. But whether we raise the questions of philosophy or sociology, it is only through the language of spirituality that we know for sure if we are
naked, standing with no alibi, on the bridge to the answer. A number of contemporary theologies have grown out of a response to the terrible human pain and suffering inflicted upon persons and communities in the modern world. Searching for
resources for addressing such suffering, they found too few in the church and turned
to the social sciences for help. What these theologies have too often failed to do,
however, is demand that the social sciences themselves be accountable to Being and

community. Accountability as answerability is the most authentic mode of spirituality, which is openness to another/Other.

Theologians seeking to answer such questions of suffering and pain, be they feminist, liberation, liberal, or traditionalist, would do well to remember that answerability means one must believe. That is how religion works. World peace, peace in neighborhoods and families, or peace with one's own self depends upon our performing the law of love. Ideologies, theologies, and theories are meaningless if they are not performed out of, and answerable to, the places where we live.

These places where we live have often been studied by theologians and missionaries who have adopted anthropological tools to translate between Bible and culture. I am suggesting here an adoption of a sociological method that will help us be as brave as Kosuke Koyama wants us to be to translate between persons. In order to be a neighbor, we must go beyond learning the indigenous languages and customs that make up the culture of the place. We must also become accountable to the culture of the place as it manifests itself in the neighbor I know—the neighbor for whose Being I am answerable to God.

NOTES

1. This article is dedicated to the Stockholm School of Theology, which occasioned a celebration of the lifetime achievements of Kosuke Koyama on January 21, 1994; and to Rector Mats Hansson, who made sure I was there to hear Professor Koyama's lectures, "Missiology of Theologia Crucis" and "Christian Mission—A Personal View." I wish to thank the Louisville Institute for the Study of Protestantism in American Culture for the summer research grant that facilitated its writing.

2. Although Koyama uses the English form of this word, I have opted for an American spelling.

3. Kosuke Koyama, *Three Mile an Hour God* (Maryknoll, NY: Orbis Books, 1980), p. 26.

4. Harold Garfinkle, *Studies in Ethnomethodology* (Cambridge, England: Polity Press, 1984).

5. Koyama, *Three Mile an Hour God*, p. 37.

6. Max Weber, "Politics as a Vocation," *From Max Weber: Essays in Sociology*, H. H. Gerth and C. Wright Mills, ed. (New York: Oxford University Press, 1958), p. 118.

7. Koyama, *Three Mile an Hour God*, p. 70.

8. Kosuke Koyama, *Waterbuffalo Theology* (Maryknoll, NY: Orbis Books, 1974), p. 132.

9. Koyama, *Three Mile an Hour God*, p. 33.

10. Ibid., p. 80.

11. Ibid.

12. Koyama, *Waterbuffalo Theology*, pp. 11, 148.

13. Koyama, *Three Mile an Hour God*, p. 11.

14. Kosuke Koyama, *Mount Fuji and Mount Sinai: A Critique of Idols* (Maryknoll, NY: Orbis Books, 1985), p. 124.

15. Ibid., pp. 118, 139. Koyama notes that such an identity formation allows European masters to draw straight lines around African "countries" in a reckless disregard for the violence done to families, tribes, and language groups. This magical control of people is aggressive self-promotion.

16. Koyama, *Waterbuffalo Theology*, p. 91.

17. Ibid., p. 93.

18. Koyama, *Mount Fuji and Mount Sinai*, pp. 119-20.

19. Koyama, *Waterbuffalo Theology*, p. 51.

20. Kosuke Koyama, *No Handle on the Cross* (Maryknoll, NY: Orbis Books, 1977), p. 20.

21. Northwestern University Settlement, *The Neighbor*, vols. 1-4 (1898-1902).

22. Ibid., 3:1 (1898): 3.

23. Nathaniel Southgate Shaler, *The Neighbor: The Natural History of Human Contacts* (Boston: Houghton, Mifflin and Co., 1904).

24. Wendy Schottman, "Proverbial Dog Names of the Baatombu: A Strategic Alternative to Silence," *Language in Society* 22:4 (Dec. 1993): 539-54.

25. For social and demographic variables that relate to reported annoyances, *see* Gary Paquin, "Specific Complaints Against Neighbors," *Sociology and Social Research* 76:3 (1992): 150-55.

26. James V. Spickard, "Environmental Variation and the Plausibility of Religion: A California Indian Example," *Journal for the Scientific Study of Religion* 26:3 (Sept. 1987): 327-39.

27. Sharon Georgianna, "Is a Religious Neighbor a Good Neighbor?" *Humbold Journal of Social Relations* 11:2 (1984): 1-16.

28. Howard M. Bahr and Thomas K. Martin, "And Thy Neighbor as Thy Self: Self Esteem and Faith in People as Correlates of Religiosity and Family Solidarity among Middletown High School Students," *Journal of the Scientific Study of Religion* 22:2 (June 1983): 132-44.

29. Barbara Michel, "The Good Neighbor and the Bad Neighbor: Sketch of a Sociology of the Ethos of Neighborhood/ Le bon voisin, le mauvais voisin: ebauche d'une sociologie de l'ethos de voisinage," *Social Compass* 28:4 (1981): 357-80.

30. Akiva Deutsch, "Social Contracts and Social Relations of Jews and Arabs Living in a Mixed Neighborhood in an Israeli Town," *International Journal of Comparative Sociology* 26:3-4 (1985): 220-25.

31. Lin Poyer, "Egalitarianism in the Face of Hierarchy," *Journal of Anthropological Research* 49:2 (Summer 1993): 111-33.

32. Hubert Cukrowicz, "Choosing One's Neighbors? / Choisir ses voisins?" *Revue francaise de Sociologie* 34:3 (July-Sept. 1993): 367-93.

33. James Dyer, Arnold Vedlitz, and Stephen Worchel, "Social Distance among Racial and Ethnic Groups in Texas: Some Demographic Correlates," *Social Science Quarterly* 70:3 (Sept. 1989): 607-16.

34. *See* Karen Campbell and Barrett Lee, "Gender Differences in Urban Neighboring," *Sociological Quarterly* 31:4 (Winter 1990): 495-512; A. J. Laite, "Paisano," *Journal of Peasant Studies* 1:4 (July 1974): 509-11; Barrett Lee, Karen Campbell, and Oscar Miller, "Racial Differences in Urban Neighboring," *Sociological Forum* 6:3 (Sept. 1991): 525-50; Gary Paquin, "Social Support as Protection: Reactions to Neighbors' Domestic Quarrels and Violence," *Free Inquiry in Creative Sociology* 20:2 (Nov. 1992): 171-77; and Carol J. Silverman, "Neighboring and Urbanism: Commonality versus Friendship," *Urban Affairs Quarterly* 22:2 (Dec. 1986): 312-28.

35. Sandra Ott, "Blessed Bread, First Neighbors and Asymmetric Exchange," *Archives Europeennes de Sociologie* 21:1 (1980): 40-58. *See also* Sandra Ott, *The Circle of Mountains: A Basque Shepherding Community* (Oxford: Claredon Press, 1981). For the sake of clarity, Sandra Ott does not claim to be an ethnomethodologist but an ethnographer.

36. Ott, "Blessed Bread," p. 42.

37. Ibid., pp. 43-4.

38. Ott, *The Circle of Mountains*, p. 75.

39. Ibid., p. 36.

40. Ibid., p. 88.

41. Ibid., pp. 48-49, brackets original.

42. Ibid., p. 50, brackets original.

43. Ibid., p. 115.

44. Thomas Dale Watts, "Ethnomethodology: A Consideration of Theory and Research," *CJSR* 9:1 (Spring 1974): 99-115.

45. Garfinkle, *Studies in Ethnomethodology*, pp. vii-viii.

46. The idea that "social life is socially constructed" is not a new idea originating with Garfinkel. What ethnomethodologists do with this idea is new.

47. Garfinkel, *Studies in Ethnomethodology*, p. 1.

48. Mark Peyrot, "Understanding Ethnomethodology: A Remedy for Some Common Misconceptions," *Human Studies* 5 (1982): 271.

49. Ibid., p. 269.

50. Ibid., p. 270.

51. Wes Sharrock and Bob Anderson, *The Ethnomethodologists*, Peter Hamilton, ed., Key Sociologists Series (New York: Tavistock Publications, 1986), pp. 42-43.

52. Ibid., p. 27.

53. To give two well-known examples: "In the beginning was the Word, and the Word was with God, and the Word was God" (Jn 1:1 RSV); "And God *said*, 'Let there be light'; and there was light" (Gn 1:3 RSV, emphasis added).

54. Garfinkel, *Studies in Ethnomethodology*, pp. 263-68.

55. Don H. Zimmerman, "Ethnomethodology," *The American Sociologist* 13:1 (February 1978): 8.

56. Ibid., p. 10. "The social interactionist finds language to be a sign of the self, the ethnomethodologist finds the self point[ing] to language as that which must be explained." Charles C. Lemert, "De-Centered Analysis: Ethnomethodology and Structuralism," *Theory and Society* 7:3 (May 1979): 298.

57. Zimmerman, "Ethnomethodology," p. 12.

58. Lemert, "De-Centered Analysis," p. 290.

59. Ibid., p. 293.

60. Ibid., p. 294; Zimmerman, "Ethnomethodology," p. 9.

61. *See* Garfinkel's pioneering categorizations in *Studies in Ethnomethodology*, pp. 263-68.

62. Paquin, "Social Support as Protection."

63. M. M. Bakhtin, *Toward a Philosophy of the Act*, trans. Vadim Liapunov, ed. Vadim Liapunov and Michael Holquist (Austin: University of Texas Press, 1993); Bakhtin, *Art and Answerability*, trans. Vadim Liapunov (Kenneth Brostom, supplement trans.), ed. Michael Holquist and Vadim Liapunov (Austin: University of Texas Press, 1990); and Bakhtin, *The Dialogical Imagination: Four Essays*, trans. Caryl Emerson and Michael Holquist, ed. Michael Holquist (Austin: University of Texas Press, 1981).

64. Bakhtin, *Toward a Philosophy of the Act*, p. x.

65. Ibid., pp. xi-xii.

66. Ibid., pp. xxi-xxiv.

67. Ibid., p. 2.

68. Ibid., p. 5.

69. Ibid., p. 9, emphasis original.

70. It is here that his editors want answerability from Bakhtin, whose philosophy of the act appears to end looking like the situational ethics Bakhtin himself deplored. There is no way to understand Bakhtin but through his life, however, a life that remained connected to the Russian Orthodox faith. Bakhtin's papers that form the content of *Toward a Philosophy of the Act* and *Art and Answerability* were discovered by his students in a woodshed and reconstructed from their draft form with many margin notes and rodent-eaten pages. They had been left in hiding through his many years of persecution under Stalinism and subsequent Soviet regimes. We know very little about Bakhtin's involvement with religious ritual, but we do know that he was active in above- and underground religious study groups. *See* the Introduction in Mikhail M. Bakhtin, *Creation of a Prosaics*, ed. Gary Saul Morson and Caryl Emerson (Stanford: Stanford University Press, 1990).

11

The Mission of Hospitality

To Open the Universe a Little More

DALE T. IRVIN

There's a beautiful image in Saul Bellow's latest novel, The Dean's December. *The central character, the Dean, Corde, hears a dog barking wildly somewhere. He imagines that the barking is the dog's protest against the limit of dog experience. "For God's sake," the dog is saying, "open the universe a little more!" And because Bellow is, of course, not really talking about dogs, or not only about dogs, I have the feeling that the dog's rage, and its desire, is also mine, ours, everyone's. "For God's sake, open the universe a little more."*

—Salman Rushdie[1]

Throughout his career, Kosuke Koyama has often found himself asking in various ways the question: What is the mission of the Christian church today? It is, of course, a question as old as the Christian movement itself, but it has taken on a special urgency at the end of the modern colonial era for Koyama and many others looking at Christianity from outside the walls of Western Christendom. Koyama has often searched for an answer to this question in the pages of Christian scriptures, from whose vantage point he has gained a critical perspective for evaluating both the Christian church and its mission. For Koyama, Jesus Christ is the person of the center who has gone to the periphery of human history, thereby locating the center of Christian faith on the peripheries of history.

The biblical tradition of persons of faith journeying to a foreign land, if not to the utter peripheries of human history, is without a doubt a richly rewarding source for contemporary missiology. But alongside this there is another biblical tradition of mission, one that Koyama has recently begun to address in greater depth.[2] It is the tradition and practice of staying at home and showing hospitality to strangers.

The theme of hospitality to strangers is represented in both testaments of Christian scriptures, and is both an ethical injunction and a means of grace.

In the pages that follow, I explore some of the implications of this tradition of hospitality shown to strangers depicted in the pages of the Second Testament. This biblical practice, I argue, is intended to create a new mode of mutuality and solidarity among persons who were previously strangers to one another. The effects of the practice have as much to do with the transformation of the ones showing hospitality as they do with the transformation of the recipients. True hospitality creates new modes of social life and options for identity for both providers and recipients. Hospitality is, I believe, near the very heart of the biblical conception of mission as transformation. At the end of the essay I will draw some of the implications I see for mission and identity of North American churches in particular. In short, I believe that the mission of the churches at the beginning of the third millennium should express, and respond to, the feeling and desire that Salman Rushdie articulates so well: "For God's sake, open the universe a little more."

THEOLOGICAL PERSPECTIVE

At the risk of sounding all too traditional, let me begin by stating that I think the mission of the church remains what it always has been: to participate with God in God's mission, which is the renewing of creation brought about by implementing a reign of love and justice. Theologically understood, mission is what God has done / is doing / will do in the world. The traditional Christian way of speaking of this mission of God is articulated as the doctrine of the Holy Trinity, specifically the economic Trinity.[3] To speak of God's mission, Christians traditionally speak of Word and Spirit, for through them God participates in creation and history. By them, the church is called to participate in God's mission, which is in turn God's active participation in the affairs of the world. The Spirit of God is already at work throughout the whole creation. The Christ of God has already come, and has been implicated in the structures and events of human historical experience. Through Jesus Christ, the Word, and the Holy Spirit, God sends forth God's own self, God's own presence, crossing over the boundary to enter into the human situation. Through their agency (Christ and Spirit) the church is called and empowered to incarnate the mission of God in its own particular historical contexts. Thus David Bosch can write, "mission is *missio Dei*, which seeks to subsume into itself the *missiones ecclesiae*, the missionary programs of the church."[4]

To be in mission is to be sent out. To carry out God's mission one must move beyond one's own self, one's own world, to enter into participatory relationships with others and with God. The result in biblical terms is a new mode of communion or *koinonia*, a new life of participation and sharing among persons who were previously alien to one another.[5] A radical decentering and self-transcending of one's own identity is envisioned as the Spirit moves to break across the boundaries of our existence and identity, enabling humanity to participate in the creation of something new. Churches are called to follow Christ, who crossed the ultimate boundaries of sin and death in order to open a new mode of community that is no longer bound by the limitations of time and location—in other words, a community which is catholic. Christian mission is thus by definition a boundary-breaking activity, and to be in mission is to be breaking boundaries and crossing over frontiers that divide us from one another and from God, in the process of creating a more inclusive *koinonia* that is characterized by relationships of love, mutuality, justice, and full participation.

The boundary-breaking activity of mission is a permanent dimension of the ministry of every church. But Christians do not break boundaries irresponsibly, as if simply wanting to hear identities shattering. We who are in churches are called instead to break the boundaries that have become idolatrous in our lives, which are keeping us from recognizing the fullness of God's image incarnated in our neighbors near and far, or which are preventing us from participating with others in communities of love and justice. In its boundary-breaking activities, the church is to be pursuing new life, not death. The boundary-breaking that is a permanent dimension of the vocation of the church requires the church to be going out of itself and receiving into itself that which is other or different, thereby giving up its own identity in order to find it in a new way on the other side of its own death. The one who loses life gains it, Jesus said. The one who takes up the challenge to participate in God's own mission in her or his location discovers life tenfold and a hundredfold richer.

Thus while the mission of the church is not necessarily something new, it is to be renewing by making new. Theologically the creation of the "new" is, of necessity, a transgression of the boundary or limit of the old. The story of the death and resurrection of Jesus Christ, which is paradigmatic for Christian life and identity, provides us with a paradigm for Christian mission as well. As Jesus broke the ultimate boundary of human experience, transgressing and thus relativizing the boundaries of death, so the Christian mission is to be a boundary-breaking practice, relativizing the boundaries of human experience and identity where ever they separate us or prevent us from experiencing *koinonia* with one another and God.

The biblical story bears witness to an ongoing mission of God, who goes outside and beyond God's self, breaking the boundary between eternity and time to cross over in a creative love. It is this God who called Abraham and Sarah to undertake a journey of faith, providing them with the promise of a blessing for all people on earth. This same God heard the cry of the oppressed community of Hebrew people held captive within Egypt's domain, liberated them, and called them into the covenant of the Law as a sign of God's mission for all people. It was this God who sent forth Jesus in Galliee, and this God who the Apostles proclaimed had raised him up from the dead. The resurrection is nothing less than the mission of God realized in a new context. The Risen Christ has broken the ultimate boundary of death itself and goes before those who are disciples to the very ends of the earth.

From the earliest days of the apostolic movement, belief in the Resurrected Christ compelled followers of his messianic way to cross the frontiers of human community and break down the walls of hostility that divided it. This fundamental impulse at the very heart of faith in the Risen Lord gave rise to the conviction and hope that where animosity and violence now divide humans from one another, there will one day be reconciliation and justice throughout the inhabited world (the *oikoumene*). A twofold praxis of boundary breaking can be discerned in the pages of the Second Testament. There we find, on the one hand, the intentional practice of some sent to cross political and cultural boundaries to proclaim the message of the Risen Lord and, on the other hand, a mandate to receive strangers with hospitality, as if entertaining angels (Heb 13:2).[6]

An interesting incident in the Second Testament in which both aspects of this boundary-breaking praxis are depicted together is found in the story of Cornelius and Peter in Acts 10. Cornelius was a Roman centurion of the Italian Cohort who feared God, gave alms to the poor, and prayed constantly to God. In the course of praying one day, he had a vision of an angel, who told him to send emissaries to find Peter. Notice who initiated the breaking of the boundary in the story. It was Cornelius, who was not a Christian though he was spoken well of by the Jews, who sent missionaries to Joppa to find the Apostle Peter (Acts 10:7-8). Meanwhile, Peter was receiving a vision of his own, of animals considered unclean and a voice telling him, "What God has cleansed you must not call common" (Acts 10:15). It was not a vision sending him on a mission, but one preparing him to receive the mission God was sending his way. Peter was being prepared to receive the Good News that the wall between Jew and Gentile had now been broken down.

While Peter was still fresh with the images of his vision, the missionaries from Cornelius appeared at his front gate. The Spirit then said to Peter, "Get up and go downstairs. Do not hesitate to go with them, for I have sent them." The Greek word used here is the perfect tense of *apostello* (to send), the root for the English word *apostle.* It was God who had sent these emissaries as missionaries to Peter, for it was Peter who was in need of being missionized and converted on this point. Two servants and a devout military officer from a Roman centurion's household were sent by God. Peter, receiving their mission, broke the boundary in his own right by inviting them into the house for lodging. Peter's hospitality was the initial act of confirmation on the part of the leaders of the Jesus community that the boundary truly had been broken between Gentiles and Jews in this new movement. The hospitality he showed these strangers was an act of opening up the early church's universe a little more.

This twofold praxis of sending forth / receiving in hospitality provides us with important signs of the wider *koinonia* that is going to be realized through that ultimate opening of the universe known as the coming Reign of God. In these signs we can discern fundamental aspects of the character of God and of God's intentions for all creation as these are manifested in the life, ministry, death, and resurrection of Jesus Christ. The mission of the church entails more than the proclamation and interpretation of these signs and indications, although it certainly includes these. It is more than sending persons across saltwater in the name of Christ, as important as this remains for the larger mission of the church.[7] As Christians, our mission remains more because God is doing more. When churches work to tear down walls of hostility constructed by racism, domestic violence, or ethnic antagonism, they are participating more fully in God's mission in the world. When churches reach out to cross the boundaries of sexual orientation, gender, or generation; when they cross the frontiers that separate communities of persons from one another or separate Christian communities from persons of other religious faiths; then the signs of God's mission become a bit clearer, and God's presence more compelling.

In the end, the sign and the promise of Christian mission point toward the communion of all people with God, to be realized in human history. Throughout the pages of the Bible, we find signs and indications pointing in the direction of a universal horizon of faith. A number of passages depict persons coming from every land and region on earth to join together in celebration and worship of God, representing the widest ecumenical horizon of mission. From the Gospels the call to a universal mission emerges from the postresurrection experience of the Risen Lord who has initiated the eschatological age (he is the firstborn of the new creation) that is expected to encompass all nations and all creation. At crucial points, the Gospels reflect an older tradition of expectation of the nations coming into Jerusalem. We read in Isaiah 60, for instance, the prophet's vision of the kings of many nations bringing their wealth as tribute into the city of Zion, in servitude to Jerusalem and the Holy One of Israel. Isaiah's vision of all nations bringing their wealth into Jerusalem is reflected in Matthew's Gospel, in the story of the Magi bringing gifts to the young Christ child, and again by the writer of the Apocalypse of John, in referring to the New Jerusalem (21:26). The historical memory of the Queen of Sheba bringing wealth and tribute before the court of Solomon and his grandeur lies behind the passage in Isaiah. In the story of Solomon, as in several of the royal psalms, we find this imperial motif at work as the kings and peoples of the earth are expected to bring tribute into Jersualem to present to its king.

This tribute is, of course, extracted wealth, and its symbolic meaning is political domination.[8] Whether it is in the form of grains, wine, money, goods, or labor, such tribute or tax was extracted from the people by their rulers, from the countryside by the city, or from a lesser political power by a greater. Rarely in the ancient world (or the modern) was it willingly given. Far more often it was extracted by violence or the threat of violence. The mode of universalism that it portends is that of extracted honor and dominion, and it leaves in place the boundaries between dominators and dominated, or the oppressors and the oppressed. In short, it is imperialistic, and even if the universal tribute depicted in these biblical passages is being paid willingly, the image of the nations and kings bringing in their wealth to the people of God is open to dangerous interpretations for churches today, given the history of the last 400 years of Western Christendom. The ambiguities of imperial power have too long gone uncriticized in ecclesial theologies of missions, leaving the churches practicing triumphalism and tribute taking under the guise of evangelism and mission.

An alternative to the mode of universalism realized through tribute can be found in the Temple economy in the Bible. The original construction of the Temple in Jerusalem under Solomon was both an expression and a strategy of state formation. Solomon's Temple was built by extracted labor, and it continued to be closely tied to the royal ideology of the kings of Israel through the period of their independent political existence. But in the postexilic period, the Temple tax that was instituted under Nehemiah became emblematic of a common religious identity among Jews scattered politically across the world. By the first century of the common era, the Temple had become the center of worldwide Jewish life, and for some an alternative to the failed nationalist political aspirations. Jews from across the world who came on annual pilgrimage to Jerusalem to worship at the Temple did not all share the nationalist aspirations held by some. All Jews were expected to pay the Temple tax or tithe as a symbol of their connection to this center.[9]

The Gospel traditions include the boy Jesus among the pilgrims who journeyed to Jerusalem and the Temple. In his adult life, the relationship of Jesus to the Temple became more problematic, however. On occasion he is remembered as having counseled those whom he healed to go to Jerusalem and present themselves to the priests according to the Law, to certify their recovery. On the other hand, the Gospel writers generally depict Jesus as rejecting the religious domination and social oppression perceived to be practiced by the Sadducee party in control of the Temple. With others of his time, Jesus appears to perceive this priestly class to be in collusion with Rome. But Jesus took his criticism further, beyond such political analysis, to encompass social, economic, and religious dimensions as well. According to the Gospels, the hierarchical nature of the Temple itself was problematic. For Jesus, and for the writers of the Gospels, the social and religious stratification established by the purity codes of the time were a fundamental problem in the life of the people, insofar as they maintained social separation and thus oppression and division. The Temple was at the institutional center of these purity codes. So John Elliott writes:

> the temple purity system established and controlled the social identity, social classifications, and social boundaries of the Jewish people as the holy people of God.... According to Luke, as well as the other Evangelists, it was this system of purity and the exclusivity and injustice that it fostered which Jesus challenged .... This challenge, so wide-reaching in its political and social ramifications, inevitably led to conflict, death, and social division.[10]

Despite his criticisms, however, Jesus appears to have entered into the Temple and participated in some manner in its economy of worship. After his death and resurrection, early Christian believers in Jerusalem continued to worship there as well, according to the Book of Acts. At least for James and his party, the Temple played a significant role in the universal messianic fulfillment they believed to be realized in Christ.

A critical shift from this Jerusalem tradition to a wider theology of mission in the early Christian movement is found in the Pauline tradition. According to Acts 21:21, Paul was suspected by some in Jerusalem of teaching Jews of the diaspora that they need no longer practice circumcision. To demonstrate his fidelity to the Law, Paul was counseled by James in Jerusalem to submit to a purification ceremony that required the services of the Temple. Several days later, according to Acts 21:28, Paul was accused by others in Jerusalem of defiling the Temple by bringing in Gentiles, a charge which resulted in his arrest and imprisonment. The possibility that Paul would have had to demonstrate his fidelity to the Law for those in the city, and that the charge of defiling the Temple with Gentiles could be lodged against him, suggests that Paul, at least according to the writer of Acts, was understood to challenge the centrality of Jerusalem and the Temple. If indeed he did so challenge them, as seems apparent elsewhere in his own writings (most notably in Galatians and Second Corinthains), Paul did so on behalf of a more egalitarian universalism. For Paul, the hallmark of this more egalitarian form of universalism would no longer be worship in the Temple (which continued to segregate and order the world of humankind hierarchically), but in table fellowship, the sharing of one loaf and one cup of blessing.

This third biblical image, that of table fellowship, offers us an alternative to the image of a universal mission symbolized through tribute or Temple tax. In the eucharistic table fellowship, Christians across twenty centuries have found access to the universal Risen Christ. In doing so they have also continued to recall the promise of a universal messianic banquet such as that depicted in Isaiah 25:6-7, to which all people will be welcomed. "Many will come from east and west and sit at table with Abraham, Isaac, and Jacob in the kingdom of heaven," Jesus is said to have told those around him in Matthew 8:11 (and today we would add "with Sarah, Hagar, Rebekah, Leah, and Rachel as well"). One can only gather that this table will be set by Abraham and his family, that it will not cost those who come from east and west, but that as Abraham and Sarah showed hospitality to the Holy One of Israel by the oaks of Mamre by providing the meal, so he will again show hospitality to those who come from east and west by providing the resources for their refreshment and the substance of the banquet. For this reason, Senior and Stuhlmueller call the messianic banquet a "more inclusive symbolization" and a "corrective to the motif of the eschatological pilgrimage of the nations to Zion." They summarize: "[Gentiles] come to Zion not in subjugation (a basic part of the traditional pilgrimage motif) but to share fully in the joy of the kingdom."[11]

The symbolism of imperial tribute held little meaning for Jesus in his ministry. Likewise Jesus had criticized—and according to the reports from his trial, had threatened to destroy—the Temple. His threat against the Temple was the immediate basis for Jesus' execution, according to the synoptic Gospels. But before this, John the Baptist had sought to open up an avenue of salvation and forgiveness which bypassed both king and the Temple. John's baptism was for the forgiveness of sins, which Crossan points out was an alternative to the offering of a sacrifice in the Temple; John's location in the wilderness put him outside the royal traditions of Zion. Apparently Jesus followed John in his practice of localizing forgiveness, offering what must have seemed to many to be an even more radical means of forgiveness through his itinerant ministry in Galilee. According to Crossan again, the main contours of Jesus' ministry in Galilee entailed astonishing feats of healing that were coupled with strange practices of table fellowship, or what anthropologists call more generally practices of commensality—eating together.

Jesus practiced an open form of commensality. He ate with those he healed, and he ate with the sinners and outcasts—making him ritually one with them in their impurity. He also ate with Pharisees, teachers, and others of a respectable social class. From the Gospels we get the impression that he was quite fond of banquet-

ing, which in the world of the first century was more than a means of social enter-
tainment. Banquets established social order. By defining who ate with whom, in
what configuration of seating or reclining, banquets were effective means of setting
social order in play and solidifying each person's place within it.[12] In his practice
of eating with unclean persons and his parables of the messianic banquet in which
those of the highways and byways are invited in, Jesus was breaking the social order
of his own day on behalf of a new social order in which all would be invited to sit
at table together.

The shared egalitarianism implied in the practice is quite striking. It is both
material and spiritual egalitarianism, the means of creating mutuality in community. Those disciples Jesus sent out ahead of him in Luke 10 to extend his work
throughout Galilee—the first missionaries of the new movement—were to follow
his practice of eating with those to whom they ministered. Crossan again summarizes the meaning of such table fellowship:

> For Jesus, however, commensality was not just a strategy for supporting the mission.
> That could have been done by alms, wages, charges, or fees of some sort. It could have
> been done, for instance, by simple begging in good Cynic fashion. Commensality was,
> rather, a strategy for building or rebuilding peasant community on radically different
> principles from those of honor or shame, patronage or clientage. It was based on an
> egalitarian sharing of spiritual and material power at the most grass-roots level.[13]

The practice of eating together would continue even after his death and resurrection. The story of his last supper, conducted in the shadow of the night of
betrayal and laden with the symbolism of the Jewish Passover, would become the
basis for the Christian churches' eucharistic supper. But there were other meals that
early Christians remembered him eating, and continued to meet him at after his Resurrection. On the road to Emmaus they listened to him speak, but only in the breaking of bread did they recognize him. By the seaside of Galilee they continued to eat
with him in open-air meals of bread and fish, a eucharistic tradition that is known
in early Christian art and writings as something of an alternative to bread and wine.

Notice in the meals by the seaside in Galilee—both the feeding of the crowds
and the postresurrection meals with the disciples—that the food for the meal is provided out of the abundance of God. In the former, Jesus receives the small contribution that is offered in the young boy's gift of loaves and fishes, offers thanks to
God, then breaks the bread. In doing so, Jesus multiplies the resources so that the
hospitality of the young boy becomes the occasion for messianic abundance. In the
latter story, the disciples respond to his call to cast their nets on the other side of the
boat and in doing so haul in an abundance of fish. But when they arrive back at
shore, he has already cooked them a meal. In both cases, the abundance of food is
coupled with the provisions of God. In both cases, those who eat do not pay for what
they receive, for it is free.

Notice as well that in these and other instances of hospitality meals in the pages
of the Second Testament, we see God's abundance manifested particularly among
the marginalized and outcasts of society. John Koenig draws our attention to this

aspect of the biblical tradition. The Second Testament's tradition of hospitality, he points out,

> welcomes marginal people because it expects them to be bearers of God's abundance or catalysts for it. Jesus ate with outcasts; Paul and Luke took strong stands on behalf of those relegated to the position of second-class citizens in the church. They did so . . . because they knew that God *by nature* recruits outsiders to be partners in providence, makes a home among them, and through them enriches the world.[14]

God enriches the world through such acts of gracious hospitality. This means that those who are members of the household of faith are enriched as well by the very hospitality they are called to show to strangers, for their existence falls within the universal (or eschatological) horizon of grace. This is why one is said to receive a blessing through offering gracious reception: the transforming effect of hospitality is mutual. According to Koenig, the biblical vision of God's loving embrace tells us that "strangers received will enlarge our total well-being rather than diminish it."[15] I would go even further and depict it as the means for the conversion of the church. Through showing hospitality to strangers, the church itself can be transformed anew to a new mode of relationship and faith. As it was for Peter, who was converted by the mission of outsiders, so this hospitality remains for the churches today both a means and a confirmation of the new thing to which God is calling us.

We need to convert our churches to those who are now unwelcomed in their midst. We need to invite to our banquet tables (the eucharist as well as the covered-dish supper) those of the highways and byways of the contemporary world. It is certainly possible that those who are comfortable with the present way things are, those who are materially well-off and believe themselves to be self-sufficient, will turn away from the church; but then there is biblical precedent for turning away a rich one who seeks to enter eternal life without walking the pathway of discipleship.

I acknowledge that this vision of mission goes against much that is written on "church growth" today and is not going to be popular with many. Were the church growth proponents to tell the parable of the messianic banquet, they would no doubt offer strategies for bringing in those wealthy invited guests ("you need to offer foods that they like; try offering an upscale brunch after your Sunday service"). Perhaps they would have offered Jesus advice, such as not having one's servant take the invitations (the guests might have misunderstood what class of people were going to be at the banquet; people respond best when "their own kind" do the calling). We can imagine all kinds of strategies that might give the parable a happier ending: sending out another note advising the invited guests that you will keep the banquet short (fifty-five minutes and out); promising that you won't challenge them with anything controversial (just a "feel-good" message).

The mission of the church lies elsewhere, however. Where ever the church is, it is to be a center of hospitality, open especially to those who are the least of the society, challenging and breaking down the barriers that separate folks from one another, creating the conditions for mutuality and a culture of forgiveness in which people can flourish. Churches are to be centers of transforming hospitality, opening up the universe a bit more by being open to those who are different: the gay and lesbian community, persons of a different "race" or culture; persons of all classes or social locations. Churches do it because God so loved the world that God sent God's dearly beloved one, Jesus, on a mission, not as a substitute for us but to institute among us a new mode of union and reunion with God.

OPENING UP THE POSTMODERN METROPOLIS

What new boundaries do we need to attend to as we face the beginning of the third millennium of the church? In recent years we have all become much more aware of the vast boundaries of difference that have characterized our societies for several centuries. In the churches we have become more attuned to the voices of difference speaking from the margins of our social and ecclesial lives. Theological schools in the North that once prized the unifying endeavors of systematicians have now discovered in the diversifying voices of contextual and liberation theologians a more complex pathway toward a universal vision of faith. For many of us, the more interesting centers of intellecutal life are to be found outside the boundaries of the modern academy, and the notion of moving toward the margins or peripheries of social life no longer seem strange.

Diversity has become a celebrated word, and although it is in danger at times of becoming indistinguishable from a virulent postmodern tribalism that is also scourging our world, in its authentic form, diversity provides us with an avenue toward community that refuses the suppression of difference while maintaining bonds of solidarity. This is to say that true diversity respects the boundaries of difference but maintains mutual bonds of accountability at the same time.[16] Here again a theological insight is of value for us in the church: God breaks down the wall of hostility not by eliminating differences but by creating community with others through acts of love and forgiveness, breaking the boundaries that separate us by instituting new bondings that can join us together.

Such a theological vision stretches the limits of both universality and particularity at the same time, affirming them both and challenging them both. It calls us to listen to the voices of those who have been excluded or who have suffered the effects of violence against them in society, but it also calls us to attend to voices we cannot yet hear or understand and seek ways to incorporate those voices into the choir we call our own. It is a vision of mission that is particularly relevant for the postmodern city, where the realities of immigration, ethnicity, diversity, and difference have all accelerated beyond anything our foreparents in the ministry could have imagined.

Recently I had a conversation with a pastor from Australia who told me that 30 percent of the churches in Sidney now use a language other than English in worship on Sunday mornings. Visitors from London tell me that the situation is pretty much the same in England, where several generations of immigrants from India, Pakistan, the West Indies, Africa, and elsewhere have permanently altered the cultural landscape and religious context of that country. In Sweden in recent years, the government of the city of Stockholm has had to address questions raised by the presence of a worshiping Islamic community in that Nordic city. No one had really anticipated the reaction of Swedes to the *adhan*, the call to prayer, being broadcast several times a day across a Stockholm neighborhood from a newly constructed mosque.

In New York, we estimate that approximately 10 percent of the Protestants of the city can be classified as white or Anglo today, in stark contrast to what most of the published Protestant theology textbooks continue to represent as the "we" and "our" of their theological communities. Every year in the seminary in which I teach we meet new students whose enthnic/racial identity is plural, mixed, or blended, and who continue to live within two or three distinctive communities of identity. Often I hear students say that when asked to check a box concerning their "racial-ethnic identity," they would like to write in, "many of the above." Our cities in the North— New York, London, or Stockholm—have become vast multicultural complexes of persons representing a bewildering array of languages, cultures, religious beliefs, and sexual orientations. Moreover, this diversity is becoming increasingly internalized within us. Few, if any, persons are just "one thing" anymore. Few of us can claim to possess singular or monolithic identities.

The impact is being felt in ecclesial communities. Black churches are becoming increasingly populated with persons who are first- or second-generation West Indian. They have always been populated by persons from both the South and the North; now there are British accents thrown in among the southern dialects and northern cadences of speech. Presbyterian and Methodist churches that once were composed entirely or almost entirely of persons of European immigrant descent are taking in Korean, Haitian, Greek, Pakistani, and Colombian members. New congregations formed amid immigrant communities are being admitted into the UCC in New York, joining older churches with distinct ethnic identities that have been a part of this fellowship for several generations.

Anyone who has looked at the history of America knows that our cities have always been diverse; today they are only becoming more so. Ronald Takaki, in *A Different Mirror: A History of Multicultural America*, compares the United States to the crew of the *Pequod* in Melville's *Moby Dick*. On deck are Captain Ahab and his officers, all white men. Below deck are European Americans, Africans, Asians, Native Americans, and Pacific Islanders. Takaki continues: "Together, we have created what Gloria Anzaldua celebrated as a 'borderland'—a place where 'two or more cultures edge each other, where people of different races occupy the same territory.' "[17] Our cities are becoming more and more each day just such borderlands— places where cultures meet each other, edge each other, and come to occupy the same space.

The border becomes internal within ourselves as we become people who internalize the multiplicity and diversities of these cultural landscapes. For many, this internalization is being manifest in border wars, however, as communities clash and engage in violence against one another. The problems we face here are often the same; there is nothing new about the racism, nativism, nationalism, and xenophobia that continue to characterize much of our urban policies. On this score the church has a mission that is highly relevant, even if as timeless as the message of the

Gospel itself. From its earliest days, the Christian movement has been one in which Jews and Gentiles, Greeks and Barbarians, Africans and Asians, people from Rome and people from Carthage have been learning how to live together in peace.

The earliest generation of Christian teachers and spiritual directors took upon themselves the tasks of teaching people who had no previous experiences with one another how to live together in friendship and communities of solidarity.[18] We must be intentional in doing the same today. How do we teach people to live together in communities of mutual accountability, solidarity, and peace? How do we learn to love one another and pray for one another and bear one another's burdens when we do not speak the same language, share the same values, or maintain the same cultural traditions? By what means, by what power, by what grace can we give up our idolatries of culture and identity in order to be converted to the neighbor who is different?

The postmodern city remains very much indebted to the modern era. The postmodern cities of the North Atlantic world in particular are products of modern colonialism that organized the entire world according to what Eric Wolf has termed the "center" and the "periphery."[19] Edward Said has called these two arenas "metropolis and colony." The primary movement of colonialism was that of the metropolis extending its control and influence over the colonies, a movement from Europe toward the World, which was from the North Atlantic to the South, West, and East. The initial stages of European colonialism witnessed the flow of political and cultural power in the direction of the metropolis toward the colony, a mode of relationship particularly true of the metropolis in Europe. Although it was predominantly a one-way movement, it was not exclusively so. The counterflow was more pronounced in the development of the metroplis in North America, however, for here the secondary colonial experience of Europeans migrating was also a factor. Eventually, in both Europe and North America, the metropolis itself began to change. We have witnessed the acceleration of those changes in the last decades in North American cities, to the point where we are now realizing that every city is a global city, every city a cultural United Nations.

In his recent work, *Culture and Imperialism*, Said has argued that the new alignments of metropolitan culture challenge static notions of identity. In this postcolonial world, "all cultures are involved in one another; none is singular and pure, all are hybrid, heterogenous, extraordinarily differentiated, and unmonolithic."[20] We live with intertwined and overlapping histories and must read them contrapuntally—that is, simultaneously aware of the history of the metropolis and the colony, of the multiple histories that have now become enmeshed in the modern arena, of the multiple histories which make up the postmodern self and church. Said's conclusion, found in the closing paragraph of the book, is arresting:

> No one today is purely *one* thing. Labels like Indian, or woman, or Muslim, or American are not more than starting-points, which if followed into actual experience for only a moment are quickly left behind. Imperialism consolidated the mixture of cultures and identities on a global scale. But its worst and most paradoxical gift was to allow people to believe that they were only, mainly, exclusively, white, or Black, or

Western, or Oriental. . . . No one can deny the persisting continuities of long traditions, sustained habitations, national languages, and cultural geographies, but there seems no reason except fear and prejudice to keep insisting on their separation and distinctiveness, as if that was all human life was about. Survival in fact is about the connections between things; in Eliot's phrase, reality cannot be deprived of the "other echoes [that] inhabit the garden."[21]

This is not just a matter of survival. It is about grace, the power of the Gospel, and the witness of the Christian movement to what it believes God is doing throughout the entire universe. It is about the connection between things or, better, the connection between persons. Connection is a theological word, because it is a theological work: covenant, reconciliation, union with God (at-one-ment), *koinonia*, *perichoresis*, communion of saints, the Holy Trinity itself. Connection is what our souls and spirits are—the inner connectedness to one another as human beings, our collective connectedness to God through Spirit.

Connection is what the mission of the churches is all about. The conversion of the churches means taking up a mission of connectedness in the context of this new cultural diversity. Instead of static, reified models of ecclesial-cultural identities, the mission of the church is to be opening persons up to that which is new. The notion of the universality in Christian faith carries with it a theological open-endedness that calls us to recognize that the future will be different. The options for the Christian future are infinitely more than the diversities of the Christian past. The universality of truth cannot be fixed into permanent, dogmatic forms. It is the task of the churches, the mission of the church, to open up more options for human community today, creating new forms of *koinonia*.

To do so, the horizon of Christian mission must be conceptualized both more locally and more globally than it has been in the past. I do not believe we need to confine our reflections to the exclusive domains of Christian theological insight and reflection. I believe that we are part of the larger experience of a world that has grown tired of the confinements of modernity, or what Max Weber so fittingly called the iron cage. We have grown tired of the iron cages of modern identities, with their debilitating effects on the human soul.

This includes the confinements of Christian exclusivism in all its forms, which make for bad neighbors and bad theologies. Two generations ago, we heard from the ecumenical movement that denominationalism was a sin and the separation of the churches an offense against God. More recently we have begun to address the legacy of Christian religious imperialism and exclusivism that seeks to eradicate other religions under the banner of missions. Today we must also assert with equal vigor that culturally exclusive churches are a sin and the separation of persons in ecclesial communions according to race, language, cultural identity, or background is an offense against the Most High. The confinements of denomination, theology, religion, ideology, or cultural identity must all be opened to the transforming grace of God's renewing Spirit. This is so because the mission of God is to open the universe a bit more.

I believe that we have the capacity to be open, because we are already more complex, interrelated, and multidimensional in our identities, communities, and faith than the politics of modernity allowed us to think. In our postmodern period, we find ourselves crossing boundaries every day: in our families, in our communities, in our selves. We have come to realize that at their deepest levels, our selves are multiple, dialogical, and perhaps better described as collective entities than a singular, reflective ego.[22] As Said said, identity is hybrid.

In this situation, the mission of the churches is to be converted themselves to new identities. We must move beyond mere celebration of diversity to commitments to efforts to work for new communities of difference. This means working to make a difference, working to open our churches and ourselves a bit more to the diversity of God's world. This finally is the mission of the church: to open itself a bit more, so as to open the universe a bit more, for God's sake.

NOTES

1. Salman Rushdie, *Imaginary Homelands: Essays and Criticism 1981-1991* (New York: Penguin Books, 1992), p. 21.

2. Kosuke Koyama, " 'Extend Hospitality to Strangers'—A Missiology of Theologia Crucis," *International Review of Mission* 82:327 (1993): 283-95.

3. *See* Katherine Mowry LaCugna, *God for Us: The Trinity and Christian Life* (San Francisco: Harper, 1993); and Jürgen Moltmann, *The Trinity and the Kingdom: The Doctrine of God* (Minneapolis: Augsburg Fortress, 1993).

4. David Bosch, *Transforming Mission: Paradigm Shifts in Theology of Mission* (Maryknoll, NY: Orbis Books, 1991), p. 519.

5. Helga Rusche, *Gastfreundschaft in der Verkündigung des neuen Testaments und ihr Verhältnis zur Mission* (Münster: Aschendorffsche Verlagsbuchhandlung, 1958), p. 5, notes that hospitality is at once the prerequisite, result, and content of the missionary proclamation of the early Christians.

6. *See* Donald Senior and Carroll Stuhlmueller, *The Biblical Foundations for Mission* (Maryknoll, NY: Orbis Books, 1983); and John Koenig, *New Testament Hospitality: Partnership with Strangers as Promise and Mission* (Philadelphia: Fortress Press, 1985).

7. Keith R. Bridston, in *Mission Myth and Reality* (New York: Friendship Press, 1965), p. 33, writes concerning the *confinement* of missions to "over-seas" work ("crossing salt water"): "It would be foolish to suggest that the geographical frontier ever was, or will ever be, insignificant in the missionary activity of the church. But if the religious significance of salt water is seen in any other than a poetic and mythical way, the whole meaning of the mission of the church is in danger of being lost, or so perverted that it would be better lost. The geographical frontier, symbolized by the seven seas, only *represents* what the Christian mission is; it does not exhaust it. Ocean trips have never made Christian missionaries, and, in itself, salt water never will."

8. On ancient tributary economy and its corresponding political practices of imperialism and social organization in city-states, *see* Norman K. Gottwald, *The Tribes of Yahweh: A Sociology of the Religion of Liberated Israel, 1250-1050 B.C.E.* (Maryknoll, NY: Orbis Books, 1981 ed.), pp. 391-434 and 461-83.

9. On the role of the Temple in postexilic and diasporic Judaism and the practice and significance of the Temple tax, *see* E. P. Sanders, *Judaism: Practice and Belief 63 BCE - 66 CE* (Philadelphia: Trinity Press International, 1992), pp. 47-169.

10. John H. Elliott, "Temple Versus Household in Luke-Acts: A Contrast in Social Institutions," *The Social World of Luke-Acts: Models for Interpretation*, ed. Jerome H. Neyrey (Peabody, MA: Hendrickson Publishers, 1991), pp. 221-22.

11. Senior and Stuhlmueller, *Biblical Foundations for Mission*, p. 153.

12. *See* Dennis Edwin Smith and Hal Taussig, *Many Tables: The Eucharist in the New Testament and Liturgy Today* (Philadelphia: Trinity Press International, 1990).

13. John D. Crossan, *The Historical Jesus: The Life of a Mediterranean Jewish Peasant* (San Francisco: Harper, 1992), p. 344.

14. Koenig, *New Testament Hospitality*, p. 126 (emphasis original).

15. Ibid., p. 5.

16. *See* Cornel West, "The New Cultural Politics of Difference," in *Beyond a Dream Deferred: Multicultural Education and the Politics of Excellence*, ed. Becky W. Thompson and Sangeeta Tyagi (Minneapolis: Univeristy of Minnesota Press, 1993), pp. 18-40; and idem., *Beyond Eurocentrism and Multiculturalism: Volume I, Prophetic Thought in Postmodern Times* (Monroe, ME: Common Courage Press, 1993).

17. Ronald Takaki, *A Different Mirror: A History of Multicultural America* (Boston: Little, Brown and Co., 1993), p. 426.

18. On the work of the early Christian desert fathers and mothers, particularly in teaching people the spirituality of solidarity and love, *see* Roberta C. Bondi, *To Love as God Loves: Conversations with the Early Church* (Philadelphia: Fortress Press, 1989).

19. Eric Wolf, *Europe and the People without History* (Berkeley: University of California Press, 1982).

20. Edward W. Said, *Culture and Imperialism* (New York: Alfred A. Knopf, 1993), p. xxv. *See also* Cornel West, *Beyond Eurocentrism and Multiculturalism: Volume II, Prophetic Reflections: Notes on Race and Power in America* (Monroe, ME. Common Courage Press, 1993), p. 163, where he writes: "because we all have multiple positions in terms of constructing our identities; there's no such thing as having one identity or of there being one essential identity that fundamentally defines who we actually are."

21. Said, *Culture and Imperialism*, p. 336.

22. *See* Jerome Bruner, *Acts of Meaning* (Cambridge, MA: Harvard University Press, 1990); and Edward E. Sampson, *Celebrating the Other: A Dialogical Account of Human Nature* (Boulder, CO: Westview Press, 1993).

12

A Place to Feel at Home

Aladura Christianity in Yorubaland

AKINTUNDE E. AKINADE

INTRODUCTION

Christianity first came to Africa in its infancy, in the story of a child named Jesus who, with his parents, were refugees in Egypt. During its early centuries, Christianity flourished in Africa as it made its home comfortably among a number of cultures on the continent. Yet eventually social and political factors stemming from the rise of Roman imperial domination of the Christian world, and the subsequent displacement of Roman Christian rule in Africa by the rise of Islam, led to the number of African Christians being severely diminished. Christianity was reintroduced to Africans in the modern era through the Western colonial and missionary incursions. The churches which were planted in Africa by Western missionaries have yet to make Africa their home, although in recent years these so-called historic churches have begun to advance in that direction. The real history of Christianity in modern Africa, however, is the history of the African Independent Churches, such as the Kimbanguist of Zaire, the Ethiopian churches of South Africa, and the Aladura churches in Nigeria.

My aim in this paper is to discuss Aladura Christianity among the Yoruba people of Southwestern Nigeria. These churches consist of the Cherubim and Seraphim Church, the Church of the Lord (Aladura), the Celestial Church of Christ, and the Christ Apostolic Church. As African Independent Churches, they are often considered under the rubric of "new religious movements" because in historical and chronological terms, they are newer than either African traditional religion or Christianity or Islam, and because of the relative "newness" of some of their beliefs and practices. New religious movements are understood here to mean those movements whose teachings, tenets, attitude, and disposition to the world are radically different from those of the established religious traditions. They have attracted much attention by scholars recently because of their continued prodigious proliferation and their phenomenal increase in membership, conditioned partly by social and economic instability and, in many instances, by a need for spiritual well-being. In Africa, the African Independent Churches can be considered as new religious movements. I have decided to concentrate on the Aladura churches because they are the dominant variety of new religious movements in Nigeria and the rest of sub-Saharan Africa.

Since the publication of Bengt Sundkler's ground-breaking *Bantu Prophets in South Africa*, a remarkable scholarly tradition has emerged concerning the phenomenon of African Independent Churches. Published materials now number into the thousands, and typologies and theories abound, yet much of the mission church is still unclear about how to relate to these new and diverse religious groups. Are they truly legitimate branches of the church universal, or are they outside? I believe that these Aladura churches have to be treated in their own right and not as separatist or syncretistic churches. African Independent Churches have been declared "the avant garde of African Christian authenticity,"[1] and Kofi Asare Opoku has said that these churches "have succeeded in stripping Christianity of its foreignness which has been a great handicap, and have shown that Christianity can be expressed and meaningfully informed by the African religio-cultural reality."[2] I believe that the most crucial issue is to recognize the theological potential of these churches and come to terms with the way African people have made Christianity their own.

Shortly after Christianity was introduced into Nigeria, indigenous impulses to this new religious phenomenon started to emerge. Early movements were Independent Churches, motivated by the desire to get rid of foreign domination in religious affairs. Known as the African churches, they seceded from the mainline Protestant missions in Lagos (Methodist, Anglican, and Baptist) from the 1880s to 1917.[3] The churches that emerged, such as the Native Baptist Church, the United Native African Church, and the United African Methodist Church, were concerned with retaining the polity and liturgy of their parent mission churches but demanded African leadership and acceptance of polygamy for both clergy and laity.

Another wave of secessions came at the end of the second decade of the twentieth century, shortly after the 1918 influenza epidemic. These secessions produced churches of the pentecostal type, locally called Aladura churches. They began as prayer groups (*egbe adura*) within the historic churches, but soon established themselves as Independent Churches. The Christ Apostolic Church broke away in 1923, led by David Odubanjo. The Cherubim and Seraphim was founded in Lagos in 1925 by Moses Orimolade Tunolase, an illiterate cripple, and a young girl, Abiodun Akinsowon. The church of the Lord (Aladura) was formed in 1925 by Oshitelu, a gifted man who broke away from the Christ Apostolic Church. The Celestial Church of Christ was founded in Porto Novo, Republic of Benin, by S. B. Oschoffa, a carpenter and former Methodist. Shortly after the church was established in Porto Novo, it spread to Nigeria, and is the most influential Aladura church in Nigeria today.

This paper discusses some of the unique characteristics of these churches and some of the ways Christianity has been reinterpreted and reappropriated by Yoruba people. My essential argument is that these churches have created a religious haven for Yoruba people to feel at home and enjoy Christianity. I also need to affirm from the outset that these churches have created the basis for a participatory ecclesiology that supports and nurtures the spiritual powers of both the clergy and the laity, providing a modest spiritual haven to "let the spirit blow where she wills."

CAUSES OF RELIGIOUS INDEPENDENCE

The most important reason for the rise of Aladura churches is the need to liberate the church from foreign domination: ecclesiastical, colonial, social, cultural, and administrative. They arose in reaction to what they felt to be spiritual emptiness associated with the historical churches. Prior to their formation, the popular feeling was that the presence of the Spirit had been greatly reduced. This spiritual aridity was aggravated by

> the prefabricated liturgies which have been imported from Europe and imposed upon this continent. . . . There are certain emotional depths which are not being reached by Africans by these liturgies. . . . Hymns are European verses sung to European tunes, the phraseology of the liturgies are either archaic, barely intelligible, or often irrelevant in Africa.[4]

J. D. Y. Peel, speaking about early African churches among the Yoruba of southwestern Nigeria, observes that "the real motive of the founders was the conviction that the mission churches were still exotic institutions, and would remain so until, led by Africans, they purged themselves of their adventitious and inessential European cultural trappings."[5]

This motive was carried into the early twentieth century and contributed to the formation of Aladura churches in Yorubaland. The call for independence was aided by the translation of the Bible into local/traditional languages. When Yoruba Christians started reading the Bible in their own language, they started interpreting Christian theological paradigms in a different way, and there arose in them a deep yearning to make the meaning of Christianity relevant to their traditional worldview and spiritual temperament.

A CHANNEL FOR CHRISTIAN CREATIVITY

The Aladura church movement is a channel of Christian creativity in the Nigerian setting. This is due to the fact that these churches are "independent" and make use of African culture, custom, and religiosity. These churches are not embarrassed for using African cultural values. If they did not utilize the African traditional heritage, on what basis would they stand as African churches originating in Africa, catering to African Christians, and concerned with African problems and anxieties? These churches are creating something new, something distinctively African—a combination of biblical and historical Christianity and African heritage in all its manifestations. One gets the feeling that members of Aladura churches want a chance to enjoy Christianity. These churches provide a place where Yoruba Christians can feel at home and worship as Africans. They are free to shout out their faith, pray at length, dance vigorously, and hold healing sessions. The most important and unique aspect of these churches is that they try to fulfill what they claim is missing in the Euro-American historic churches, that is, to provide ways of worship that are satisfying both spiritually and emotionally.

Aladura churches have definitely created a place to call home. They have created a vibrant living faith solidly rooted in African realities and striving to come to terms with biblical truth. In these churches, human problems are confronted with the power of the Holy Spirit.

The sense of feeling at home is also exhibited in worship services, which are characterized by joyfulness, spontaneity, and excitability. According to Adrian Hastings:

> Africa is a continent of song, dance and musical instruments. It is a continent of language and languages. Here lies the heart of its communal artistic inheritance and nothing was sadder than the missionary failure to open a door whereby at least some of this wealth might pass across into the worship of the young churches. The drum was not heard in most churches, only the harmonium accompanying carefully translated European hymns sung to the tunes of the West.[6]

It is noteworthy that many Christian songs in Aladura churches have been copied by many historic churches and slowly African musical instruments are being reclaimed for use in worship. Also, listening to Aladura churches can help the West recover a lost spiritual heritage that would include the prospect of communicating with God through dreams and visions.

SPIRITUALITY AND THE SENSE OF THE HOLY

The Yoruba word *Aladura* needs some explanation. In Yoruba, *adura* means prayer. The prefix *Al* means the owner/possessor/doer of something. Therefore *Aladura* literally means one who prays. *Adura* (prayer) constitutes the basis of both the doctrine and practice of African Independent Churches. Aladuras believe in the power of prayer. Prayer brings both material and spiritual benefits. Thus, prayer can cure illness, protect against enemies, bring financial success, and so on. Aladuras believe that for prayers to be successful, they must be in compliance with the known ways of God and must correctly state and take into account the numerous seen and unseen forces at work in the world. The ways of God are described in the Bible, hence its study and interpretation are of crucial importance for spiritual wholeness. The forces at work in a particular situation are discovered through dreams, visions, and the words of people possessed by the Holy Spirit. Aladuras also believe that the efficacy of prayer is conditional on the observance of certain taboos, of which the most important are those on the consumption of alcoholic beverages, contact with menstruating women, and wearing of shoes in prayer houses. Most Aladura prayers are extempore and made with remarkable forcefulness. The effectiveness of prayer is reinforced by the use of palms and other symbolic objects such as candles, perfumes, incense, and water.

The sense of the holy is expressed through belief in the intervention of the divine and the spirits in life situations and belief in and use of sacred times, places, and objects. Dreams, visions, and gifts of prophecy enable people to identify the type of spiritual antidotes appropriate for different situations. For the Celestial Church of Christ, the land around its church building is usually fenced and is called *Ile Aanu*—the mercy land. Anyone who enters this area must be barefoot, for it is holy ground, as God told Moses about the ground near the burning bush (Ex 3:5).

One paramount concern in all Aladura churches is how to obtain, retain, and use spiritual power. According to Harold Turner, "spiritual power is the inspiration by the Holy Spirit through spiritual power over spiritual enemies."[7] Aladura churches follow the teaching of St. Paul (1 Cor 12:13) that spiritual gifts are gifts of grace and given by God's will, regardless of experience, age, education, or status. Spiritual power is equated with direct contact with God. There are constant warnings from the pulpit that this line would be broken if moral standards are not maintained.

Aladura spirituality is deeply rooted in the African understanding of the Christian community. The New Testament concepts of fellowship (*koinonia*) and the church as a called-out assembly (*ekklesia*) are taken seriously by these churches. David Barrett remarks that Africans have always been community oriented and so have an advantage over the individualistic societies of Europe and America.[8] Barrett's analysis of African Independent Churches comes to the conclusion that their appeal is primarily in the realm of brotherly love and community. Aladura churches assume the form of "a community relatively small for the members to cultivate and maintain a knowledge of one another, a warm philadelphia among themselves and face-to-face relationship."[9]

Aladura churches are different from traditional or mission-oriented churches. They started as indigenous churches founded by indigenous people and are under indigenous leadership. Harold W. Turner, one of the leading authorities in the study of new religious movements, defined African new religious movements as movements "founded in Africa, by Africans, and primarily for Africans."[10] The late Kofi Appiah Kubi also described these movements as having "all African membership as well as African leadership."[11] I believe this description is slightly off the mark because Aladura churches such as the Celestial Church of Christ and the Cherubim and Seraphim regard the whole world as their mission field. These churches have branches in Europe, the United States, India, and the West Indies, and they now believe that it is Africa's turn to evangelize the world. In most cases, Aladura churches are referred to as Independent Churches, with emphasis on the word *Independent* to signify the claim of these churches that they are independent of foreign control in organization, administration, and liturgy. The word *Independent* should not be construed in pejorative terms.

Aladura churches are the fastest-growing churches in Nigeria, a testimony to their compatibility with African worldviews and spirituality. This situation confirms the observation of the sociologist of religion, Hans Johannis Mol, who notes that "religious forms can be relevant only when they grow together with the culture in which they find themselves."[12] Christianity is culturally neutral. It cannot be tied to the apron strings of any one race or culture. Nigerians have encountered Christ in a unique way. Consequently they are demanding that in order for Christianity to be meaningful, it must be expressed through concepts and constructs that are familiar to them. Yoruba Christians want a Christianity in which at least some of the essentials of Yoruba religiosity—dreams, visions, belief in the world of spirits, the use of holy water or holy oil for spiritual healing—continue to have a legitimate place. This is what is provided by Aladura churches. Professor Akin Omoyajowo has attributed the immense evangelistic success of African Independent Churches to their use in divine service of drums, singing, dancing, and clapping. Omoyajowo further states that "apart from their aesthetic nature and their sociological significance, and despite their great 'emotionalism' which is an essential characteristic of any religious form, these religious expressions are reminiscent of the traditional way of worship."[13]

Aladura churches are concerned with this-worldly, immediate salvation, and are involved with matters germane to the total well-being of human beings. The Yorubas have traditionally worshiped God to obtain concrete, material benefits—more children, avoidance of calamities, success in trade, and a big harvest. The intention of Aladura churches is to provide religious structures that can ensure such things. Here, mission churches are challenged to think through their ways of worship. Harold Turner is correct in his assertion that Independent churches are not so much concerned with correct doctrines as they are with "power to deal with the practical problems of daily living—security, good relations with others, prosperity, success, and especially the problems of fertility for women and health for all."[14] In Africa, human liberation is conceived in both spiritual and material terms.

Nathaniel Ndiokwere has recognized these aspects specifically as reasons why Nigerians join the country's new religious movements:

> The sense of insecurity is perpetuated in the African milieu by fears of evil spirits, the phenomenon of "poisoning"... the unlimited anxiety over fruitfulness in marriage.... It is the urge to have these problems solved which drives people to the doors of the Aladura prophets.... If there were no healing mission there would be no meaningful Independent Churches; if there were no sick people or individuals craving for security, there would be no followers.[15]

In the same vein, J. Akin Omoyajowo has explored the message and work of the Aladura churches. I quote him at length:

> Africans generally fear the power of witches and the evil spirits, who beset them in their dreams; they worry about their future and want to know what it has in store for them. Orthodox Christianity repudiated this practice and substituted abstract faith for it. The Aladuras take the problems as genuine and offer solutions in the messages of the Holy Spirit given through the prophets and visionaries. They give candles for prayers, incense to chase away evil powers and blessed-water for healing purposes.

Consequently, the Christian suddenly finds himself at home in the new faith, and Christianity now has more meaning for him than before, for it takes special concern for his personal life, his existential problems and assures his security in an incomprehensibly hostile universe. That is what has endeared the Cherubim and Seraphim to the hearts of the cross-section of our society, irrespective of creed, status and class.[16]

There is no doubt that people join the Aladura churches because they see something worthwhile in them. One member of the Cherubim and Seraphim is reported to have testified: "since I joined the Cherubim and Seraphim, I have always seen good things; if there is any difficulty, once you pray, it will go away. Since I joined I have enjoyed life."[17] Another member of the Christ Apostolic Church is also reported to have witnessed thus: "If someone joins the Christ Apostolic Church, he will have rest of mind. There is no need to use medicine if you join; if you ask something from God, immediately you will get the result."[18] In research I conducted on Aladura churches in Ile-Ife in December 1993, I asked some professional people on several occasions why they left their former church to join the Aladura type of church. Their attraction ranged from the belief that Aladura churches can protect them from invisible powers that operate through witchcraft and sorcery to a desire for what Bryan Wilson has called "this-worldly, proximate salvation."[19]

I believe that the fear of people is well-founded, because Yorubaland is a home of fear. It is believed that every person lives in the midst of enemies, seen and unseen. The society is full of spirits, good and bad; thus one has to seek protection against malevolent spirits. Aladura churches' practice of healing is based on the example of Jesus, whose earthly ministry was dominated by preaching and healing. Through his healing ministry, Jesus demonstrated God's will to deliver people from the shackles of sickness and dis/ease.

The growing interest in Aladura churches arises from the fact that they appear to have developed a form of Christianity with a spirituality that is "truly Christian and truly African." David Barrett testifies in the same spirit thus:

In varying degrees there are in virtually every movement (African Independent Churches), a central confession of Christ as *Kyrios* (using the traditional vernacular term for chiefship), a marked resurgence of traditional African custom and worldview, and a strong affirmation of their right to be fully Christian and fully African, independent of foreign pressure.[20]

CONTRIBUTION TO CHRISTIANITY
AND AFRICAN THEOLOGY

Africans have a lot to contribute to Christianity for its enrichment and continued relevance within Africa itself and the rest of the world. What is going on in Aladura churches is that Nigerians are enriching Christianity with what they regard as the best in their cherished tradition. The indigenization of the church in Africa expresses the desire of Africans to communicate the gospel in their own language and use their cultural worldview to convey our Christian identity. Culture is the basis of the creativity and way of a people. It is the foundation of their collective identity.

It expresses their worldview, their conception of the meaning of human existence, and their conception of God. It involves the historical manifestations of people's creativity—such as their language, art, philosophy, religion, and theology.

The indigenization of the church in Africa is a call for self-determination and an affirmation that it is possible to be Africans and Christians at the same time. Aladura churches provide good examples of how the church has been indigenized in Africa. These churches have enabled Nigerians to think theologically, enjoy Christianity, and feel at home. Members of these churches dance, drum, and can be themselves, without any interference from any other church. I can attest to the fact that there is a feeling of joy and pleasure in worshiping in these churches. The Bible does not authorize religious imperialism or spiritual dependence. Nigerians have to speak their faith with words of their languages and signs of their cultures. We don't have to be culturally uprooted in order to be Christians. While Aladura churches are making significant contributions to African theology, they are also rescuing the African cultural worldview from the morass of neglect.

The urgent moral necessity for the church in Africa is to affirm that God is not a stranger in African culture. This is not to say that African culture is impeccable in the sight of God. I believe all cultures are under the judgment of God. However, it is imperative for the church to affirm African cultural identity in order to restore dignity and a sense of wholeness to a deeply wounded African psyche. The church does not have to turn people into strangers in their own land. In spite of the cultural raid that has taken place under a combined missionary and colonial era, African Christians still live and breathe African culture and cannot completely move away from their cultural background. It is from this a priori affirmation that a genuine African expression of Christianity can emerge, in order to give meaning to who we are as Africans, both individually and communally. Aladura churches are providing tools through which the selfhood of the church can be attained in Nigeria in particular and Africa as a whole. It is abundantly clear that the negation of the African experience and the attempt to deemphasize the traditional culture have shut the church's eyes and ears to many chances for enriching its own life and contributing to a more just and humane society. The late Bolaji Idowu has this to say about the earliest missionary attitude in Africa:

> It was a serious mistake that the church took no account of the indigenous beliefs and customs of Africa when she began her work of evangelization. It is now obvious that by a misguided purpose, a completely new god who had nothing to do with the past of Africa was introduced to her peoples. Thus there was no proper foundation laid for the gospel message in the hearts of the people and no bridge built between the old and the new; the church has in consequence been speaking to Africans in strange tongues because there was no adequate communication.[21]

Also, according to Professor Emmanuel Ayandele:

> missionary activity was a disruptive force, rocking traditional society to its very foundations denouncing ordered polygamy in favour of disordered monogamy, producing disrespectful presumptions and detribalised children through the mission schools,

destroying the high moral principles and orderliness of indigenous society through denunciation of traditional religion without an adequate substitute, and transforming the mental outlook of Nigerians in a way that made them imitate European values slavishly whilst holding in irrational contempt valuable features of traditional culture.[22]

These are strong words. I do support the present trend of Christianity exhibited in Aladura churches, but I also believe that mission/historical churches have had a glorious history within Nigeria and helped millions of Yoruba Christians find a well-meaning spirituality. John Mbiti has rightly said that "when African Christians take the microphone on the church platform, they exhaust themselves with harping on the ills and mistakes caused by missionaries or Western Churches."[23]

African Independent Churches (Aladura churches belong to this group) are invaluable sources for African theological reflection. According to Kofi Asare Opoku, African Independent Churches "have succeeded in stripping Christianity of its foreignness which has been a great handicap and have shown that Christianity can be expressed and meaningfully informed by the African religio-cultural reality."[24] Adrian Hastings regards African Independent Churches as "the avant garde of African Christian authenticity,"[25] while the late Fashole-Luke from Sierra Leone believed that the innovative insights of African Independent Churches will prevent African theology from "becoming sterile academic exercises divorced from the life situation of Africa."[26]

It would be a pathetic position for World Christianity, as well as for religion in Africa, if it started from the premise that there is or should be one universally adequate expression of the Holy. Aladura churches have helped many Christians find genuine indigenous spirituality. What God is doing in these churches should be given due recognition. Genuine Christian theology is not based solely on past formulations, but on what God is doing in the present, here and now. Aladura churches are thriving on a combination of African heritage and Christian tradition. This is a theological necessity in Africa.

PUBLIC RESPONSE AND OTHER LITURGICAL ATTRACTIONS

It is not unusual to find many secret admirers of the Aladura churches in Nigeria, including ministers, state governors, university professors, and top civil servants. Many of these classes of Nigerians are members of various Aladura churches, although many have not openly declared their membership. Peel cites the example of one civil servant he interviewed who confessed that he "played the part of a Nicodemus in the sense that he occasionally attended Aladura Churches in secret, because he liked their services (he was an Anglican), and had in fact been secretly baptised by an Aladura minister."[27]

The numerical and physical growth of Aladura churches is there for everyone to see. In many Nigerian towns and cities, Aladura church buildings match those of the historic churches in size and attendance. This increased recognition, which many, although not all the churches, enjoy has enabled people from the upper echelon of society to openly join or publicly associate themselves with churches they had previously ridiculed as being too sectarian or unsophisticated for their social position.

One major problem in the historic churches is that of participation. The clergy are in control of the worship throughout the service. The reverse is the case in Aladura churches. Both clergy and laity are active participants, and there is no room for passive observers. Consider the Celestial Church of Christ, for example. Members file into the church in a procession, thus creating a sense of communal call to priesthood. The division between the clergy and laity is very tenuous in Aladura churches, and spiritual activities, such as seeing visions and interpreting dreams, are not the sole prerogative of the ordained clergy. In Aladura Christianity, the laity play significant roles as vehicles of divine revelation.

MISSIOLOGICAL IMPLICATIONS

The rise of Aladura churches points to a change in what Andrew Walls calls the center of gravity of Christianity. No longer is Europe or North America considered the determinant of what the church should be. Today the focus is shifting to Asia, Latin America, and Africa. The West has a rich theological heritage to share with Africans, but this process of sharing should not stifle the voices of the indigenous churches in Africa. The problem lies in the generational metaphor of older/younger churches used so often in ecumenical theology. Western churches are described as parents, and non-Western churches as their children. But even so-called children can come of age and have a life of their own. I quote here an opening passage from Walbert Bruhlmann's book, *The Coming of the Third Church*:

> The First Church, then, will be the oriental church, possessing the rights of the first born (the eight ecumenical councils were held on eastern soil) but now become, in large measure, the church of silence. The Second will be the Western Church, which in the course of history has more and more come to be thought of as the church without qualification and, by this token, as mother of her offspring in the world. Finally, the Third Church will be that of the new nations, now entering as a new element into the history of the church, who will be the "surprise packets" of the near future.[28]

By AD 2000, there will be over 393 million Christians and over 695 million evangelized people in Africa. It would seem obvious that the future of Christianity depends to a large extent on how African Christianity evolves. Aladura churches have proved that Christ is not against African culture. Whatever may be said for or against the Aladura churches, they continue to be an expression of a vibrant, powerful Christian witness in Nigeria. They reflect in many areas the failure of Western Christianity to socialize the Nigerian mind completely to Western culture and the Christian tradition. They are a distinctive expression of the disturbing tension that exists between the Christian mythos and Nigerian culture.

RELATIONSHIP WITH OTHER CHURCHES
AND OTHER OBSERVATIONS

The attitude of mission/historic churches toward Aladura churches is very ambivalent, despite the decrease in initial hostility. At the level of the Christian Council of Nigeria, there are signs of ecumenical unity, especially since the 1970 admission of the Church of the Lord (Aladura) into the World Council of Churches. On the local level, some of the historic churches are paying close attention to the contribution of Aladura churches to African Christianity. However, prejudices still abound, and Aladura churches are labelled as the back door through which paganism has re-entered African Christendom. My own position is that these churches should be treated in their own right and should be approached without any preconceived negative ideas. I'm suggesting a kind of phenomenological approach to the study of Aladura churches in Nigeria. It is more profitable to analyze these churches as they are, without beclouding our analysis with any jaundiced and unsubstantiated ideas and notions we may have about these churches.

Aladura churches must be in constant dialogue with the Church Universal. They cannot live in a world of their own; they must stretch their hand of fellowship to mission churches. Kosuke Koyama talks about the dangers of exchanging the universal God of Christianity for what he calls a tribal god.[29] The tribal god, an example of extreme indigenization, is only interested in one people/nation and not in the rest of the world. It is an uncritical and limited god, which is different from the God revealed in the Bible. Aladura churches must be wary of anti-ecumenical self-righteousness and steer clear of sin described by Paul in 1 Corinthians.

Aladura churches must be concerned with the challenges of inner renewal and growth. Being the church means basically being "on the way," following Jesus. The church must always be in process of being reformed. In 1961, the third assembly in New Delhi said:

> The assembly wishes only to urge that those who know themselves to be called to the responsibility of Christian witness in their own locality should examine afresh the structures of their new church life with a view to meeting the challenge and opportunity of a new day. In a spirit of penitence and of willingness to be led by the Spirit of God into new ways of witness, the whole church must recognize that its mission calls for the most dynamic and costly flexibility. . . . Thus the church may become the pilgrim church, which goes forth boldly as Abraham did into the unknown future, not afraid to leave behind the securities of its conventional structures, glad to dwell in the tent of perpetual adaptation, looking to the city whose builder and maker is God.[30]

CONCLUSION

The contribution of Aladura churches is a pointer to the fact that traditional African spirituality is an essential ingredient for the revival of an African Christian spirituality. There is no gainsaying the fact that the spirituality of Aladura churches appeals to a large section of the Nigerian population. The Aladura church movement has a future for Africans because it is African, independent, and Christian. It is a movement of the Spirit. The rise of Aladura churches is an appropriate challenge to a Christianity that so often gives the appearance of lackluster antiquarianism incapable of arousing people's feelings, emotions, and dispositions. The future of these churches is bright and replete with possibilities for growth and renewal. These churches will continue to challenge our faith convictions as Africans.

NOTES

1. Adrian Hastings, *African Christianity* (New York: Seabury Press, 1979), p. 54.

2. Kofi Asare Opoku, "Issues in Dialogue Between African Traditional Religion and Christianity," paper presented at the World Council of Churches' subunit on Dialogue with People of Living Faiths Consultation, Kitwe, Zambia, September 22-25, 1986.

3. For a full account of this movement, *see* Lamin Sanneh, *West African Christianity: The Religious Impact* (Maryknoll, NY: Orbis Books, 1983), and Ogbu U. Kalu, *The History of Christianity in West Africa* (London: Longman, 1980).

4. E. Bolaji Idowu, "The Predicament of the Church in Africa," in *Christianity in Tropical Africa*, ed. C. G. Baeta (London: Oxford University Press, 1968), p. 417.

5. J. D. Y. Peel, "Syncretism and Religious Change," *Comparative Studies in Society and History* 10:2 (1968): 128-29.

6. Quoted in A. Osotsi Mojola, "Vernacular and the African Independent Churches," *Africa Theological Journal* 22:2 (1993): 114.

7. Harold W. Turner, *African Independent Church*, vol. II (Oxford: Oxford University Press, 1967), p. 317.

8. David B. Barrett, *Schism and Renewal in Africa: An Analysis of Six Thousand Contemporary Movements* (Nairobi: Oxford University Press, 1968), p. 170.

9. John S. Mbiti, *New Testament Eschatology in an African Background* (Oxford: Oxford University Press, 1971), p. 186.

10. Harold W. Turner, "A Typology for African Religious Movements," *Journal of Religion in Africa* 1 (1967): 17.

11. Kofi Appiah Kubi, "Indigenous African Churches: Signs of Authenticity," in *African Theology en Route*, ed. Kofi Appiah Kubi and Sergio Torres (Maryknoll, NY: Orbis Books, 1979), p. 117.

12. Hans Mol, *Identity and the Sacred: A Sketch for a New Social-Scientific Theory of Religion* (Oxford: Basil Blackwell, 1976), p. 73.

13. J. Akin Omoyajowo, *Cherubim and Seraphim: The History of an African Independent Church* (New York: NOK Publishers, 1982), pp. 164-65.

14. Harold W. Turner, "Religious Movements in Primal (or Tribal) Societies," *Mission Focus* 9 (1981): 50.

15. Nathaniel Ndiokwere, *Prophecy and Revolution: The Role of Prophets in the Independent African Churches and in Biblical Tradition* (London: SPCK, 1981), pp. 256, 279.

16. J. Akin Omoyajowo, "The Cherubim and Seraphim Movement: A Study in Interaction," *Orita: Ibadan Journal of Religious Studies* 4:2 (1970): 134.

17. J. D. Y. Peel, *Aladura: A Religious Movement Among the Yoruba* (London: Oxford University Press, 1968), p. 212.

18. Ibid.

19. Bryan R. Wilson, "The New Religions: Some Preliminary Considerations," *Japanese Journal of Religious Studies* 6:1-2 (1979): 196.

20. David Barrett, "African Independent Church Movement," s.v., *Contemporary Encyclopedia Dictionary of Religion*, ed. P. K. Meager (Washington, DC: Corpus Publication, 1979).

21. Idowu, "The Predicament of the Church in Africa," p. 423.

22. E. A. Ayandele, *The Missionary Impact on Modern Nigeria 1842-1914* (London: Longmans, 1966), p. 329.

23. John S. Mbiti, "Faith, Hope and Love in the African Independent Church Movement," *Study Encounter* 10:3 (1974): 19.

24. Quoted in Emmanuel Martey, *African Theology* (Maryknoll, NY: Orbis Books, 1993), p. 76.

25. Hastings, *African Christianity*, p. 53.

26. E. W. Fashole-Luke, "Footpaths and Signposts in African Christian Theologies," *Scottish Journal of Theology* 34:5 (1981): 401.

27. Peel, *Aladura*, p. 214.

28. Walbert Bruhlmann, *The Coming of the Third Church: An Analysis of the Present and Future of the Church* (Maryknoll, NY: Orbis Books, 1978), pp. 3-4.

29. Kosuke Koyama, "Tribal Gods or Universal God?" *Missionalia* 10 (1982): 106.

30. Quoted in Philip Potter, "Doing Theology in a Divided World," in *Doing Theology in a Divided World*, ed. Virginia Fabella and Sergio Torres (Maryknoll, NY: Orbis Books, 1985), pp. 16-17.

13

The People Next Door

An Essay in Honor of Kosuke Koyama

MERCY AMBA ODUYOYE

"And who is my neighbor?" was the question posed to Jesus by one who had fulfilled the requirements of the law. What more does one have to do to express the fullness of life we are expected to live before God? The reflections offered in this essay are based on a view of life which affirms that the concentric circles of relationships experienced by all human beings require a sensitivity to the presence of the other and to the center which is Ultimate Being, God. Life in community is for me a spiritual matter, hence the centering on God. Secondly, community is a web that links all together and, as such, underlines interdependence and mutual accountability of neighbors.

This study of neighborliness will call attention to three of the strands in this complex web of life and conclude with a suggestion of what it means to love the neighbor as one's self. It will begin with what I consider to be the marks of neighborliness and then move into a reflection on the earth as a neighborhood with an environment to be respected and taken care of. This is followed with a discussion of the world of human beings as a neighborhood. Thirdly, I call to the center various unacknowledged neighbors. In all the discussion, I shall be drawing upon my experience of Africa, the neighborhood I know best, although for a total of fifteen years I have had substantial residence in Europe and North America and have interacted with persons of varying geographical locations as friends, colleagues, and worshipers.

WHO IS MY NEIGHBOR?

The marks of neighborliness were defined by Jesus in the parable of the Good Samaritan whom I name the Compassionate Other. The parable sets the scene with the evil of violent exploitation of an Other, and the sanctimonious notions of purity and pollution that result in an inadequate understanding of what religion demands. We are presented with a scene of good people who are so intent on fulfilling their religious duties that they could not stop to recognize the work of evil or counter it with life-giving moves. They were tuned into a type of righteousness that will be frustrated by getting mixed up with "ritual pollution." Acting as neighbor called for a different type of righteousness. With Jesus' understanding of life, one can raise the question: How can you say you worship, love, and hold God worthy when you despise, ignore, or leave God's handiwork to perish?

Neighborliness, for Jesus, consisted of stopping by the scene of disaster, caring for what faces perdition, using one's resources and one's time to restore life where death threatens to take over. It is going out of one's way to seek the well-being of the other. The parable of Luke 10:29-37 is replayed in Matthew 25:31-46, the parable of the Last Judgment, set in an eschatological dimension. The thirsty, the hungry, the homeless, and the captive are neighbors, persons calling on our resources of compassion, people whose sufferings are ours by virtue of their humanity and the humanity of Jesus of Nazareth.

The neighbor is not only the person who is geographically "next door" but whoever and whatever is threatened with annihilation and a return to chaos. The planet earth exists in a "heavenly" neighborhood, the world is a neighborhood of the created, among whom are human beings with their classification into races, classes, and communities of faith. Human existence takes place within concentric circles of relatedness: family, nurture, culture, nationality, and racial identification make us into particular human beings. The question of who is my neighbor signifies the fact that often we live oblivious of the existence of the other, yet the unacknowledged neighbor is still a neighbor.

THE EARTH, A NEIGHBORHOOD

The earth is our home. We have no other, and our survival depends on its health and wholeness. Studies of environment have called our attention to the larger neighborhood within which our human communities develop. Planet earth belongs in a heavenly environment that it responds to and to which we in turn relate. As earth dwellers, our lives are in constant relationship with the sun, the moon, and the atmosphere around us. On earth, other beings are our neighbors—plants, animals—some too small for eyes to behold and others much larger than we are. Mountains and rivers are so imposing we sometimes feel them as the habitation of being that is different and more potent than us. Minerals, solid, liquid, and gaseous, are all our neighbors. Contemporary ecological sensitivities have underlined the principles of connectedness, interdependence, and mutual sustainability. When air and water and vegetation are in danger, human life too is endangered. With the awareness of ecology, human vision of neighborliness has begun to expand to include all creation, seen and unseen. Loving our neighbor has come to mean recycling, reforestation, and cleaning up the waters around us. It is interesting that the African biologist Wangari Maathai sees "the environmental movement as part and parcel of the pro-democracy movement." Wanton exploitation of the other goes with the marginalization of the other through decision making. It imposes silence on all and takes away the voices of humans while it refuses to hear the groanings of the rest of creation.

The world of human beings, land masses, regions, and nations is linked together by human conquest of space. This geographical world has become a neighborhood bound together by political links and communication technology. The human species, now divided into races, does not live in geographically separate spaces. Few human communities can claim uniformity of physical features. Having created a United Nations, all races find themselves in the position of neighbors and face the challenge of working out their interactions and relationships across round tables. The classification of humans on the basis of socioeconomic status, which remains with us, does not nullify the fact that we are in constant interaction, even when we prefer to operate as cliques. Even grouping human beings into faith communities no longer circumscribes neighborhood, though we may prefer not to have to recognize the validity and power of other religions. The earth is willy-nilly our common neighborhood.

In the three circles of neighborhoods—planetary, geographical, and human—the last two challenge us to review our understanding of neighborliness. Our environment is full of unacknowledged neighbors, all who are in need of survival, healing, or affirmation and call for our understanding and practice of neighborliness. We know who our neighbor is. The challenge is how to live as neighbors in the family and culture that has made us and how to derive and cultivate resources for nurturing global neighborliness from these primary experiences. Christians believe that God was agitated enough about this to come and physically join our earthly neighborhood.

A COMMUNITY OF NEIGHBORS

Associating with Europeans and Americans, I have very often come up against the hurdle of what family is. Is your family with you? Or, even more strange to my ears, do you have a family? Whatever meaning we assign to the word *family*, its value to human development is undoubtedly high. What we are today depends to a large extent on whom we had for family when we were growing up. There is an adage in Akan that is popularly translated as "Alone is miserable." *Baako ye yaw* captures the African rejection of individualism and aloneness. To lose one's place in or touch with one's family is the worst possible misfortune. Worldwide, the smallest human community that makes us social beings with power to communicate and gifts and skills to contribute is the family. We developed relationships and learned who is who in that smallest of communities. From there we were launched toward our nearest neighbors, the people next door. We were nurtured and socialized and acculturated. We became conscious of difference and nationality. We learned citizenship and nationalism. We learned what is expected of us in the various subgroups that make up our world.

For Africans, religion and ethics are high on the agenda of socialization. A respected member of the Akan community, to which I belong, is a good person who thinks and lives by what is good. A person with *adwenpa*, a good mind or brain, is not simply an intelligent person but a good person, humble, generous, and brave, a community-minded person. Without these qualities, an Akan community will not make one a leader.[1] However, if a person has all these but has any physical disability or wound, he or she cannot become a king or queen. Royalty is symbolic of excellence and security. They, more than everybody else in the community, should exhibit the benedictions for which the Akan pray: God's grace, peace, good visual and auditory powers, fertility, and prosperity.[2] These high ideals create their own marginalization, for the community is extremely adamant about its definition of fullness and wholeness. Families will spend their all to enable one to regain one's health of mind and body or overcome impotence and infertility, but would not think of the possibility of changing traditional attitudes toward such "handicaps." These handicaps are disgraceful, and *animguase mfata okaniba* ("to be dead is better than to be alive and disgraced"). Applying the principle to fertility, Okyeame Amoateng of Kumasi concludes that to be impotent or sterile is worse than death.[3] Therefore neighborliness requires that one is helped to overcome these symbols of death, but there the compassion ends. No transformation is envisaged, and so in this most caring community, one finds unneighborliness arising from the fear of ritual impurity.

The ethics that govern relationships and neighborliness among the Akan are expressed in symbols, proverbs, and maxims. The traditional symbols are printed on Akunintam cloth (the cloth of the great warriors) and on Adinkra cloth (the parting cloth traditionally meant for funerals and memorials). The symbols of the latter have been very much popularized, hence their use here to highlight what an Akan community expects of its members and those with whom it deals. The most central idea of community is that of unity in diversity. This is represented by two crocodiles who share one stomach (Siamese twins). The symbol points out that it is unnecessary for people whose destinies are joined together to struggle for a larger share of the available resources. Community of property and mutual aid used to be a cardinal principle among the Akan. As a people, the Akan abhor covetousness, greed, and all egocentrism and believe that affluence and power are the result of togetherness.

"One's neighbor's day is one's day"; one's trouble is bound to affect one's neighbor. Many proverbs, sayings, and folktales underline this principle. The Adinkra symbol of four hearts joined together teaches togetherness and unity in thought and deed. There is a recognition that disharmony is possible in a community, but the symbol and proverb relating to tongue and teeth says that although they quarrel occasionally, that is never a reason for parting company. The community warns its members not to bite one another and presents them with the qualities of fair play, peace, forgiveness, unity, and harmony. The need for cooperation in situations of interdependence is represented by a chain which also marks the unity that is the strength of a community.

The solidarity and security one expects to find in a community is captured in the symbol of the enclosed compound, the traditional quadrangle housing several generations that belong to a lineage, as well as some who are related as clients and spouses. This safety and care is also symbolized by a fence. Within the fence are one's closest neighbors; outside the fence, diplomacy and caution are needed. Within the fence, one is expected to be truthful, strong, brave, ingenious, creative, loving, wise, patient, just, intelligent, generous, alert, obedient, and so on, but all these qualities are to be available for the maintenance of the health, security, and welfare of the community.

The community disapproves of all that brings death or negates the above qualities. Sins and taboos are made known so that offenders have themselves to blame for the punishment they get, for what they do or fail to do brings negative influences that affect the whole community and have to be expiated with rituals and sacrifices.[4] The Akan abhor murder, suicide, stealing, insincerity, and hypocrisy. They frown upon pride and ostentatiousness. Ingratitude, selfishness, laziness, filthy habits, lasciviousness, and sorcery are all things that break or undermine community and therefore are to be avoided. A healthy neighborhood will vigilantly monitor interpersonal relationships to ensure good neighborliness.

These community norms, mores, and ethics are rooted in a common culture that includes the belief in a Supreme Being, Onyame, who sanctions all the ethical requirements. People believe that they live under the keen eyes of their ancestors, who are concerned that traditions that have enabled the community to survive are diligently kept. In other words, neighborliness is guided by religion and culture. The concept raises critical questions for intercommunal relations. Here one could say that our parable does not help us, for we do not know the ethnic origin of the person who lay brutalized. On other hand, Jesus could be interpreted as saying the ethnic origin of the neighbor is immaterial. Of no consequence also is the ethnic origin of the robber or robbers, the exploiters and other agents of death. The critical root here is their common origin in the one God.

Continuing with the Akan as model community within the national neighborhood of Ghana, we can ask: Do the Akan see and behave toward their neighbors to the north, the Hausa, as children of the one God? Do Ghanaians extend neighborliness to other Africans? Do Africans extend neighborliness to Europeans? In all cases, one should ask, Is this neighborliness reciprocated? From the geographical/spatial model, one could ask other types of questions. Is there reciprocal neighborliness between Hindus and Moslems, across racial fences, between homosexuals and heterosexuals, rich and poor, young and old? How do we respond to variety and difference? Does neighborliness stop at the fence? This brings us to our second locus of hospitality, the world.

We began by assuming that the particular label of the one in need is of no consequence. But supposing the wounded man was a Jew. A Jew, taught to have no dealings with a Samaritan, allowed himself to receive the neighborly act of "the Filthy other." The people we despise, those of "lower rank," those with unmentionable diseases, those we label as causing social problems—they too can be neighborly. But can we bring ourselves to let *them* touch *us*? Jesus, the paradigm shifter, asked water from a Samaritan woman. Those we have been taught to avoid because they are less than we are have it in them to be neighborly. They too are made in God's image. They have a womb that becomes agitated at the sight of suffering and injustice.

When the Samaritan saw the wounded Jew, he had compassion on him. Like God, his womb turned and so he did what God does to people who have been cast aside to die. Those our religion and culture teach us to ostracize, God draws back into the orbit of compassion and neighborliness, whether they are wounded Jews or marginalized Samaritans. The neighborly act is a Godlike act. Imagine, the wounded Jew woke up to discover that his survival had been assured by the compassion of a Samaritan. Does he feel polluted by this touch and try to forget it?

THE WORLD AS A NEIGHBORHOOD

Jet travel, communication, and the information explosion have joined the traditional trade routes and patterns of migration to make the world into one neighborhood. Here we would like to discuss race, class, and faith communities as the loci of variety that could either threaten or enrich the practice of neighborliness. The African communal ideology illustrated above does not produce a closed community. It is a flexible entity that expands to include those who prove themselves hospitable and understand life as a continuum and human relations and humanity as in process of evolving and becoming. We have all been children, but none has a prior experience of adulthood. We are all learning together.

Nobody has seen it all before, so there is always room for new ideas, as well as for benefiting from the experience of others. For this reason, membership in the community is not closed. There is always room for one more person, as long as the person is ready to participate in creating the community and has not come with inflexible dogmas. Welcoming difference, diversity, and variety demands a sensitivity to the needs of the whole community as well as respect of every member, irrespective of the difference that marks them. There is no one who has nothing to contribute to the community, hence hospitality is expected from all and due to all.

One identification mark that distinguishes persons in the global community is what we have come to label "race." Humans, as a biological species, have been subdivided into races on the basis of physical characteristics. Color, broadly described as Black or White, has been a fundamental issue in human relations since Europeans overran Africa, the Americas, Australia, Aotearoa/New Zealand, and other islands in the Pacific Ocean and the Caribbean Sea in search of land, wealth, and fame. Africa, the nearest neighbor to Western Europe (the home of early European adventurers), took the brunt of the absence of neighborliness that governed the minds of these early Europeans. To be able to perform the atrocities that gave them land and wealth, they convinced themselves that the "Dark Races" were not human and therefore could be exploited and disposed of with impunity, in the same fashion as the rest of earth's resources, which they claimed God had put at the disposal of the white race of Europe. It is inconceivable that Black people and White people, dark people and pale people could live together as neighbors. Racism is the antithesis of neighborliness. When one is not of your race, you owe them nothing but contempt.

THE SATIATED NEIGHBOR

Where race was not the barrier to neighborliness, social location took over, especially as class based on the economic status of persons. In many human settlements, "birds of the same feathers flock together," the rich on one side, the poor on the other. In between, grades of wealth and poverty divided people. The African communal ideology succeeded in curbing the tendency for social location—royalty, access to land, education, and training—to develop toward a rigid class system that is identified by wealth. The principle of hospitality undermines it. The Akan say "It is one person who hunts down the elephant to provide meat for the whole village." Abundance is for sharing. With this view of hospitality, Europeans were made at home in Africa, and Africans were surprised that the Europeans turned out to be predators. They turned out to be people whose eyes are shut to the humanity of the other. "If you hate me, close your eyes." The Akan believe that you cannot do evil to one whose eyes you can see. It seems, however, that the coming of class with westernization has meant that people can close their eyes and not see the humanity of the people they wrong. One who is not of your class ceases to be in your neighborhood.

In the global neighborhood, class and race seem to coincide at many points. In Africa, apartheid has crystalized this for us. The phenomenon operates globally. Most of the countries whose people have to swallow the humiliating pill of structural adjustment programs (SAP) imposed by moneylenders are also predominantly Black. The moneylenders are predominantly those of White, European, or European descent who got an economic lift on the backs of the peoples they colonized or whose lands they appropriated. The terms Black and White, North and South are being used here to mark the economic equator that divides the world and is also found in every state. The South is poor, and its inhabitants are Black and exploited. The North is rich, and its inhabitants are White and comfortable. The nuances to this caricature are many, for on the one hand, there exist in wealthy countries people who are structurally marginalized and cannot dip into the wealth that is available. On the other hand, there are a few in the poor countries who are, by the standards of the North or in comparison with their immediate neighbors, wealthy because they participate directly in the wealth of the North or off the crumbs that fall from the master's table. In Africa, hardship continues to have its ripple effect while the wealthy become increasingly unneighborly, ridding themselves of the African culture that obliges them to share.

In this analysis, Africa as a whole becomes the underclass in the world's economic neighborhood. African expertise is underutilized, while designated experts are flown in (and maintained by African economic resources at colossal expense) to monitor the SAP these same moneylenders required the African governments to set in place as a condition for the lending. These experts help to pile up debts that African peasants and minor technicians are called upon to pay, and the interest of which the undercompensated primary products go to defray. This rejection of local expertise is both dehumanizing and demoralizing. (And, by the way, Church structures are not above SAP-type relationships.) SAP has no human face, thus it presents itself as another phase of the scramble for Africa. It is an attempt to complete the task initiated by nineteenth-century policies of colonial exploitation and land alienation, by so-called policies of cooperation through the financing of extractive industries. SAP has built into it a notion of surplus population, meaning those who are not avid consumers. They do not count for the market that produces profits that capital so urgently demands.

Increasingly the money world makes inroads into Africa's agricultural economy, not only by the traditional utilization of land for export crops, but now by the control of what Africa can plant to eat, through plant genetic manipulation that spreads hybrids around the world. How will peasant farmers manage if they cannot safeguard next year's crop by this year's harvest? Africa's loss may be immediate, but the fact that we are eliminating certain plant and animal species is bound to affect the global ecology in the long run. The earth remains a neighborhood, and in the end, the environmental hazards associated with the extractive industries, disposal of industrial waste, and the increasing use of chemicals in food farming will have a negative effect on our common home and its environment. The New International Economic Order proposed by the Third World in Algiers (1975), the Brandt commission (1980), and the 1995 summit on world poverty all cry for a recognition that economics is about human relations and not how individuals and wealthy neighbors can hold on to the competition in consumerism while the poor strategize continuously for survival.

FAITH COMMUNITIES

No survey of human neighborhoods can ignore the factor of religion. Faith is a mark of human existence that affects relationships in a very real way and at a very deep level. For Christians, biblical exegesis presents one with the existence of many faiths and one source of all being, God. A good deal of the scriptures of the Christian religion teach exclusivism, but within the scriptures there are also teachings that urge us to liberate ourselves from such biblical texts. The prophets and Jesus direct us to the points at which our paradigms need to shift—the people next door that we label pagans and idol worshipers. We do so from a selective and uncritical approach to scripture that has become an idol for us. Often we do so from doctrinal positions and phrases that we learned by heart, never stopping to ask ourselves, Do you understand what you are saying? Unexamined religion can and does constitute a danger to neighborliness.

Beyond the biblical traditions are many more faiths. One is led to ask, Can we say we have the same God? What is the reason for our mutual prejudices? For what reasons do neighbors support or frustrate the marriage of persons who hold different religious faiths? The African neighborhood is full of these challenges. The people next door in many African countries, and increasingly elsewhere, may be practitioners of a religion other than what one adheres to. We seem to have come to terms with the fact that the global neighborhood is multireligious, but we have yet to actively appropriate this experience for promoting community life.

Generally speaking, Africa enjoys a live-and-let-live attitude in this neighborhood. Often there is sharing of a neighbor's joy during religious festivals and mutual respect for religious observations. This remains true until there is a scramble for economic resources or political power. Nigeria and Sudan remain supreme examples of this struggle, but history attests to the fact that religion can be a force that rips apart neighborliness. We have even used religion to promote violence against the other. The mutual suspicion between Christian and Muslim, Muslim and Hindu, and the contempt poured on primal religions by Christians and Muslims alike, have not made for dynamic learning and affirming neighborhoods. There are few efforts around the world like Birmingham, England's, multireligious program and Africa's Programme for Christian Muslim Relations, based in Nairobi, where active practical attempts are made for a positive recognition of the neighbor's religion. The efforts of the World Conference of Religion and Peace call for local manifestation of a dialogue of life in people's immediate neighborhood. Religious chauvinism from whatever quarters is not a recipe for good neighborliness. It presupposes a monopoly of truth and of God and so undercuts the roots of our common humanity in a way that prevents our acting humane toward the other. The practice of neighborliness is anchored in a spirituality of care and respect for the other's spiritual resources.

Sharing spirituality across religious boundaries will make us neighbors who honor each other's specificities while at the same time seeking mutual caring and sharing and learning together.

GENDER

One's neighbor is often not even the people next door but the people of one's home, household, workplace, and religious community. One's neighbor is the person of the opposite gender. Gender can and does destroy hospitality and hence human relationship and community health. The relationship can move from being healing circles in a wounding world, to a prison of gender definition. Communities in which one's gender as a female takes precedence over one's humanity can generate dehumanization and marginalization. In the past thirty or so years, many women have pointed out and protested against sexism and other social operations along the gender divide that do violence to the humanity of women, tear up community, and distort hospitality. We cannot avoid having persons of other gender as our neighbors, except by deliberate institutional separation. The challenge is how to create a neighborhood that is affirming and nurturing and for which all contribute their gifts, irrespective of gender. Very often we have overlooked gender as a hermeneutic principle in our understanding of and our journey toward Christlike neighborliness, and the silence has meant the marginalization of women in the process of history making.

Our social definitions of gender, of what constitutes masculine and feminine, generate enough oppressive and disempowering relations to constitute walls of separation. When we add to this a phobia of same-sex love relations, we create situations of marginalization, active antagonism, and even cruelty that one does not expect among human beings. Our humanity, we are learning, exhibits a variety of expressions of sexuality. The Christian religion fights shy of human sexuality, negating and devaluing it with its dogma of virgin birth and the association of sin with sex. Having presented sexuality and sexual activities in a negative light, Christianity has provided no way of positively celebrating eros. Anyone in our neighborhood who does not adhere to the understanding of sexual relations as illicit outside of procreation is courting censor and marginalization. At best, we prefer not to know that anything else exists, but when we really get going, we can even use bumper stickers that say "Kill a queer for Christ's sake." Homosexuals were in many communities "the invisible or unacknowledged neighbors."

The objectification of the female body and the location of sin in sexual relations, accompanied by the institutions of female prostitution and sexual slavery, have put a mantle of invisibility around sex tourism that is shattering human relations in many places around the world. Moreover, sex tourism highlights the power that money wields in the shaping of human relations. Money runs our neighborhoods. Persons are not neighbors, they are tools, instruments, objects for feeding the ego of the neighbor who can "pay" for the services of others who have no bargaining powers. Human beings cease to be persons with whom to relate in mutual dialogue and empowerment. They only exist to be used. They are not our neighbors, they are simply at our service, available for our use. They are at our disposal, and by that very fact disposable.

THE UNACKNOWLEDGED NEIGHBOR

Absence of community and hospitality develops when we do not acknowledge the existence of the other. The people next door become invisible and inaudible to us. The many isolated and hidden persons whom we simply ignore or actively marginalize are put beyond the bounds of our neighborliness. When we pass by on the other side, we cannot even tell who it is we are avoiding. We simply deny their existence. All who are in need of affirmation, survival, and healing tend to exist for us as unacknowledged neighbors or as social problems—never as fellow humans.

In our neighborhood are children, persons with visible mental and physical disabilities, persons who are homeless and landless and nameless. All these and many more are human beings we prefer not to see because they are not of our race, class, religion, or whatever is the name of the fence we have erected to mark our in-group. They are persons we do not need and who, in our view, are dispensable—or even worse, a burden to the neighborhood. We set up neighborhood watches to ward off crime, but we do not set up neighborhood watches to look out for the hungry, the homeless, the sick, and the housebound. They are either invisible or we prefer not to know of their existence.

Being a neighborhood does not preclude conflicts. A history of animosity and exploitation breeds a legacy of cyclical strife, resistance, and often bloodshed. Jews and Arabs, Hutu and Tutsis, Moslems and Croats yearn unsuccessfully for neighborliness, and the rest of the world looks on, wringing its hands. Compassion should result in life-giving action. An agitated womb should give birth to new life. The challenge is how this endemic conflict is managed. Difference is a fact in human community, but being white or male should not become equated with having hegemony over others, for "power over," whatever its source or destination, is an enemy of neighborliness. How do we get at the roots of endemic conflicts? We would like to affirm that these experiences of how community works encourage us to accept variety as an opportunity for widening our circles of relationships so our own humanity would be enriched, but how can we extricate ourselves from biting one another?

There is another angle to this diversity, variety, and inequality that presents an acute challenge to our sense of neighborliness. We often hear this articulated as one's responsibility to one's self and to one's kind. In situations of injustice and exploitation, does one cover up the evil to shield or safeguard the interests of the immediate neighbor? If the exploitation of primary producers means higher interest that pays for me and my kind, do I work against this exploitation and subvert my primary circle's interest? Is every person a neighbor? How and to what extent do I prove myself a neighbor to the isolated or violated persons named above? Having acknowledged the presence of hidden persons among us, how do I stay close to the victims of these societal fences that prevent neighborliness and block the spread of qualitative living to all? Jesus did throw a challenge to his followers: "If you do good only to your kind, what right living have you exhibited beyond human wisdom?" (my understanding of Mt 5: 43-48).

THE NEIGHBOR AS THE SELF

A study of neighborliness beginning with the parable of the Good Samaritan underlines for us how God makes the invisible visible. We are led into God's own method of becoming our neighbor in Jesus of Nazareth. The challenge is, what do we do after we have become aware of who is our neighbor? What does it take to love one's neighbor as one loves one's self? God is indeed agitated by our lack of recognition of the divine presence. Your closest neighbor is yourself—the self that is in the image of God. In this parable, God is revealed as the Compassionate One, the One who suffers with us. In the idiom of the Akan and the Hebrews, God is the one whose womb becomes agitated at the sight of suffering and meanness. The call to be a neighbor is a call for the demonstration of compassion, on the model and the pattern of God. God does not simply hear cries, God responds with appropriate action for transformation that brings with it peace, justice, and fullness of life. Hence the call to perfection at the end of the above passage. To be perfect in love is to love your neighbor as yourself.

NOTES

1. Kofi Abrefa Busia, *The Position of the Chief in the Modern Political System of Ashanti* (London: Oxford University Press, 1951), p. 9.

2. Kofi Antubam, *Ghana's Heritage of Culture* (Leipzig: Koehler and Amelang, 1963), p. 42.

3. Ibid., p. 52.

4. Ibid., p. 48.

14

Oikos and Cross

LARRY L. RASMUSSEN

It's a complicated sentence, but that is what it takes to say what Kosuke Koyama has done: perhaps no theologian and ecumenist or student of comparative religions has so profoundly engaged the theology of the cross as basic orientation in a quest for global community that begins with the integrity of local forms of culture and religious practice. In doing so, *oikos* and *cross* have become key symbols in Koyama's "neighborology." What follows is not an exegesis of his writings on these, however, but an exploration inspired *by* his work and directed to neighborhood issues in an age of social-environmental jeopardy.

EARTH AS *OIKOS*

Symbols speak truth (and falsehood) in their own way. *Oikos* is an old symbol with the feel of new truth.

The numbers are stunning, both the big ones and one very small one. There may be 100 billion galaxies, each with billions and billions of stars. Surely planets circle some, perhaps many. But so far as we know to date, earth is the only one supporting life in the universe. Its thin, living envelope is its distinctive signature. Apparently good planets are hard to find.

The *oikoumene* is indeed "the whole inhabited world" or "the inhabited globe." All things belong to an all-inclusive form upon which the life of each depends. Humankind and otherkind are fit together in an undeniable, if precarious and sometimes downright mean, unity of life and death. We are not so much *at* home *on* earth as we *are* home *as* earth.[1] This is the first truth of earth ecumenics and ethics—"the integrity of creation," by another name. In light of it, the ecumenical task is basic and clear: to help life not only survive but thrive together indefinitely—"sustainability," by another name.

But what are the dimensions of *oikos*, or earth, as life's habitat in the cosmos as we know it?

Many religious traditions, Judaism and Christianity included, understand the inner secret of creation to be the indwelling of God within it. Creation is the place of God's presence, and the purpose of the *Shekinah* (a Jewish way of speaking of God's indwelling), or the work of the Holy Spirit (a Christian way of speaking), is to render the whole creation the very house of God. The "economy of God" (*oikonomia tou theou*) is the ancient way of speaking about this redemptive trans-formation. For the moment, however, the point is the underlying notion of *oikos*: earth (and all creation) is the house of God's presence and indwelling. God is "home" here.[2]

The word *oikos* itself is from classical Greek and the "street Greek" of the New Testament (*koine*). It was recently revived by Daniel Bell. Bell ended his study of the world coming apart, *The Cultural Contradictions of Capitalism*, in search of a unifying vision.[3] He sought direction for society and culture, United States society especially. *Oikos* offered this social vision. We will return to it after noting some-thing even more basic that eluded Bell and most other treatments of *oikos*.

What is most decisive for the whole inhabited earth (*oikoumene*) is that it be hab-itable! The first and basic meaning of *oikos* is simply "Habitat Earth." Habitat is the core meaning of all "eco" words. *Oikos*—earth as a vast but single household of life—means the capacity for survival, i.e., sustainable habitat. It means space and the means for the living of all living things. Without adequate hospitable habitat, nothing lives. Not only humans, but all life-forms require habitats carefully fitted for them.

This foundational fact that we all need a space for the basics is the one great ele-ment of democracy in life, a kind of first equality of all creatures. Whatever we choose to call it, the point is that without that which good space provides—pro-ductive land, a hospitable atmosphere, safe water, the numberless forms of life that provide sustenance for one another in astounding ecosystems—*none* of the other "household" goods we treasure, including educational, artistic, and spiritual ones, are possible. This is finite, bounded space, to be sure. The earth is curved, well wrapped, a closed sphere. But the boundaries are those of life itself and what life requires to stay in place.[4]

Habitation in this closed space (sunlight is the *only* life element not permanently resident within the biosphere) rests on further understandings. *Oikos* carries these. It is the root and common unity of economics, ecology, and ecumenics, the "eco" of each. Economics is *eco* (habitat as the household) and *nomos* (the rules or law). Eco-nomics means knowing how things work and arranging these "home systems" (ecosystems) so the material requirements of the household of life are met and sus-tained. The household is established as hospitable habitat. The basic task of the economy, then, is the continuation of life, though no economist has put it that way for ages, perhaps since Joseph himself. Joseph says to his brothers in Egypt: "God sent me before you to preserve your lives . . . to make sure that your race would have survivors in the land and to save your lives, many lives at that" (Gen 45:5,7).[5]

In fact, the kind of economics generating the present ecocrisis made three decisive moves *away* from *oikos* economics. One was to consider nature as inter-changeable parts and machinelike, rather than organic. Another was what Guy Beney calls the "genius" of the West always "to flee towards the exterior"; i.e., the propensity to generate affluence by expanding to new worlds until the globalized West became a full "planetary wave." (Beney also notes that this wave now doubles back on itself, having come up against the closed nature of the *oikos* and "fusing" with it; what we then have left are vulnerable systems with little room for error.[6] It is the foolishness of pursuing frontier economics in a postfrontier world.) The third departure was to shift economic attention from the household and its community to the firm or corporation. The founders of modern economics chose the corporation or firm rather than the household (*oikos*) as the basic unit of economic agency and focus. The long-term interests and perspectives of corporations or firms are very different from those of households and the communities which households constitute and which in turn sustain households. The household seeks to maximize the quality of life and benefits of its members. Corporation and firm measures of success are maximized profits and market share. The aggregation of household interests approaches the collective interest of the community. The aggregation of corporation and firm interests has very little to do with the interests of even their own geographical area, however, and represent instead the interests of those who own, control, and decide about capital.[7] Because firm and corporation perspectives are potentially global, attachment and loyalty to households and communities run a very poor second, third, or fourth. These three changes in economics in the modern period—nature as parts, globalization, and the firm or corporation as the basic unit of economic agency and analysis—all revise radically the inherent eco-economics of *oikos*, even when household and community may, in a contracting world, take on many different dimensions, from a literal single household to the earth community itself as an all-inclusive life form.[8]

In New Testament usage, the one who knows the house rules and cares for the life of household members is the *oikonomos*, the householder. English customarily translates *oikonomos* as steward, which derives from "sty warden," the keeper of the pigs—a fine image, though at first blush somewhat less attractive than householder! Whether as steward or householder, *oikonomos* signals trusteeship. It means broad human responsibility for the world we affect, including deep and far-reaching impact on nonhuman nature. It means wise management of life's household, including knowledge of human limits, together with the rest of nature's.

Ecology is "eco" plus "logos"—the "doctrine of the house" or knowledge of the logic and structure of the household, how it has been configured and runs. Ecology thus means knowing, from inside, the interrelationships that make up the total life of the household and the requirements for "good housekeeping." This is to respect the integrity of creation and live life in accord with it. English usage is recent, apparently initiated by Ernst Haeckel in 1870. "By ecology," he wrote, "we mean the body of knowledge concerning the economy of nature—the investigation of the total relations of the animal both to its inorganic and to its organic environment; including, above all, its friendly and inimical relations with those animals and plants with which it comes directly or indirectly into contact."9 In short, ecology as a dimension of *oikos* is the knowledge of life systems, including the economy of nature, necessary for good home economics.

Oikos members were themselves *oikeioi*, household dwellers. Their tasks together comprised what the Apostle Paul called simply "the upbuilding of community." In the full vision of *oikos*, however, building up community includes all that belongs to *oikodome*, yet another *oikos* word. *Oikodome* is the continual upbuilding of the *oikos* as a whole,10 what we might term world citizenship or earth patriotism, with all the attendant duties of "choosing life" (Dt 30:19) and living in accord with the choice.11 This includes restoration of damage suffered and done. Yet for all the attention to global stewardship, *oikodome* never loses its focus on the particular community at hand and its well-being. It is a neighborhood notion. The global does not substitute for the local but, like the understanding of ecumenical in the early church itself, means the whole church in each place. Neighborhood and community—this is the basic unit *of* the global. This Christian notion is similar to the Stoic one. Stoics, too, considered themselves citizens of a world which transcended their immediate locale. Yet transcendence of the local was not contempt of it or a way of leaving it behind; rather a way, through local responsibility, of gathering the whole world together as community over time. For the Stoics, humans, gods, animals, and vegetation were all included and understood by way of the *theologia naturalis*—knowledge of the essence of things.

It is important to underscore this relationship of local and global and distinguish it from others. *Oikos* as a vision is not the Enlightenment project of an earth ethic grounded in the universally human as some core that can be stripped of particularity and exist independently of differences generated by race, gender, class, and culture. Nor is the *oikos* an earth ethic held together by universal norms and procedures secured through the power of shared universal reason as a capacity that somehow leaves the passions (and treasures) of time and place, of culture and locale, behind. In the Enlightenment tradition, the provincialities of communities and cultures, of local time and space, are held in a kind of veiled contempt as tribal residues impeding a developing cosmopolitanism, rather than the finite units *of* a greater community to which they intrinsically belonged. *Oikos* is also at odds with the globalism of the presently globalizing economy, even an ecologically sensitized global economy. Such global thinking has disregard for local community loyalties and needs and, by virtue of globalism itself, necessarily oversimplifies and reduces, often with cruel results. *Oikos* earth ethics is instead closer to Wendell Berry's contention that

> properly speaking, global thinking is not possible. Those who have "thought globally" have done so by means of simplifications too extreme and oppressive to merit the name of thought.... Unless one is willing to be destructive on a very large scale, one cannot do something except locally, in a small place. Global thinking can only do to the globe what a space satellite does to it: reduce it, make a bauble of it.... If you want to *see* where you are, you will have to get out of your spaceship, out of your car, off your horse, and walk over the ground. On foot you will find the earth is still satisfyingly large and full of beguiling nooks and crannies.12

Berry's is an *oikos* earth patriotism and world citizenship, *through* local in-habitation of Habitat Earth, a kind of "neighborology" that takes neighborhood seriously.

The ancient *oikos* vision includes instruction for all this. *Peri oikonomias*, "on household management," was a steady theme of philosophers and rhetoricians from Plato's time until the waning of the Roman Empire. Essentially practical moral instruction for the conduct of different family members, the circle was often enlarged to include societal duties and roles as well. *Peri oikonomias* was the rationale for, and articulation of, such duties. (Here is Bell's quest for a coherent stipulation of society and the moral education necessary for life together.)

Early Christians took over this instruction in household management on their own terms. Their new communities were originally conceived as *oikoi* themselves ("households of faith" in this case), partly because the early church was literally a house church movement. Community instruction came in numerous forms, some of them demanding and lengthy. Catechumens, for example, normally studied for two years and were subjected to rigorous examination leading to the rite of baptism and their first eucharist. The purpose of instruction was to learn the way of life and belief of these congregations, including the respective roles and responsibilities of different community members. It was concrete instruction for *oikos* living as a visible way of life.

Ecumenics was another early Christian *oikos* notion. It meant recognizing the unity of the household—all belonged to the same family—and nurturing this unity, both within each community and across the collective household of faith scattered on three continents around the Mediterranean basin. It included a conscious effort to stand for the whole church in each place.

The Stoics, too, had their take on the venerable *oikos* tradition of instruction. They taught *oikeiosis*—"appropriation" (in the sense of making something one's own). *Oikeiosis*, like Christian catechesis, included practical moral instruction and its supporting rationale. To become what one might as a human being, the Stoics taught, meant care of the self and nurturing the divine spark that by nature lived within each person. The primary means was cultivated reason, employed to tutor and order human appetites and actions. This was not care of the abstracted individual, however, but each person as a member of the *oikos*. Such membership might refer to membership in the familial household, society, the human race collectively, or the *cosmos* (world) as a whole. Underlying all was the Stoic conviction that we owe reciprocal duties which express the law of nature. (Western natural-law traditions have deep roots in the Stoic *theologia naturalis*.) Taking these duties on and living them out "realized" one's true nature. Appropriation (*oikeiosis*) followed from, and issued in, right living.[13]

But *oikos* also includes homelessness, if only as a way to mark that which violates the vision and its implicit earth ethic. (Koyama's work speaks increasingly of homelessness and understands it in this way.)

The forms of homelessness are at least two—deprivation and alienation. Each in turn has multiple expressions, but for the moment our attention is to deprivation and alienation through the destruction of home as habitat and the literal economic, cultural, and spiritual uprooting of people from their homes.[14]

In a manner anticipating the Chiapas revolt in Mexico, testimony to homelessness in our time was given at a public hearing of the World Commission on Development. The Krenak people, a living continuation of early agricultural peoples, were protesting a resettlement from their traditional home in the valley of the Rio Doce, which was planned for development. "The only possible place . . . to weave our lives is where God created us," their elder explained to blue-ribbon commissioners. "It is useless for the government to put us in a very beautiful place, in a very good place with a lot of hunting and a lot of fish. The Krenak people . . . die insisting that there is only one place for us to live." The elder finished by saying: "I have no pleasure at all to come here and make these statements. *We can no longer see the planet that we live upon as if it were a chess board where people just move things around. We cannot consider the planet as something isolated from the cosmic."*[15]

First colonization, then development and commerce, spelled alienation and deprivation for the Krenak. The prospect of relocation meant homelessness of both spirit and place, a homelessness different but no less real than any encountered on the streets of New York or Calcutta. Many peoples long at home in their world, like the Krenak, have been rendered strangers in their own land as globalizing intruders from elsewhere decided how their earth space, their habitat, their *oikos*, would be used. The Krenak did not understand that space and traditional borders mean nothing to the porous ways of a global economy, including land and its native treasures, both now rendered commodities. Chief Seattle's claim in 1854 that you cannot "buy the sky" or "the warmth of the land," or "own the freshness of the air and the sparkle of the water," turns out not to be true at all. But the Krenak did not comprehend the commercial and industrial globalization of the past few centuries, even when they sensed clearly enough what it asked of body and spirit, culture and religion. Thus even another very beautiful place with a lot of hunting and a lot of fish was no substitute. Homelessness is alienation from the land of one's forebears, where one's own spirit still lives with those who have gone before in near-biblical fashion—generation by generation by generation by generation.

Masses of people are homeless now, and not only indigenous peoples and the poor. *Oikos* as the experience of belonging somewhere intimate to one's bones eludes most moderns. The homeless mind, Peter Berger argues, is a condition of modernity itself, accompanying development and modernization as their own sure offspring.[16] But even apart from homelessness as a matter of mind, it is quite literally displacement of one kind or another. The highly mobile rich, living from hotel to suburban lot to condo and hotel again, hardly have a community they call their own and, even less, binding commitment to it. All the advertisements and job descriptions, the trade and tourism, declare the world itself as their oyster—but no particular locale is home in a deep, settled sense. The uprooted but formerly settled poor also move about in search of new places to sustain them or their families back home via money and the mail. The lucky ones live in places alien to them, the rest in refugee camps. The biggest issues of the coming decades will likely include refugees and internally displaced persons near the top of the list. "It's a privilege to be exploited now" is already the going humor of the 1990s. The alternative to bad employment is none. Homelessness, then, is both a physical and psychic condition, a reality spun off the global marketplace and development. It affects both rich and poor, though hardly in the same way![17]

CROSS AND COMMUNITY

Unlike the discussion of *oikos* in much literature, including Christian literature, in Koyama's work it is never far from the discussion of the cross and Jesus as the one who makes the periphery the center.

In his presentation of Jesus and the cross, Koyama draws deeply from Luther's theology of the cross. That theology itself assumes and asserts Luther's contention that "the finite bears the infinite" (*finitum capax infiniti*). This is the reason for Luther's sacramental panentheism, nicely summarized in one of his meditations on the body of Christ: "God in his essence is present everywhere, in and through the whole creation in all its parts and in all places, and so the world is full of God and God fills it all, yet God is not limited or circumscribed by it, but is at the same time beyond and above the whole creation."[18] Cross theology, then, is earthbound and limited. Incarnate finitude is God's way, among us. The body, nature, is God's path. God is not a separate item, even a very large one, on an inventory of the universe. The universe itself is God's "body," the abode of God's dwelling (to necessarily risk metaphor, as all religious language must). To be sure, God is not wholly encompassed by the creaturely, but the creaturely is the one and only place we know the divine fullness in the manner appropriate to our own fullness. Of itself, such a notion—the finite bears the infinite—would lead us to Wisdom tradition themes for guidance. This one, for instance.

> But ask the animals, and they will teach you;
>   the birds of the air, and they shall teach you;
> ask the plants of the earth, and they will teach you;
>   and the fish of the sea will declare to you.
> Who among all these does not know
>   that the hand of the Lord has done this?
> In [God's] hand is the life of every living thing
>   and the breath of every human being. (Job 12: 7-10)

Is not such wisdom enough? If we learned this and no more, would we not have everything necessary for an adequate ecojustice and neighbor ethic for earth as *oikos*? Some religious environmentalists think so; Luther thinks not. Is he right, or they?

Finitum capax infiniti certainly does express itself as a rich panentheism. Yet Luther never makes nature or the creaturely as such *the* focal reality of God's revelation. Rather, *the* compelling glimpse of God is in the humanity of a particular poor Jew from Nazareth in the region of Galilee during the season when Augustus happened to be the Roman Caesar. What we can most reliably know of God's own way, we know in the way of this man Jesus. God is like this Jesus. God is not more divine than God is in Jesus' humanity, Luther insists. God is not more powerful than God is in the power seen in this Jesus. God is not more majestic than God is in the *keno-*

sis (the self-emptying) of God in this Jesus. God is not greater than God is in this servant.[19] As this particular Jesus is, so also is God. God is the ultimate life source of the entire universe but, in the manner appropriate to human experience and knowing, this life source is disclosed most compellingly in Jesus.

Though Luther's is a New Testament claim in this respect, the pattern is an older Hebrew one. Just as the Hebrews moved from the experience of a redeeming God to the awesome realization that this very One was also the Creator of the Universe and of life itself, so Luther moves from the redemptive presence of the transcendent God in the human Jesus, as testified to by his followers and experienced by Luther himself, to the awesome presence of this God in all things great and small. The universe is itself the primordial revelation of God. But the path to understanding God as Creator comes by way of the distinctive, though not exclusive, revelation of the suffering and redeeming God seen in Jesus and his way.[20] Redemption's scope is all creation. But its route for earth is via the formation of a people whose mission is to display redeemed creation as just community. Such is the pattern for both the formation of Israel and "the People of the Way" of Jesus (Acts 4:32-35).

This Jesus is not a fleeting docetic visitor, nor a ghostly bearer of gnostic truth, but real, mortal flesh and blood from the countryside, indeed from a village so peripheral it didn't even merit notice on the maps of the day. Joseph tickles his bare belly button and covers his bare bottom, Mary puts his hungry mouth to her bare breast. (These are Luther's images.)

Jesus is, to be sure, not the *exclusive* revelation of the ubiquitous immanence of God. *All* creation manifests God. But he is the most compelling and single most definitive revelation, argues Luther. Thus while "God is [always] in the facts themselves" (D. Bonhoeffer), including the facts of nature, the facts are best comprehended via God-in-Jesus. In Jesus we see the kind of God God is.

This is so with special power in Jesus on the cross. Yet Jesus on the cross is a very strange revelation. In one sense, a dying Jesus is akin to all revelation of God in that it is only indirect—itself a rather strange attribute for revelation. But that's the way it is with God, Luther insists. Just as Jesus is a human male, so *all* evidence of God and God's presence is *masked*. It is hidden in something else, always something finite and creaturely, borne of nature itself. We have no *direct* evidence of God at all, no manifestation that is not via nature. All divinity is mediated by finite nature. So we see only what Luther calls the "rearward parts" of God (*posteriori Dei*). (The reference is to Moses and the Jewish notion that no one would survive a direct encounter with the Holy One in full majesty.)

Yet the cross is not only indirect exposure of God, it is God's presence *sub contrario*—under the opposite. This is not only the rearward parts, it is the indecent exposure and scandal of a God who is crucified as well as hidden (*Deus crucifixus et absconditus*). God is concealed in a vilified and broken human being. Jesus is God made poor and abused. This is God revealed not only indirectly in nature, but in a particular, broken, and scandalous condition.

Reason and all theologies of glory expect and insist upon something else of God, namely, God in power, majesty, and light, in triumph, ecstasy, mighty deeds, and wild success. God is found, however, says Luther, in weakness and wretchedness, in darkness, failure, sorrow, and despair. God is not found *only* there, but God *is* found there in a special, crystallized, and *saving* way. God is present in a certain kind of suffering love and as a certain kind of power on the home turf of deadliness and degradation itself. God is present in twistedness and pain, and not in beauty and health alone, precious blessings though these be. God is internally affected by creation's travail. When finite nature suffers, God suffers.

What does a crucified and hidden God mean for *oikos* ethics, a God sufferingly present in degraded nature? And what might an apparent preferential option of God for the suffering mean? Gazing from the foot of the cross to the man of sorrows, how does the heart of the universe manifest itself here for the well-being of all creation? Isn't Wisdom's way of discerning God in common experience of the world sufficient?

Jesus, as the way of God among us and as "a model of the godly life" (*Lutheran Book of Worship*), shifts our attention in ethics decisively in a way the opening verses from Job of themselves do not, even if read in a panentheistic manner. ("In God's hand is the life of every living thing, and the breath of every human being" (Job 12:10). Or, for that matter, most other ethical systems. The standard attention in modern ethics concentrates upon our own limited resources to effect good, to see what we might do to leave the world less a mess than we found it. The attention is to my capacities as a morally autonomous and responsible agent armed with natural powers. The way of Jesus, however, means entering into the predicaments of others who are suffering—as the *starting point*. There is a major moral and theological assumption here, but they merge so as to be indistinguishable in practice. The moral assumption is that the farther one is removed from the suffering present in creation, the farther one is from its central moral reality; the closer one is to the suffering, the more difficult it is to refuse participation in that afflicted life, human or extrahuman. Compassion (suffering-with) is the passion of life itself, in this view, even as joy is. Both are a corollary of the fact that the only way we can be human is to be human together and with otherkind; this includes the pain of unredeemed relationship. In fact, compassion is not, as we often think, something high and "religious." Compassion, as the Dalai Lama says, is

> the common connective tissue of the body of human life. . . . Without it children would not be nurtured and protected, the slightest conflicts would never be resolved, people probably would never even have learned to talk to one another. Nothing pleasant that we enjoy throughout our lives would come to us without the kindness and compassion of others. So it does not seem unrealistic to me: compassion seems to be the greatest power.[21]

"A-pathy" contrasts with compassion. It is the denial of the senses and of our inherent connectedness to all things. It is a rejection of our constitutional sociality and the pathos of life. The corrective is a return to our senses and to "the imaginative ability to see strange people as fellow sufferers," in Richard Rorty's words. (Rorty's "strange people" should be extended to include other strange creatures.)[22]

The theological assumption of the way of Jesus is that discipleship or, for that matter, simply being human, means to participate in God's sufferings in and for the life of creation itself as "Habitat Earth." That is where and how God is a saving God, and that is the way of the cross as a human and divine way.

This renders compassion (suffering-with) the key virtue for a Christian ethic and an earth ethic as well, and solidarity (standing-with) the key means. The quest of earth faith in this understanding is precisely for a power that overcomes suffering by entering into it and leading through it to abundant life for all (the sabbath condition of redeemed creation). God's goal is newness of life. God's means is overcoming by undergoing. And God's way is seen in Jesus, who is the full compassion of God in human form.

What is discovered via Jesus, then, and is experienced in imaging him, is this: Only that which has undergone all can overcome all. In this sense, cross ethics is an utterly practical necessity. Suffering, in any of its many expressions among any of its creatures, will not be redemptively addressed apart from some manner and degree of anger,[23] compassionate entry into its reality, some empowerment from the inside out, some experience of it as both a burden and a burden to be thrown off, some deep awareness of it as unhealed but not unhealable suffering. Of course it's frivolous simply to call this "no pain, no gain" ethics! But it's not frivolous to recognize, with Koyama's teacher Kuzoh Kitamori, that until our pain is intensified at the sight of creation's pain, as God's is, there is no movement toward redemption; until we enter the places of suffering and experience them with those entangled there, as God does, our actions will not be co-redemptive.[24]

The simple logic here is that any power which does not go to the places that community and creation are most obviously ruptured and ruined is no power for healing at all. This is the impotence of what we wrongly call power—wealth, fame, legions of soldiers and ships, triumphalist ideologies, and arrogant, wasteful ways of life. Such power does not truly know the disasters of the spirit, the catastrophes of the psyche, the acidity of rain, soil, mind, or household, and thus cannot help work wounds back to health from within battered flesh itself. Or, if such power does recognize the normal pathologies of everyday life—they are, after all, as unavoidable as death itself—it treats them as rabid leprosies and sectors of life to be quarantined out of sight, beyond notice and beyond feeling. These powers are not the powers of the senses and deep bonds, but abstracted powers that violate them.

The only power which can truly heal and keep the creation[25] is power instinctively drawn to the flawed places of existence, there to call forth from the desperate and needy themselves extraordinary yet common powers which they did not even know they had. This is the power seen in Jesus. It is strength in weakness, life in the midst of death, joy within suffering, and grace where only wrath and pain and the rearward parts of God are most obvious. The ironic thing, one worthy of reversing standard accounts of wisdom and foolishness, is that this weak kind of power, learned in suffering, expressed as compassion, and deeply sensed and felt, is what wins space for joy and abundant life. Perhaps this is why, in "the emotive region of the cross"[26] and in the awful silence before a dying Christ, one hears the seismic whisper of none other than the power of God. It feels like that. Even temple curtains are torn from top to bottom in that moment, and the stones themselves cry out (Mt 27:51). Hope surges from the mended places.

In short, the kind of earth ethic that reads the presence of the divine from the flourishing of nature on its better days, or which reads the presence of the divine off the beauties of nature as we observe or imagine those (Jb 12, e.g.), speaks of God in true but limited ways. God is here present to us in creation's beauty; the holy is mediated via nature's grandeur. But God is also present in the cross of pain and twistedness and whatever other ways by which creation is violated.[27] If God were only present in the beautiful and graced but not the blighted and disgraced, then broken creation would not be healed and the only creation saved will be that rare portion that does not stand in need of it! And if we are only present in a saving way to creation's flourishing but not to its plunder and rape, then we absent ourselves from the very reality for which we are responsible. Such absence numbs the very senses that are the surest signs we are alive; absenting ourselves from earth's pain— eco-social and psychic pain—leaves us despoiled as well.

Koyama, Kitamori, Soelle, Bonhoeffer, and Sobrino have all explicated in profound terms the way of the cross and its relationship to suffering, pain, justice, and peace.[28] That need not be further discussed here. The point here is another, namely the connection of earth as *oikos* to cross. While true, it is not enough to say simply that joining the gracious God means loving earth. If Luther is correct, we must also say that joining the gracious God means loving Jesus. This means Jesus on the cross and the way of the cross as God's ethic and ours. Love earth as *oikos*, yes, but redeeming the planet with God means embracing its distress. It means going to the places of suffering to find God and God's power there. God in Jesus strangely, offensively, makes the margin the center and hefts the rejected stone to set the corner itself. The cross is erected "outside the gate" (Heb 13:12), beyond the zone where salvation is commonly expected, in the place of the damned. There renewal, redemption, restoration begins, the unexpected appearance of new life "after its evaporation has left us desolate."[29] It is not less than resurrection from the dead.

NOTES

1. *See* Shannon Jung, *We Are Home: A Spirituality of the Environment* (Mahwah, NJ: Paulist Press, 1993), esp. chapt. 4, "The Earth: God's Home, Our Home."

2. *See* Jürgen Moltmann, *God in Creation: A New Theology of Creation and the Spirit of God* (San Francisco: Harper & Row, 1985).

3. Daniel Bell, *The Cultural Contradictions of Capitalism* (New York: Basic Books, 1976), esp. the last chapter.

4. *See* Konrad Raiser, *Ecumenism in Transition: A Paradigm Shift in the Ecumenical Movement?* (Geneva: World Council of Churches, 1991), pp. 84-91.

5. The Jerusalem Bible.

6. Guy Beney, " 'Gaia': The Globalitarian Temptation," in *Global Ecology: Conflicts and Contradiction in Environmental Management*, ed. Wolfgang Sachs (London and Atlantic Highlands, NJ: Zed Books, 1993), pp. 181-82.

7. Herman E. Daly and John B. Cobb, Jr., *For the Common Good: Redirecting the Economy Toward Community, the Environment, and a Sustainable Future* (Boston: Beacon Press, 1989). Note this shift as one from *oikonomia* to *chrematistics*. The distinction between the two is Aristotle's, but both refer to the discipline of economics. *Chrematistics* casts the work

of economic practices as the "manipulation of property and wealth so as to maximize short-term monetary exchange value to the owner." *Oikonomia*, by contrast, "is the management of the household so as to increase its use value to all members of the household over the long run." With the shift in industrial economies from the household to the firm came also the shift from *oikonomia* to *chrematistics* as the substance of economic ends. Daly and Cobb go on to say that "if we expand the scope of household to include the larger community of the land, of shared values, resources, biomes, institutions, language, and history, then we have a good definition of 'economics for community,' " (138). This is the direction the discussion above takes—*oikos* as the symbol for an understanding of sustainable development as "economics for community."

8. *See* David C. Korten, "Sustainable Development: A Review Essay," *World Policy Journal* 9:1 (Winter 1991): 183-84.

9. Charles Birch and John B. Cobb, Jr., *The Liberation of Life* (Denton, TX: Environmental Ethics Books, 1990, 1981), p. 27. Birch and Cobb cite this date and definition but not the source in Haeckel's writings.

10. This discussion of various meanings of *oikos* and its derivatives is in part indebted, as noted above, to Raiser, *Ecumenism in Transition*, pp. 102-11.

11. I was reminded of this, not by slow social-environmental degradation, but the historical reality of genocide. At the United States Memorial to the Holocaust, there is a Hall of Remembrance. It is a stark, open, octagonal, marbled space that gathers only silence and has only an eternal flame, an inscription about remembrance, and two biblical verses, one high to the left, the other high to the right. To the left is Genesis 4:10: "And the Lord said: 'What have you done? Listen; your brother's blood is crying out to me from the ground!' " To the right is Deuteronomy 30:19: "I call heaven and earth to witness against you today that I have set before you life and death, blessings and curses. Choose life so that you and your descendents may live." Life is increasingly a matter of human choosing, as is death.

12. Wendell Berry, *Sex, Economy, Freedom and Community: Eight Essays* (New York and San Francisco: Pantheon Books, 1993), pp. 19-20.

13. *See* Alasdair MacIntyre, *Whose Justice? Which Rationality?* (Notre Dame, IN: University of Notre Dame, 1988), pp. 147-50; also Wayne Meeks, *The Origins of Christian Morality: The First Two Centuries* (New Haven, CT: Yale University Press, 1993), pp. 77-79.

14. Maria Mies and Vandana Shiva, *Ecofeminism* (London and Atlantic Highlands, NJ: Zed Books, 1993), pp. 103-4.

15. Ibid., p. 104. The emphasis is theirs.

16. Peter Berger, et al., *The Homeless Mind: Modernization and Consciousness* (London: Pelican Books, 1981).

17. Mies and Shiva, *Ecofeminism*, p. 98.

18. Martin Luther, "That These Words of Christ—This is my Body, etc. Still Stand Firm Against the Fanatics," *Luther's Works*, Vol. 37 (Philadelphia: Muhlenberg, 1959), p. 59.

19. This is a paraphrase of Jürgen Moltmann's *The Crucified God: The Cross of Christ as the Foundation and Criticism of Christian Theology* (New York: Harper & Row, 1974), p. 205. I am grateful to Lisa Stoen Hazelwood for bringing this passage to my attention anew.

20. While I respect the experience of both Luther and the Hebrews, the fallout has often been, for some streams of Christianity, to make the second article of the Creed the first, i.e., to obscure the fact that creation is primary and redemption is wholly the redemption *of* creation. God is first "maker of heaven and earth"; God is redeemer in order to save and serve creation's destiny.

21. H. H. the Dalai Lama, "Tissue of Compassion," *Cathedral* 5:1 (December 1989): 5.

22. As cited in Anthony Walton, "Awakening After Boston's Nightmare," *The New York Times*, 10 January 1990, A27.

23. The reference is to the line from Augustine that "hope has two lovely daughters, anger and courage; anger at the way things are, courage to set them right." For a profound treatment of this in Christian ethics, *see* Beverly Wildung Harrison, "The Power of Anger in the Work of Love: Christian Ethics for Women and Other Strangers," in *Making the Connections: Essays in Feminist Social Ethics*, ed. Carol S. Robb (Boston: Beacon Press, 1985), pp. 3ff.

24. Kuzoh Kitamori, *The Theology of the Pain of God* (Richmond, VA: John Knox Press, 1965).

25. Presbyterian Church, *Keeping and Healing the Creation* (Louisville: Committee on Social Witness Policy, Presbyterian Church [U.S.A.], 1989).

26. Kosuke Koyama, *Mount Fuji and Mount Sinai: A Critique of Idols*, Preface (Maryknoll, NY: Orbis Books, 1985).

27. *See* John Shea, *Stories of God: An Unauthorized Biography* (Chicago: The Thomas More Press, 1978), pp. 148-61.

28. *See* Dorothee Soelle, *Suffering* (Philadelphia: Fortress Press, 1975); Dietrich Bonhoeffer, *Letters and Papers from Prison* (New York: Macmillan, 1972); Kitamori, *Theology of the Pain of God*; Koyama, *Mount Fuji and Mount Sinai*; Jon Sobrino, S.J., *Christology at the Crossroads* (Maryknoll, NY: Orbis Books, 1978). For a discussion of Bonhoeffer's themes, *see* Larry L. Rasmussen with Renate Bethge, *Dietrich Bonhoeffer: His Significance for North Americans* (Minneapolis: Fortress Press, 1989), chaps. 7 and 8, "Divine Presence and Human Power" and "An Ethic of the Cross."

29. Landon Gilkey, *Nature, Reality, and the Sacred: The Nexus of Science and Religion* (Minneapolis: Fortress Press, 1993), p. 135.

An Afterword

A Personal Tribute to Kosuke Koyama

DONALD W. SHRIVER, JR.

The Pacific is our widest ocean. Culturally considered, it is wider by far than the Atlantic. My first conversation with Kosuke Koyama was via a New York-New Zealand telephone call in which I invited him, on behalf of Union Seminary, to join our faculty. In sheer mileage, it was perhaps the longest long-distance phone call of all my years as president of that faculty.

But it was long in another sense. After fifteen years of colleagueship with this remarkable Christian intellectual, I have had to reckon anew with an experience that members of almost any faculty are likely to recognize and which T.S. Eliot described in one of his Four Quartets:

> We shall not cease from exploration
> And the end of all our exploring
> Will be to arrive where we started
> And know the place for the first time.[1]

Like almost any of our human neighbors, faculty colleagues get to know each other very gradually and very imperfectly. Kosuke Koyama has been the first full-time, tenured Asian member of the Union Seminary faculty in all of its 160-year history. Returning to the moment when our personal connections began, I am moved to reflect that our long long-distance call presaged another kind of distance that communication satellites are not likely to overcome anytime in the near future: the distance between Western and Asian cultures, religions, ideologies, and political-economic interests.

As the essays in this *festschrift* demonstrate, Professor Koyama is one of this century's pioneers in the bridging of such distances. Just how long they are was symbolized in one incident, humorous in retrospect, that occurred just before his arrival at Union Seminary in the summer of 1980. In the hall outside our distinguished theological library there appeared, on a "Discard" shelf, a paperback book entitled *Waterbuffalo Theology*. Something about the title must have convinced a cataloger that the book was not serious enough to belong in our library. Soon after, word went around that its author was a newly elected member of our faculty, and theology-in-the-context-of-people-who-plow-with-buffalos—i.e., in Thailand—entered the permanent collection of books housed at Union Theological Seminary.

But it takes more than books on a shelf for an intellectual contribution to become truly integrated into an institutional heritage. One does not have to be around Kosuke Koyama very long to realize that his is a uniquely innovative intellect, as profound as it is agile and playful. Mining the riches of that intellect is a demanding task, especially for those of us whose ears are ill-tuned for hearing voices from outside the two-millennia-old thought world of western Christianity. Asked to conclude this volume with a personal tribute to Kosuke Koyama, I gladly do so, but with the sober realization that in his books, lectures, conversations, ecumenical outreach, and personhood, Kosuke Koyama is a man whom we shall have to go on appreciating for many years to come, if we are to understand how much he has already done to fortify the hope that Asia and the West are capable of becoming a spiritual neighborhood.

I can suggest my own present sense of debt to him in three dimensions.

A JAPANESE CHRISTIAN

This is a more remarkable first identification of Koyama than most Christians around the world are likely to surmise. Christians in Japan are a small, historically persecuted, culturally suspect minority. They were notably so during the Pacific War of the 1940s. Yet it was early in that war, in 1942, that twelve-year-old Koyama accepted baptism in a church in Tokyo, a member of the third generation of his family to do so.

Two aspects of that youthful decision, he has often reminded us, stand out in his memory. In prebaptism instruction, the local pastor said to his confirmation class: "Remember, the God of Jesus is one who cares for Americans as much as for the Japanese." Wartime reminders of such a claim are remarkable in any country at war. In Japan of 1942, it was astonishing. As a slightly older American Christian of fourteen in 1942, I do not remember being offered the complementary instruction on any church occasion of those years.

Three years later, at age fifteen, Koyama had vivid, terrifying reason to wonder if the God of Jesus really loved Americans, at least those who on March 10-11, 1945, firebombed Tokyo with a loss of life (88,000) approximating the coming death toll in Hiroshima. Two months later, as bombs continued to fall on Tokyo, Koyama was running for shelter when a bomb fell squarely in front of him with a *thunk* as it hit the earth. It was a dud. "That is why I survived the war," he says.

The war, he always adds, was the womb in which his theology came to birth even as his life was saved. "In my mind an outer event, the destruction of proud, violent Japan, and an inner event, my baptismal death in the hope of new life in the risen Christ, coincided. What happened in 1945 to Japan has become a part of my Christian identity."[2]

Koyama's lucid English prose is suffused with an Asian accent. Christian identity for him is a compound of the awesomely universal and the intimately local. As a Japanese Christian, he owes allegiance to Mount Fuji and Mount Sinai. Contrasts between the two mountains and the relation of both to the cross and resurrection of Jesus became the great motif of his theological vocation. That vocation linked his calling to that of the prophets of Israel, especially Jeremiah. In the linking, his exploration of the idolatries of Israel and Japan has brought him equally into collision with the idolatries of western and American culture. His theological criticism of his own native culture has profound, painful relevance for the Christians of America. Like Bonhoeffer, Koyama shows us what it is to will the defeat of idolatries in the history of one's own nation. This hard lesson most of us American Christians have scarcely begun to learn. Do we not live in the world's best country? Is it not lack of patriotism to protest, these fifty years later, the firebombing of Tokyo and the nuclear bombing of Hiroshima? Homeborn critics of America swim upstream against these rhetorical questions. One does not have to read many pages of Koyama's works to know why he thinks of Jeremiah as his model prophet, or why neither he nor that ancient troubler of Israel find an easy home in America.

A BIBLICAL, ECUMENICAL THEOLOGIAN

From his years as a missionary of the Kyodan in Chienmai, Thailand, through every year of his teaching in New York, Koyama has traveled to many a country and engaged in many an ecumenical dialogue with the churches of every continent. If he has been able to enter so many conversations with so wide a cross section of the global Christian community, the major reason—he would be the first to say—has been his dependence theologically upon the Bible. Both personally and academically, he has a high doctrine of scripture. He sees it as the churches' unique resource for protection against their own idolatries. In this he is not hostile to the scriptures of other religious, especially Asian, traditions; but now and again he insists that the Bible is a unique window to the love, judgment, and active presence of the Lord of human history. Over our human history and in it: that is the Holy One to whom the Bible bears witness.

More carefully and regularly than most theologians whom I know, Koyama practices what Karl Barth used to preach: that "Christians should sleep over neither their Bibles nor their newspapers." It is not just today's papers that he refuses to sleep over. Koyama is constantly exegeting his own lifetime and the history of the countries he has worked in. Those histories are replete, he believes, with the Word of God spoken through biblical word and traumatic human events. For him, all of human history is full of God's love, judgment, and holy presence. If he does practice Barth's "analogy of faith," he does so in constant back-and-forth connecting of biblical narrative and contemporary circumstance. What other twentieth-century theologian has had the courage to accuse Elijah of overkill in his treatment of the priests of Baal and to accuse the Americans who firebombed the civilians of Tokyo of the same excess?[3] Typically, in discussing the parable of the Prodigal Son, he connects it with the disasters of prodigal wartime Japan. "I cannot read the story of the prodigal son without thinking of that time in 1945."[4] So agile a leap from the usual personal-perennial interpretations of that parable in Christian pulpits to the context of historical world conflict is breathtaking. Few theologians of our time have been so adept at such maneuvers or so exemplary in their insistence on combing the Bible for clues to what it means to perceive God at work behind today's news. "We learn to see the saving message of the name of God in the light of scripture as we live through history today."[5]

For this reason I would nominate Koyama as one of this century's great biblical theologians. Unfortunately, however, his career exemplifies a certain crisis in the relation of contemporary biblical scholarship to theological education in seminaries and in many churches around the world. A few years ago in Indonesia, I heard church leaders from several continents complain that they had great difficulty making use of western biblical scholarship for purposes of teaching in their local churches. A hundred years of critical work on the origins and history of the Hebrew and Christian Bible surely has its place in the life of the church and its seminaries. But what is that place? Who has the right to say, "The Bible says . . . "? Seminaries themselves have not yet answered these questions with a wisdom that is transferable to many a pulpit and Bible study group across the world.

One reason for this problem is the faculty organization of the seminaries themselves. Is intense, disciplined study of the Bible the exclusive province of those who are professional biblical scholars? How often does an entire seminary faculty engage in Bible study together? More momentously, how much intervention, if any, does the ordinary church congregation require from technical biblical scholarship? Do guilds of biblical scholars and ministers of congregations have some mutual responsibility to each other for discerning the Word of God in the words of the Bible? Can anyone pretend to be a biblically grounded theologian without first being a specialized biblical scholar? Currently there are no easy academic answers to these questions.

Not so easily, but with great intellectual courage, Koyama has blazed some new trails in connecting the historical world of the Bible to our own histories. In any final reckoning with this achievement, tribute has to be paid to his faithful, not to say relentless, willingness to bring the Bible and his experience of his own century into fruitful, illuminating relationship. Every student of biblical hermeneutics has something to learn from his writings.

One may say that his courage has been that of a bridge builder. A more accurate metaphor for his career to date might be: bridge-crosser. But even better: Koyama displays an uncanny knack for standing still in the busy crossroads of contemporary world cultures and learning from the hubbub there.

A THEOLOGIAN OF THE GLOBAL CROSSROAD

It seems natural to entertain a prolixity of images for describing this man because, if one feature of his mind stands out on first impression, it is his talent for fashioning metaphors. He had not been at Union Seminary long before he told us that Mount Fuji and Mount Sinai were embodied in the architecture of our place. One of our entrances is crowned by a graceful sweep of round arches rightly named the Rotunda. Down the hall are classrooms where "square" rational discourse goes on, and, in another wing of the Quadrangle, the arches of our Gothic chapel strain upward severely toward a dark roof that seems to go infinitely upward. In our Rotunda he saw the smooth slopes of Fujiyama, symbol of religion oriented to a cosmos. In classrooms and chapel, he saw historically oriented faith and the ruggedness of Sinai pointing beyond itself to the transcendent holiness of God.

This ability to mix, juxtapose, and interrelate old and new images of world cultures is the heart of Koyama's genius as a teacher. He once imaged the imperial mindcast in the stretch limousine, with its one-way windows, permitting its privileged passengers to look out at others who are not permitted to look in at them. The human experience of the future, he remarks, is best imaged among the Maori, who see themselves as backing into the future while fixing their eyes on the past, in contrast to the brave presumption of the West that "faces the future" as though we can predict what it will be. Buffalo-level theology, a frog jumping into a cosmic pond in an exercise of "plop spirituality," traveling with the Three-Mile-an-Hour God, seeing the Lincoln Memorial in its proper historical contrast to a Shinto shrine, the Golden Calf of Exodus and Emperor worship in Japan as kindred idolatries—hundreds of such arresting images crowd his books and lectures. His is a prodigious talent for making us think, and think again, about what our symbols symbolize.

His aim in the exercise of this talent is to facilitate a new level of empathy between the inhabitants of diverse cultures living and yet to be born. I have on occasion identified Union Seminary itself as "a crossroads sort of place." But in my years as his colleague, I can confidently say that no one on our faculty has been a more stunning example of a crossroads sort of *intellectual* than Kosuke Koyama. As a teacher and curriculum developer in the cross-disciplinary field of ecumenical studies, he has literally visited many a crossoad: in midnight visits with students to hungry and homeless street people in New York, in Caribbean study tours, and in three-week "immersions" in the cultures of peoples of developing countries. Quite unforgettable, for both of us, was an overnight visit we shared in 1992 in the homes of South African families living on the fringes of Tembisa, a Johannesburg township. There we had reaffirmed to us the dignity, intelligence, and hospitality that characterize so many poor people around the world in defiance of the ravages of oppressive social systems. Like him, I suspect, that direct experience of the culture of the poor was more educational for us both than many an abstraction of social theory, ideology, and theology.

Our new global humanity has no surplus of members who listen to each other in the places where cross the crowded ways of our increasingly common life. Once, in an interview, Karl Barth was asked what profession he might have preferred if he had not become a theologian. Barth answered that he rather liked the job of the traffic police—standing in the intersection and directing folk in this direction and that. The image has in it a touch of domination, and, as Christian theologian, Kosuke Koyama might have some trouble with it as an image of himself. I think he might prefer the image of interlocutor: one who stands silently for a while in the midst of conflictful conversations and enters occasionally to suggest what the conversants have to say and contribute to each other.

In the role of interlocutor, Kosuke Koyama has become one of our century's eminent ecumenical theologians. In this and the coming century, we cannot have too many of the likes of him.

NOTES

1. T. S. Eliot, "Little Gidding," in *Four Quartets* (New York: Harcourt, Brace, and Company, 1943), p. 39.

2. Kosuke Koyama, *Mount Fuji and Mount Sinai: A Critique of Idols* (Maryknoll, NY: Orbis Books, 1985), p. 31.

3. Ibid., p. 218.

4. Ibid., p. 30.

5. Ibid., p. 207.

Bibliography of Kosuke Koyama

BOOKS

1965

In the Land of Mendicant Monks and Waterbuffaloes (in Japanese). Tokyo: The Christ Weekly, 1965, 223pp.

1966

Commentary on Karl Barth's Dogmatics in Outlines (in Thai). Bangkok: Christian Literature Society, 1966, 50pp.

Commentary on the Lord's Prayer (in Thai). Bangkok: Christian Literature Society, 1966, 57pp.

Gospel and Law (in Thai). Bangkok: Christian Literature Society, 1966, 68pp.

What Did the Apostle Preach (in Thai). Bangkok: Christian Literature Society, 1966, 40pp.

What the Bible Says about Work (in Thai). Bangkok: Christian Literature Society, 1966, 36pp.

1974

Pilgrim or Tourist. Singapore: Christian Conference of Asia, 1974, 108pp.

Waterbuffalo Theology. Maryknoll, NY: Orbis Books / London: S.C.M. Press, 1974, 239pp.

1975

Theology in Contact. Madras: Christian Literature Society, 1975, 87 pp.

1977

No Handle on the Cross. Maryknoll, NY: Orbis Books / London: S.C.M. Press, 1976, 120pp.

1979

50 Meditations. Belfast: Christian Journals L.T.D., 1975 / Maryknoll, NY: Orbis Books, 1979, 191pp.

1980

Three Mile an Hour God. Maryknoll, NY: Orbis Books / London: S.C.M. Press, 1979, 146pp.

1984

Biblical Meditation on Contemporary Issues. Vol. I (in Japanese). Tokyo: Doshin Publishing House, 1984, 238pp.
Biblical Meditation on Contemporary Issues. Vol. II (in Japanese). Tokyo: Doshin Publishing House, 1984, 146pp.

1985

Biblical Meditation on Contemporary Issues. Vol.III (in Japanese). Tokyo: Doshin Publishing House, 1985, 250pp.
Mt. Fuji and Mt. Sinai: A Critique of Idols, Maryknoll, NY: Orbis Books / London: S.C.M. Press, 1984, 267pp.

ARTICLES

1962

"Strengthen the Discernment of the 'Christocentric.' " *South East Asia Journal of Theology* 4:2 (1962): 52-60.

1963

"Imitatio Christi in Luther's Theology of Faith." *Indian Journal of Theology* 12 (1963): 59-65.

1964

"Eating with Human Brokenness We Meet God the Paraclete." *The South East Asia Journal of Theology* 5:2 (1964): 54-65.
"From Waterbuffaloes to Asian Theology." *Japan Christian Quarterly* 30 (1964): 167-69; and *International Review of Mission* 53 (1964): 457-58.
"God is Disturbed." *Frontier* 7 (1964): 107-10.
"McGilvary Theological Seminary and Ministry in Thailand." *The South East Asia Journal of Theology*, 5:1 (1964): 38-41.
" 'Wrath of God' vs. Thai Theologia Gloriae." *The South East Asia Journal of Theology* 5:1 (1964): 18-25.

1966

"Prelude to a 'Neighbourology': Confessing the Faith in Thailand." *The South East Asia Journal of Theology* 8:1-2 (1966): 171-75.

1967

"Aristotelian Pepper and Buddhist Salt." *Practical Anthropology* 14 (May-June 1967): 97-102.

1968

"Bangkok, Wittenberg and Jerusalem" (guest editorial). *South East Asia Journal of Theology* 10:1 (1968): 3-5.

"Christian Presence in the Light of Our Theme: In Him All Things Hold Together." *South East Asia Journal of Theology* 10:1 (1968): 12-22.

"Missiology in South East Asia." *South East Asia Journal of Theology* 10:3-4 (1968): 3-8.

"The Role of Theology in Asia Today." *Indian Journal of Theology* 17: Supplement (1968): 1-22.

1969

"Appetiser and Main Course." *Frontier* 12 (August 1969): 193-96.

1971

"A Letter to Murray Rogers from Kosuke Koyama." In *Missionary Service in Asia Today*. Singapore: East Asia Christian Conference, 1971, 130-41.

"Brief Reflections on Theological Education in South East Asia," *The South East Asia Journal of Theology* 14:1 (1971): 96-8.

"Gun and 'Ointment' in Asia." In *The Future of the Christian World: Studies in Honor of R. Pierce Beaver*. William J. Danker and Wi Jo Kang, eds. Grand Rapids, MI: Wm. B. Eerdmans, 1971, pp. 43-55.

"Theology in the Time of Acute Complexity in History." *South East Asia Journal of Theology* 12:1 (1971): 5-9.

1972

"Director's Presentation to the Executive Committee of the Association of Theological Schools in South East Asia." *South East Asia Journal of Theology* 13:2 (1972): 68-87.

"The Lord's Controversy with Thailand." *International Review of Mission* 61:243 (July 1972): 229-35.

"The Place of Australia in South East Asian Affairs—Theologically Speaking." *South East Asia Journal of Theology* 15:1 (1972): 48-56.
"The 'Wrath of God' and the Thai Theologia Gloriae." Reprinted in *Christ and the Younger Churches*. Georg F. Vicedom, ed. London: SPCK, 1972, pp. 42-50.

1973

"The Mad Man Sits Down." *The South East Asia Journal of Theology* 14:2 (1973): 3-12.
"Ten Key Theological Issues Facing Theologians in South East Asia." *South East Asia Journal of Theology* 15:1 (1973): 1-11.
"Theological Statement." *International Review of Mission* 62:246 (April 1973): 224-25.

1974

"Barefoot in an Ascending Elevator: A Meditation." In *On Language, Culture, and Religion in Honor of Eugene A. Nida*. M. Black and William A. Smalley, eds. The Hague: Mouton, 1974, pp. 213-36.
"Reflections on the Association of Theological Schools in South East Asia." *The South East Asia Journal of Theology* 15:2 (1974): 10-35.
"Theological Reflections on the Bamboo Room and the Oil Room." *Lutheran World* 21:3 (1974): 266-71.
"What Makes a Missionary: Toward a Crucified Mind, Not a Crusading Mind." Reprinted in *Mission Trends No. 1: Crucial Issues in Mission Today*. Gerald H. Anderson and Thomas F. Stransky, eds. New York: Paulist Press, 1974, pp. 117-32.

1975

"Christianity Suffers from 'Teacher Complex.' " Reprinted in *Mission Trends No. 2: Evangelization*. Gerald H. Anderson and Thomas F. Stransky, eds. New York: Paulist Press, 1975.
" 'Not by Bread Alone . . . ' How Does Jesus Free and Unite Us?" *The Ecumenical Review* 27:3 (July 1975): 201-11.

1976

"Asian Christian Contribution to 'Jesus Christ Frees and Unites.' " *The South East Asia Journal of Theology* 17:2 (1976): 63-71.
"Att kunna bli stilla." *Svensk Missionstidskrift* 64:4 (1976): 205-17.
"Thailand: Points of Theological Friction." In *Asian Voices in Christian Theology*, Gerald H. Anderson, ed. Maryknoll, NY: Orbis Books, 1976, pp. 65-86.
"Theological Dimension of Technological Culture: Why Jahweh not Baal?" *Anticipation* (March 1976): 38-41.

"Theological Situations in Asia and the Mission of the Church." In *What Asian Christians Are Thinking: A Theological Source Book with Supplementary Bibliography*. Douglas J. Elwood, ed. Quezon City: New Day Publishers, 1976, pp.16-40.

"Three Theological Perspectives to 'Jesus Christ Frees and Unites.' " *The North East Asia Journal of Theology* 16 (March, 1976): 34-45.

1977

"Interpreting Religious Situation in the Technological Age." *Colloquium of Australia New Zealand Society of Theological Studies*. Melbourne, 1977, pp. 27-37.

"Traditional Cultures and Technology." In *Today's Church and Today's World: With a Special Focus on the Ministry of Bishops*. J. Howe, ed. London: CIO Publishing, 1977, pp. 64-72.

1978

"Adam in Deep Sleep." In *The Human and the Holy: Asian Perspectives in Christian Theology*. Emerito Nacpil, ed. Maryknoll, NY: Orbis Books / Manila: Makati, 1978, pp. 36-61.

"Covenant: Some Issues." *Reformed World* 35 (1978): 169-74.

1979

"Bangalore: A Theological Travelogue to Five Intelligible Words." *Mid-Stream* 18:1 (Jan. 1979): 44-51.

"Evangelism in the Reign of God." In *Witnessing to the Kingdom*. D. Preman Niles and T. K. Thomas, eds. Singapore: Christian Conference of Asia, 1979, pp. 17-23.

1980

"The Crucified Christ Challenges Human Power." In *Your Kingdom Come: Mission Perspectives*. World Conference on Mission and Evangelism. Geneva: Commission on World Mission and Evangelism, W.C.C., 1980, pp. 157-70.

"Religion as a Critical Attitude Towards Illusion." In *From Cosmos to Daily Life*. Paris: Unesco Press, 1980, pp. 11-19.

1981

"Ritual of Limping Dance: A Botanical Observation." *Union Seminary Quarterly Review* 36, Supplement I (1981): 91-104.

1982

"The Ambiguity of History: Help from the Maker of Heaven and Earth." *Currents in Theology and Mission*, 9:3 (June 1982): 149-56.

"Christ at the Periphery." *The Ecumenical Review* 34:1 (Jan. 1982): 67-75.

"Kagawa," "Little Flock Movement," "Christian Mission," "Mukyokai," "Watchman Nee," "Matthew Ricci," and "Uchimura." S.v. in *Abingdon Dictionary of Living Religions*, Nashville: Abingdon Press, 1982.

"Religion in Global Village." *The Drew Gateway* 52:3 (Spring 1982): 39-48.

"A Search for Ecumenical Theology" (in Japanese). *Fukuin To Sekai* (*The Gospel and the World*) (1982): 10-16.

"Tribal gods or Universal God." *Missionalia* 10:3 (Nov. 1982): 106-12.

1983

"Asian Spirituality" and "Indigenous Theology." S.v. in *The Westminster Dictionary of Christian Theology*, Philadelphia: Westminster Press, 1983.

"Violence and Theology" (in Japanese). *Fukuin To Sekai* (*The Gospel and the World*), (1983): 6-18.

1984

"The Asian Approach to Christ." *Missiology* 12:4 (Oct. 1984): 435-47.

"The Ecumenical Movement as the Dialogue of Cultures." In *Faith and Faithfulness: Essays on Contemporary Ecumenical Themes. A Tribute to Philip A. Potter*. Pauline Webb, ed. Geneva: W.C.C., 1984, pp. 40-51.

"Pilgrim or Tourist." Reprinted in *Epiphany* 5:1 (Fall, 1984): 6-7.

1985

"Christianity and East, West, South, North" (in Japanese). *Japan Christian Almanac*, (1985): 58-60.

"Evangelism in the Light of a Vulnerable God." *Faith and Mission* 2:2 (Spring 1985): 70-75.

1986

"Ecumenical and World Christianity Center, Union Theological Seminary, New York City." *Theological Education* 22:2 (1986): 132-37.

"Gate." In *Whither Ecumenism?* Thomas Wieser, ed. Geneva: W.C.C., 1986, pp. 94-97.

"Gospel and Japanese Spirituality" (in Japanese). *Fukuin To Sekai* (*The Gospel and the World*) (Jan. 1986): 61-71.

"Interplay with Other Religions." In *The Study of Spirituality*. Cheslyn Jones, Geoffrey Wainwright, and Edward Yarnold, eds. London: SPCK, 1986, pp. 554-61.

"Reflections on War and Peace for an Ecumenical Theology 40 Years after Hiroshima." *Mid-Stream* 25:2 (April 1986): 141-54.

1987

"An Analysis of Idolatry." *International Christian Digest* 1:1 (Feb. 1987): 34-36.
"The Hand Painfully Open." *Lexington Theological Quarterly* 22:2 (April 1987): 33-43.
"The Suffering God." *Perspective: A Journal of Reformed Thought* (March 1987): 4-6.
"Theocentric Christology: A Response to Mark Heim." *Journal of Ecumenical Studies* 24:1 (Winter, 1987): 37-41.

1988

" 'Building the House by Righteousness': The Ecumenical Horizons of Minjung Theology." In *An Emerging Theology in World Perspective: Commentary on Korean Minjung Theology*. Jung Young Lee, ed. Mystic, CT: Twenty-Third Publications, 1988, pp. 137-52.
"The Mountain of the Lord: Micah 4:1-7." *International Review of Mission* 77:306 (Apr. 1988): 194-200.
"Simple World, Complex World" (in Japanese). *The Japan Christian Year Book*, 1988, 44-49.

1989

"American Church History from a Third World Perspective." In *Altered Landscapes: Christianity In America 1935-1985. Essays in Honor of Robert T. Handy*. David W. Lotz, Donald W. Shriver, and John F. Wilson, eds. Grand Rapids, MI: Eerdmans, 1989, pp. 171-85.
"Asian Theology." In *The Modern Theologians: An Introduction to Christian Theology in the Twentieth Century*, Vol II. David F. Ford, ed. Oxford and New York: Basil Blackwell, 1989, pp. 217-34.
"Creative Mutuality." *Horizons* [Presbyterian Women] (July/August, 1989): 4-5, 28.
"For the Sake of Ten." *The Christian Century* 106 (July 19-26, 1989): 683.
"He Had Compassion." *The Christian Century* 106 (July 5-12, 1989): 651.
"I am Jesus, Whom You Persecute." *The Christian Century* 106 (April 5, 1989): 347.
"If You Give a Feast, Invite the Poor." *The Christian Century* 106 (Aug. 16-23, 1989): 747.
"May God Continue to Bless Us." *The Christian Century* 106 (April 26, 1989): 442.
"So They May See My Glory." *The Christian Century* 106 (May 3, 1989): 467.
"Speak My Word Faithfully." *The Christian Century* 106 (Aug. 2-9, 1989): 716.
"The Word Became Flesh and Dwelt Among Us." *Mission Focus* (Dec. 1989): 65-69.
"They Are a Stiff-Necked People." *The Christian Century* 106 (Aug. 30-Sept. 6, 1989): 779.

"Who is God for Us Today?" *Thinking Mission Series Two* (July 1989): 3-7.
"Yahweh Is Generous to All." *The Christian Century* 106 (April 19, 1989): 411.
"You Prepare a Table for Me." *The Christian Century* 106 (April 12, 1989): 379.

1990

"The Role of Translation in Developing Indigenous Theologies—An Asian View."
In *Bible Translation and the Spread of the Church: The Last Two Hundred Years*.
Philip C. Stine, ed. Leiden and New York: E.J. Brill, 1990, pp. 95-107.
"Union of Ethical Walking and Theological Beholding: Reflections from an Asian
American." In *Yearning to Breathe Free: Liberation Theologies in the U.S.* Mar
Peter-Raoul et al., eds. Maryknoll, NY: Orbis Books, 1990, pp. 111-19.

1991

"Jesus Christ Who Has Gone to the Utter Periphery." *The Ecumenical Review* 43:1
(Jan. 1991): 100-6.
"Religion in the Global Village." In *The Contribution of Carl Michalson to Modern
Theology: Studies in Interpretation and Application*. H. Thompson, ed. Lewiston,
NY: E. Mellin Press, 1991, pp. 227-42.
"Theological Reflections." *Lectionary Homiletics* (Feb. 1991): pp. 2f, 8, 28, 35.

1992

"Challenges the Church Faces in the World" (in Japanese). *The Christian Almanac*
(1992): 45-47.
"The Eucharist: Ecumenical and Ecological." *The Ecumenical Review* 44:1 (Jan.
1992): 80-90.
"Forgiveness and Politics, Japanese Experience." *Asia Journal of Theology* 6:1
(April 1992): 10-30.
"Missiology." S.v. in *A New Handbook of Christian Theology*. Donald W. Musser and
J. L. Price, eds., Nashville: Abingdon Press, 1992, pp. 312-14.
"Sharing the Good News of What God is Doing Today." In *The Scandal of the Cross:
Evangelism and Mission Today*. W. S. Robins and G. Hawney, eds. London: The
United Society for the Propagation of the Gospel, 1992, pp. 36-42.

1993

"Blessed Are Those Who Mourn, for They Will Be Comforted." *Currents in The-
ology and Mission* 20 (June 1993): 204-6.
"Christ's Homelessness." *The Christian Century* 110 (July 14-21, 1993): 702-3.
"The Crucified Christ Challenges Human Power." Reprinted in *Asian Faces of Jesus*.
R. S. Sugirtharajah, ed. Maryknoll, NY: Orbis Books, 1993, pp. 149-62.
" 'Extend Hospitality to Strangers' —A Missiology of Theologia Crucis." *Interna-
tional Review of Mission* 82:327 (1993): 283-95.

"Monde nouveau, creation nouvelle." *Spiritus* (Mai 1993): 129-48.

"Neue Schopfung—Neue Welt: Mission in der Kraft des Glaubens." *Jahrbuch Mission* (1993): 123-40.

"New World—New Creation: Mission in Power and Faith." *Mission Studies* 10:1-2 (1993): 59-77.

"Participation of Culture in the Transfiguration of Humanity: Forms of Ecumenical Theology in Asia." *Asia Journal of Theology* 7:4 (Oct. 1993): 214-30.

"Theological Education: Its Unities and Diversities." *Theological Education* 30: Supplement I (Autumn 1993): 87-105.

"The Tradition and Indigenisation." *Asia Journal of Theology* 7 (April 1993): 2-11.

1994

"The Book That Can Speak to All Peoples." In *The Bible in Theology and Preaching: How Preachers Use Scripture*. Donald K. McKim, ed. Nashville: Abingdon Press, 1994, pp. 169-71.

"Listening to the Spirit." *Hear What the Spirit Says to the Churches: Towards Missionary Congregations in Europe*. Gerhard Linn, ed. Geneva: WCC Publications, 1994, 126-32.

"The Theology of the Cross and the Self-Consciousness of the Church." *Asia Journal of Theology* 8:2 (April, 1994): 2-12.

1995

"Father, Forgive . . . ," *Ecumenical Review* 47:3 (July 1995): 268-77.